Tourism and Hospitality in the 21st Century

Edited by

A. Lockwood and S. Medlik

OXFORD   AUCKLAND   BOSTON   JOHANNESBURG   MELBOURNE   NEW DELHI

Butterworth-Heinemann
Linacre House, Jordan Hill, Oxford OX2 8DP
225 Wildwood Avenue, Woburn, MA 01801-2041
A division of Reed Educational and Professional Publishing Ltd

A member of the Reed Elsevier plc group

First published 2001

British Library Cataloguing in Publication Data
Tourism and hospitality in the 21st century
   1.   Tourist trade   2.   Hospitality industry
   I.   Lockwood, Andrew   II. Medlik, S. (Slavoj), 1928–
337.4'7'91

ISBN 0 7506 4676 4

Composition by Florence Production, Stoodleigh, Devon
Printed and bound in Great Britain by MPG Books, Bodmin, Cornwall

Contents

Preface

Throughout the world more people than ever travel and stay away from home. Tourism and hospitality are the world's major industries, which are in large part responsible for much economic growth, balance of payments, employment and regional balance in their countries. They are also important socially, culturally and environmentally – for those who become tourists and for their hosts. The future of tourism and hospitality is of interest to many businesses and other organizations, as well as governments.

This volume contemplates the future of these activities. It draws on invited contributions to the first international conference of the millennium year on 'Tourism and Hospitality in the 21st Century' at the University of Surrey in Guildford, England, in January 2000. The authors' original contributions have been edited at the discretion of the editors because of limitations of space, the need to conform otherwise to the issued guidelines, or for other reasons.

Many authors are from Britain but more than half come from the rest of Europe, North America and other parts of the world. They represent a wide range of interests involved in tourism and hospitality, and while many come from universities, most work in business, consultancy and other organizations. Their profiles are given in the list of contributors, where affiliations shown are those at the time they submitted their papers.

The book follows the successful structure of the conference programme of three main parts. Part One, consisting of nine chapters, reflects the conference plenary sessions and deals with global views. Part Two, comprising seven chapters, corresponds to the conference regional workshops and is concerned with global regions' futures and prospects. Part Three, with eleven chapters, covers most of the conference sectoral workshops and examines the futures and prospects of the component sectors. The concluding chapter reviews the problems and challenges and highlights some thoughts expressed in the three main parts of the book.

Like the conference, the book sets out to introduce educators and practitioners as well as others with an interest in the future, to the new century and the shape of things to come.

Written as it was by an international team of contributors for an international conference, and coming as it does from an international publishing company, it is aimed at an international audience. It would not have been possible without the cooperation of the authors, conference organizers or publishers, and to all of them we express our appreciation.

A. Lockwood
S. Medlik
Guildford, 2000

Principal contributors

Daniel Affolter

Daniel Affolter graduated with a law degree from the University of Zurich, was admitted to the Bar, and had some twenty years' varied professional legal experience. Since 1990 he has been chairman and member of several boards of directors. Over that ten-year period he has been a member, non-executive chairman and since July 1999 executive chairman of the Board of Directors, Kuoni Travel Holding Ltd, based in Zurich. His other appointments include membership of the Executive Committee of the World Travel and Tourism Council (WTTC).

Maggie Bergsma

With more than fourteen years' experience in tourism, the last eight as an international expert in tourism marketing, Maggie Bergsma has worked as a consultant for international organizations and countries, including both public and private sector clients. In 1996 she joined Interface International based in Brussels which specializes in tourism marketing, as Director of the Consulting Department. In this position she has undertaken major projects with a particular focus on tourism from Germany and the UK to Poland and on European tourism to Bulgaria.

Richard Butler

Richard Butler is currently Professor of Tourism at the University of Surrey and Emeritus Professor at the University of Western Ontario, Canada, where he previously held a Chair in the Department of Geography. He has been employed as a researcher and adviser by government and other public as well as private sector agencies in the UK, Canada, USA and Australia. Professor Butler received his doctorate from the University of Glasgow, is a Fellow of the Royal Geographical Society and Royal Society of Arts, past President of the International Academy for the Study of Tourism and the Canadian Leisure Studies Association.

Marvin Cetron

Dr Cetron is the founder and President of Forecasting International based in Virginia, USA, and is one of the foremost forecaster-futurists. As a pioneer in corporate, industry, demographic and lifestyle forecasting, he has structured the company to provide industry and government with the benefits and insights of an international group of experts in a wide range of activities. He is an author and co-author of books, articles and papers on American and global contemporary and future scenes. Over the years he has been a consultant to more than 150 firms, government agencies and other organizations.

Kenneth Chamberlain

Ken Chamberlain studied history at Oxford and transportation management at Stanford University, USA. His business career spans more than forty years. His posts with P&O (North America) Inc. as Vice President Marketing and Executive Vice President of the cruise line were followed by senior posts with Pacific Asia Travel Association (PATA), including eleven years as Chief Executive. In the 1990s he was Executive Director of the PATA Foundation managing grants for the environment, cultural heritage and education, and he continues working as a tourism consultant.

Colin Clark

Colin Clark is a director of Horwath UK, a member of Horwath International, consultants to the tourism, hotel and leisure industries. There he was responsible for the Leisure Time Study commissioned by the World Tourism Organization (WTO). He is also a member of the WTO Business Council Leadership Forum of Advisers, Chairman of the British Standards Institute Committee on Tourism Standards and UK representative on the European Committee on Tourism Standards. Previously he was a director of the British Tourist Authority and English Tourist Board, executive agencies for tourism promotion and development.

Robert Cleverdon

Robert Cleverdon has worked for more than three decades as a travel, tourism and leisure consultant on the development of the tourism sector in the UK and overseas, trends in future demand and the market for particular products. After many years with the Economist Intelligence Unit and the UNDP/WTO Programme in the South Pacific, in the 1990s his consultancy activities have focused mainly on tourism sectors in developing countries. He is also the WTO adviser on its global tourism forecasting research and holds a senior lecturer post in the Centre for Leisure and Tourism Studies at the University of North London Business School.

Suzanne Cook

Dr Cook is the Senior Vice President of Research for the Travel Industry Association (TIA), responsible for overseeing the work of the US Travel Data Center, the TIA research department, where she directs a major multi-faceted programme of research. Prior to joining the Center in 1977 she held the position of Senior Project Director for the Arbitron Company, a major broadcasting research firm. *Travel Agent* magazine named her as one of the 200 most powerful women in the travel industry and recently she received the Lifetime Achievement Award, the highest and most prestigious award of the Travel and Tourism Research Association (TTRA).

Bryony Coulson

Bryony Coulson has nearly twenty years' experience in the travel industry and training. She joined Saga Holidays as a graduate management trainee in 1980 where she had varied responsibilities for various aspects of tour operating, reaching the position of Quality Control Manager. Over the following five years she developed quality improvement programmes at Stena Line, Hoverspeed and Utell International. Her current role as Assistant Director of the Passenger Shipping Association (PSA) and General Manager of PSARA (the training and education arm of the PSA) is to oversee and develop the seminar training programme aimed at travel agents to sell cruises.

Douglas Frechtling

Dr Frechtling is Chair of the Department of Tourism and Hospitality Management in the George Washington University's School of Business and Public Management. He began his career as an economist for the US Congress and later served as deputy assistant to the Secretary of the US Treasury. He was founding Director of the US Travel Data Center and served as its chief executive officer for fourteen years. Later he was President of GuestPlus Inc., founded to market independently owned luxury hotels to frequent travellers. He is a past president of the Travel and Tourism Research Association and for more than a decade he has been a consultant to the World Tourism Organization.

John Heeley

After graduating with Masters and PhD research degrees in tourism, Dr John Heeley was for a number of years senior lecturer in tourism in the Strathclyde Business School, Glasgow. There he authored numerous reports and articles and did extensive consultancy work for both the public and private sectors of the Scottish tourist industry. Between 1990 and 1996 he was Director of Tourism for the City of Sheffield and Managing Director of Destination Sheffield; since 1997 he has been Chief Executive of

Coventry and Warwickshire Promotions. He has developed both organizations from scratch and also played an important role in city development.

Nelson Hitchcock

Nelson Hitchcock is Group Managing Director for RCI Europe, part of the world's leading timeshare exchange organization, having previously held several key senior management positions with RCI, both at European headquarters and within the European operating units. Before joining RCI, he worked in senior marketing and management positions for several major American consumer and financial services companies, which included Citicorp in the United States and Europe. American-born, Nelson Hitchcock has an MBA from the Harvard University Graduate School of Business Administration and holds a Bachelor degree in Economics and English from Allegheny College.

Peter Jones

Professor Jones holds the Charles Forte Chair of Hotel Management and is responsible for the work of the Centre for Hospitality Industry Productivity Research in the School of Management Studies at the University of Surrey. Prior to joining Surrey in 1997 he was the Assistant Dean of the Brighton Business School. Professor Jones holds an MBA degree from London Business School and a doctorate from the University of Surrey, is a Fellow of the HCIMA, author or editor of nine textbooks and numerous journal articles. He was the first President of EuroCHRIE and serves as CHRIE's adviser to the Board of the IH&RA.

Walter Leu

Walter Leu graduated in law from the University of Zurich and had an extensive professional career in the banking, trust company and insurance sector before making a major contribution to tourism. Between 1979 and 1994 he was Director General of the Swiss National Tourist Office and since 1996 he has been Executive Director of the European Travel Commission (ETC), which represents national tourist organizations of most European countries. He has also been chairman of ETC, chairman of the Alpine Tourist Commission and member of several Swiss governmental commissions on tourism.

Martin Lohmann

Dr Lohmann is managing and research director at NIT, Institute for Tourism and Recreational Research in Northern Europe, based in Kiel, Germany. He studied psychology, sociology and philosophy at several German universities and was a researcher at the University of Würzburg where his doctoral thesis was on stress and recreation. Before joining the Kiel

Institute he was for a number of years research director at Studienkreis für Tourismus in Starnberg, Germany, responsible for a number of projects, including the annual national travel survey 'Reiseanalyse' and studies of holiday areas.

Victor Middleton

Professor Middleton is an independent academic, consultant and author who currently holds visiting appointments at the Universities of Central Lancashire and Oxford Brookes in the UK. His career bridges international commercial organizations, tourist boards, local authorities and academic institutions over thirty years and he has undertaken visiting professor roles and consultancy assignments in many countries worldwide. As an author of more than 100 articles, books and reports, his major published contributions have been in tourism marketing and measurement, museums and heritage management and sustainable development.

Hansruedi Müller

Professor Müller teaches leisure and tourism at the University of Berne, Switzerland, where he heads the Research Institute for Leisure and Tourism (FIF). He started his academic career at the University in the early 1980s and has a wide range of publications to his credit. His most important ones dealing with leisure, tourism, ecology and quality management draw mainly on Swiss and to a lesser extent Austrian and German experience. They include a Delphi study of travel to 2005 which covers the three countries.

Michael Olsen

Michael Olsen is a Professor of Strategic Management in the Hospitality Industry at Virginia Polytechnic Institute and State University, Director of Research for the International Hotel & Restaurant Association, President of Michael D. Olsen and Associates (MDO) and Chairman of the Olsen Group Inc., a subsidiary of MDO. During more than thirty years of industry and academic experience he has served on many national and international associations, authored/co-authored/edited books and manuals as well as over 200 articles in the professional and trade press, given more than 250 presentations in some forty countries, and held a number of visiting appointments world-wide.

Auliana Poon

Dr Poon graduated with a Masters degree in Economics from the University of the West Indies and a doctorate in tourism from the University of Sussex, England. She is managing director of Caribbean Futures, based in Bielefeld, Germany, and Port-of-Spain, Trinidad, a travel and tourism consultancy with a particular expertise in the Caribbean. Her recent clients have included a number of governmental bodies, including the European Union. Her publications include, as editor and publisher, *Tourism Industry Intelligence*, a leading travel and tourism industry newsletter.

Regina Schlüter

Dr Schlüter is Professor at the Universidad Nacional de Quilmes and co-founder and Director of the Centre for Tourism Studies and Research (CIET) in Buenos Aires, Argentina. She graduated in demography and tourism and received her doctorate in social psychology from the Universidad Argentina J. F. Kennedy. She is editor-in-chief of the social science journal *Estudios y Perspectivas en Turismo*, author of and contributor to, several books and author of articles in Latin American, North American and European journals.

John Seekings

Although brought up in South Africa, John Seekings' working life has been based in Britain. After transport-related studies at Capetown and the London School of Economics, his first appointments were in the airline business, before moving into aviation journalism as editor of *Aeroplane* and then of *Airways*. In 1975 he set up Tourism International to extend his interests into the wider world of tourism and in the early 1980s he teamed up with Steve Wheatcroft as senior partner in the consultancy Aviation and Tourism International.

Victor Teye

Dr Teye is an Associate Professor of Tourism and co-ordinator of the Travel and Tourism Programme at Arizona State University. He received his degree from the Universities of Ghana and Manitoba in Canada and was a Research Associate with the Universities of Zambia, Ghana and Manitoba, before joining Arizona State University. He served as a tourism consultant with the UNDP/ILO in Ghana, USAID in the Gambia and the Mid-Western University Consortium in Ghana's Central Region. In 1996 and 1997 he was a Fulbright Scholar at the University of Cape Coast in Ghana.

Graham Todd

With over thirty years' experience as an economist and consultant, and following ten years' specialization in international travel and tourism, Graham Todd co-founded Travel Research International Limited (TRI) in 1998 to provide research services and publications to the industry. Earlier he spent five years with the Economist Intelligence Unit (EIU), ten years with Coopers & Lybrand Associates and two years with Job Creation

Limited. He then started a career as an independent consultant, in parallel with more than ten years as managing editor of EIU travel and tourism publications, which became Travel & Tourism Intelligence.

Salah Wahab

Professor Wahab is Professor of Tourism at the University of Alexandria School of Tourism and Hotel Management, Founder and Chairman of Tourismplan and Chairperson of the Tourism Division of the National Council on Productivity and Economic Affairs in Egypt. Formerly he was Head of the State Tourism Administration, First Under Secretary of State for Tourism, Chairman of the National Organization of Tourism and Hotels, and Chairman of public and private sector investment companies. He is the author, co-author and co-editor of many books, articles and papers on tourism.

Betty Weiler

Dr Weiler is Associate Professor in the Department of Management, Monash University, Melbourne, Australia, where she heads up a small team of tourism lecturers and researchers. She completed an MA at the University of Waterloo and PhD at the University of Victoria in Canada, both with a focus on tourism, and has spent twenty years lecturing, researching and publishing in tourism. She has a strong track record in completing externally funded research and working on industry-based research projects. Since migrating to Australia ten years ago, she has focused mainly on special interest tourism, with an emphasis in recent years on ecotour guiding and interpretation.

Michael Willmott

Michael Willmott is co-founder of the Future Foundation, a research-based business 'think-tank' which he set up in July 1996 with fellow director Melanie Howard, and which has established itself as the leading independent futures research and consultancy organization in Britain. It helps organizations improve their performance through anticipating how society and marketplaces are likely to develop in the future and developing a better understanding of current customer demands and needs. Formerly Michael Willmott was Deputy Chairman and Director of Research at the UK Henley Centre for Forecasting.

Stephen Witt

Stephen Witt is Professor of Tourism Forecasting in the School of Management Studies at the University of Surrey, UK, and in the Department of Applied Economics at Victoria University, Australia. Previously he was Professor of Tourism Studies in the European Business Management

School at the University of Wales, Swansea, having started his academic career at Bradford University Management Centre. Recent visiting appointments include research posts in Australia, Denmark and Sweden.

Part

I

Global Views

1

World travel and tourism today

Graham Todd

This chapter examines the current global dimensions and patterns of, and the recent trends in, travel and tourism, in order to provide a framework within which to consider the likely future of this global industry. It highlights the main generators of tourism demand, the main destinations of tourists and the main international tourism flows. Reference is made to the three leading tourism regions – Europe, North America and the Pacific Rim – and comments are also offered on the position of Africa, Asia and Latin America. The main trends of the 1990s are examined and the chapter concludes with some indicative pointers to the issues likely to influence tourism in the coming decades.

Definitions

It is important to acknowledge at the outset that the measurement of tourism is both an imprecise science and is increasingly susceptible to definitional problems. The central source of data on international tourism, and the one upon which this chapter primarily draws, is provided by the World Tourism Organization (WTO) using data drawn from government sources. These data are largely concerned with two common measures of tourism – the number of arrivals registered in each country, and the levels of expenditure made by visitors. They also permit some analysis of the main generators of international tourism demand. However, as Edwards and Graham (1997) point out, destination countries use ten different measures of tourism, and origin countries use a further five, and there are often quite wide discrepancies between different data sources. They conclude that expenditure measures are the most reliable in assessing tourism's magnitude, yet it is immediately obvious that most countries, in discussing, planning and promoting their tourism industries, tend mainly to refer to arrivals numbers as if these were a reliable economic indicator. Clearly, without accurately analysing the types of arrivals, they are not.

Furthermore, international tourism traffic is the tip of the iceberg. Domestic travel, in terms of the number of trips taken, far exceeds the level of international trips. Domestic travel is rarely measured with much accuracy other than through macro-economic estimations and/or sample survey data. However, to provide just one indication of the magnitudes involved, the Prime Minister of China, Li Peng, in his opening address to the Pacific Asia Travel Association conference held in Beijing in 1997 reported that the Chinese had made 640 million domestic tourist trips in the previous year. This is 45 million more than the global total of international tourist arrivals in that same year.

It is obvious that the magnitude of domestic tourism in the industrialized world is vast – notably in North America and Europe. The oft-quoted statistic that less than 10% of Americans hold passports (despite the fact that the USA is the world's largest spender on international tourism, excluding transport costs), hints at just how massive this domestic business can be. However, the main thrust of this chapter is to focus on international tourism on which, notwithstanding data problems, information is most readily available.

Growth and magnitudes

Today's massive tourism industry has been driven by a number of factors – and these are the factors whose future directions need to be considered. They are:

- growth in real incomes;
- the advance in personal wealth as expressed in the ability of individuals to generate resources beyond those needed to pay for life's basic needs –

food, housing, clothing, education, health and, in more recent times, 'essential' consumer goods – in other words, the expanding ability for discretionary expenditure on non-essential items;

- increases in leisure time;
- peace amongst nations;
- freedom from administrative restraints on international travel;
- freedoms within international currency markets;
- expansion of fast, efficient and widely affordable public transport, coupled with wide access to private transport.

In a word, tourism depends upon economic development and open, free societies. It can be immediately seen that, measured against these basic criteria, much of today's world fares very badly. Such a comparison reveals two important facts. First, the majority of the world's population has yet to attain what we in the industrialized world would regard as a minimum level of supply of these elements. Second, and as a consequence, if the world's under-privileged can reasonably hope to attain access to these elements during the next century, the capacity for demand growth in national and international tourism is, for all practical purposes, unlimited.

For the advocates of tourism, this is wonderful news. For those concerned about wider issues of environmental integrity, it is potentially terrifying. For pragmatists, it raises issues to explore and elucidate.

The basic facts of the modern international tourism industry are well known and can be briefly stated. According to WTO data, in 1950 there were 25 million international tourist arrivals and the value of tourism receipts was US$2.1 billion. In 1998 international arrivals had risen to an estimated 635 million and the value of receipts to US$439 billion. Over those 48 years, the average annual increase in arrivals was around 7%; in terms of (current) tourism receipts, the average was just over 11.5%. The temptation to conclude that international tourism is subject to uninterrupted exponential growth is thus obvious but, as this chapter will show, it is also misleading, since there is clear evidence that rates of growth are now slowing down.

This chapter concentrates on the trends evident during the 1990s. As Table 1.1 shows, the rate of growth in international tourism arrivals averaged just over 4% a year between 1990 and 1998, but with very wide differences by region. The world's two major tourism regions – Europe and North America – both exhibited below-average growth. The fastest growing regions were Latin America, the Middle East and Africa – all relative back-markers in volume terms.

5

Table 1.1   International tourist arrivals by region, 1990–98 (mn)

	1990	1995	1996	1997	1998	% change from 1990 to 1998[a]	Annual average % change
Africa	15.1	20.1	21.5	23.2	24.7	63.9	6.3
North America	71.7	80.5	85.2	84.7	85.0	18.5	2.2
Caribbean	11.4	14.0	14.3	15.3	16.0	40.0	4.3
Latin America	10.4	15.8	17.2	18.9	21.7	75.1	9.6
East Asia/Pacific	54.6	81.4	89.2	88.0	86.6	58.7	5.9
Europe	282.3	333.9	349.0	369.8	381.1	35.0	3.8
Middle East	9.0	13.5	14.1	14.9	15.0	67.8	6.8
South Asia	3.2	4.2	4.4	4.8	5.0	59.4	6.0
Total[b]	**457.6**	**563.4**	**595.0**	**619.6**	**635.1**	**38.8**	**4.2**

[a]Calculated on unrounded data.
[b]Totals may not add due to rounding.
Source: World Tourism Organization

Table 1.2   Regional shares of international tourist arrivals, 1990–98 (%)

	1990	1995	1996	1997	1998
Africa	3.3	3.6	3.6	3.7	3.9
North America	15.7	14.3	14.3	13.7	13.4
Caribbean	2.5	2.5	2.4	2.5	2.5
Latin America	2.3	2.8	2.9	3.0	3.4
East Asia/Pacific	11.9	14.4	15.0	14.2	13.6
Europe	61.7	59.3	58.7	59.7	60.0
Middle East	2.0	2.4	2.4	2.4	2.4
South Asia	0.7	0.7	0.7	0.8	0.8
Total[a]	**100.0**	**100.0**	**100.0**	**100.0**	**100.0**

[a]Totals may not add due to rounding.
Source: World Tourism Organization

In terms of market share, Europe remains the dominant influence on international tourism by the arrivals measure, accounting for 60% of all international arrivals in 1998, with East Asia/Pacific and North America next in importance. Together, these three regions account for almost nine out of every ten arrivals globally.

Table 1.3 International tourism receipts by region, 1990–98 (US$ bn)

	1990	1995	1996	1997	1998	Annual average % change 1990/98
Africa	5.3	7.5	8.7	9.0	9.6	7.7
Americas	70.0	102.7	112.4	118.9	120.0	7.0
East Asia/Pacific	39.2	74.2	82.0	76.4	68.6	7.3
Europe	146.8	207.6	222.2	220.5	228.9	5.7
Middle East	4.4	7.5	8.2	9.1	8.0	7.7
South Asia	2.0	3.5	3.9	4.3	4.3	10.1
Total[a]	**267.8**	**403.0**	**437.6**	**438.2**	**439.4**	**6.4**

[a]Totals may not add due to rounding.
Source: World Tourism Organization

Looking now at tourism receipts, during the 1990s these grew in current US dollar terms at an average annual rate of 6.4% to 1998. Only Europe was below average during this period, with South Asia leading the pack, and Africa and the Middle East being the next best performers.

However, the major earners in terms of the volume of total receipts remain again Europe, the Americas (of which North America accounts for almost three-quarters) and East Asia/Pacific. The fastest growing regions are the small ones, and it should also be noted that the rate of growth in receipts in East Asia/Pacific until 1996 was 13.1% – by far the fastest – before the first hints of a slowdown in Asia's economies became apparent. Europe's

Table 1.4 Share of international tourism receipts by region, 1990–98 (%)

	1990	1995	1996	1997	1998
Africa	2.0	1.9	2.0	2.1	2.2
Americas	26.1	25.5	25.7	27.1	27.3
East Asia/Pacific	14.6	18.4	18.7	17.4	15.6
Europe	54.8	51.5	50.8	50.3	52.1
Middle East	1.6	1.9	1.9	2.1	1.8
South Asia	0.7	0.9	0.9	1.0	1.0
Total[a]	**100.0**	**100.0**	**100.0**	**100.0**	**100.0**

[a]Totals may not add due to rounding.
Source: World Tourism Organization

share of total tourism receipts has hovered around the 50% mark since the mid-1990s, having eroded slightly in the face of the rapid expansion in Asia in the early 1990s but recovering slightly thereafter. Similarly, the share of the Americas has remained broadly stable, the slight increase in the latter years being attributable partly to accelerated growth in Latin America, while the share of East Asia/Pacific fell back.

Europe is, of course, unique in international tourism owing to its geography. Most of its countries are accessible to most of its citizens by the simple means of taking a private car or train across borders. Where distances are too great for surface transport, air transport offers a short journey time alternative – rarely in excess of a 3-hour flight. The development of mass international tourism in the post-war era largely took place within Europe, based on these factors and assisted, of course, by the progressive liberalization of air transport markets. This allowed charter flights to drive leisure tourism forward, coupled with the development of the inclusive tour which took care of anxieties, inexperience and uncertainties arising from taking a holiday in another country where a foreign language and customs prevailed.

No other region of the world has such characteristics, so it is of little surprise that Europe is so massively important. It is, however, worth reverting for a moment to definitional issues in tourism measurement. Historically, Europe has consisted of some 30 independent states, each with normal border controls and each with its own currency. As the European Union proceeds with economic integration, these characteristics will fade. A common currency will soon be sufficiently widely in use for foreign exchange measures of tourism expenditure and receipts with the EU to become first increasingly difficult to make and ultimately irrelevant. In economic terms, intra-European tourism is on the way to becoming a domestic market. Already, border formalities between signatories to the Schengen Agreement are negligible, making the measurement of tourism flows also increasingly difficult. If the EU continues over, say, the next half century, on its path to create a European super-state, for all practical purposes intra-European tourism will become as domestic in its nature as is already the case within the USA. The point at which this becomes widely recognized is debatable, of course, but if and when it does, Europe will no longer be the dominant force in what will then be termed 'international tourism'.

The leading origin countries

Looking at the level of expenditure on international tourism, excluding fares, four countries – the USA, Germany, Japan and the UK – account for over 40% of global tourism. The ranking of these countries has not changed during the 1990s. Indeed, there has been little change in the rankings of the top eight countries since then. It is noticeable that the world's largest country – the Peoples' Republic of China – has leapt from fortieth to ninth place in 7 years, with newly liberated Poland (not shown in Table 1.5), also rising from forty-sixth place to fourteenth in the rankings over the same period.

Table 1.5 Top 12 international travel origin markets by expenditure abroad (excluding transport costs), 1997

Ranking 1990	1997	Country	Expenditure 1997 (US$ mn)	% share of world total
1	1	USA	51 220	13.5
2	2	Germany	46 200	12.2
3	3	Japan	33 041	8.7
4	4	UK	27 710	7.3
5	5	Italy	16 631	4.4
6	6	France	16 576	4.4
7	7	Canada	11 268	3.0
9	8	Netherlands	10 232	2.7
40	9	China	10 166	2.7
8	10	Austria	10 124	2.7
–	11	Russian Fedn	10 113	2.7
13	12	Belgium	8 275	2.2
Sub-total			**251 556**	**66.5**
All other			128 201	33.5
World total			**379 757**	**100.0**

Source: World Tourism Organization

The leading destination countries

The ranking of tourism destination countries is different according to the measure used. In terms of international arrivals, France, Spain, the USA, Italy and the UK form the top five and account for 35% of all international

Table 1.6   Top 15 destinations by arrivals totals, 1990–98 (mn)

	1990	1995	1996	1997	1998	% change 1990/98
France	52.5	60.0	62.4	67.3	70.0	33.3
Spain	34.1	38.8	40.5	43.3	47.7	40.1
USA	39.4	43.3	46.5	47.8	46.4	17.9
Italy	26.7	31.1	32.9	34.1	34.8	30.5
UK	18.0	23.5	25.3	25.5	25.8	43.0
China	10.5	20.0	22.8	23.8	25.1	139.2
Mexico	17.2	20.2	21.4	19.4	19.8	15.3
Canada	15.2	16.9	17.3	17.6	18.8	23.8
Poland	3.4	19.2	19.4	19.5	18.8	453.5
Austria	19.0	17.2	17.1	16.6	17.4	−8.7
Germany	17.0	14.8	15.2	15.8	16.5	−3.3
Czech Republic	7.3	16.5	17.0	16.8	16.3	124.3
Russian Federation	7.2[a]	9.3	14.6	15.4	15.8	119.5
Hungary	20.5	20.7	20.7	17.2	15.0	−26.9
Greece	8.9	10.1	9.2	10.1	11.1	24.8
Sub-total	**296.8**	**361.8**	**382.3**	**390.2**	**399.3**	**34.5**
% of world total	64.9	64.2	64.2	63.0	62.9	—

[a]Former USSR.
Source: World Tourism Organization

arrivals. Again, China and Poland have made rapid progress up the league table since 1990 to take sixth and ninth place respectively by 1998. The UK has moved from seventh to fifth place, while Austria and Hungary have lost ground.

Ranked in terms of tourism receipts, however, the order at the top of the league table is different. The USA emerges as the largest earner of non-transport tourism revenues (as well as being the largest spender on international tourism), followed by Italy, France, Spain and the UK. These top five – the same as those in arrivals terms – accounted for 41% of global tourism receipts in 1998, and it is noteworthy that the USA earned over twice the level of receipts of Italy in second place. The main winners during the 1990s by this measure were China, Turkey and Poland, and the main loser in the rankings was Switzerland, albeit falling only from eighth to eleventh place.

Table 1.7   Top 15 international tourism destinations by value of receipts (excluding transport), 1990–98

Ranking 1990	1998	Country	Receipts 1998 (US$ mn)	% share of world total
1	1	USA	71 116	16.2
3	2	Italy	30 427	6.9
2	3	France	29 700	6.8
4	4	Spain	29 585	6.7
6	5	UK	21 233	4.8
5	6	Germany	15 859	3.6
5	7	China	12 600	2.9
7	8	Austria	11 560	2.6
9	9	Canada	9 133	2.1
21	10	Turkey	8 300	1.9
8	11	Switzerland	8 208	1.9
65	12	Poland	8 000	1.8
10	13	Mexico	7 897	1.8
11	14	Hong Kong, SAR, China	7 109	1.6
23[a]	15	Russian Fed.	7 107	1.6
Sub-total			**277 834**	**63.2**
All other			161 559	36.8
World total			439 393	100.0

[a] former USSR
Source: World Tourism Organization

Country-to-country flows

Analysing the principal bilateral travel flows again raises some problems of definition. For example, China records 24 million arrivals in 1997, but most of these were related to cross-border travel from Hong Kong, often work-related, and can lead to misleading conclusions. What might be considered as 'genuine international tourists' to China may not number many more than 5 million. Day trips are sometimes included in countries' arrivals counts and sometimes excluded. The potential for distortions in the data in the case of contiguous countries is high in such cases.

Although some of the data in Table 1.8 are a little out-of-date, they indicate the broad magnitude of current tourism traffic (including the day trip/excursionist business in some cases, such as France to Spain). Nearly all of

Table 1.8 The world's leading country-to-country tourism flows (mn)

	Arrivals	Year
France to Spain	20	1995
USA to Mexico	18	1997
USA to Canada	15	1998
Germany to France	13	1996
Canada to USA	13	1998
UK to France	12	1998
Germany to Spain	12	1998
UK to Spain	12	1998
Germany to Austria	10	1998
Mexico to USA	9	1998
Switzerland to Italy	8	1997
Germany to Italy	8	1997

Source: Travel & Tourism Intelligence, *International Tourism Forecasts to 2010*; World Tourism Organization data; International Passenger Survey, UK; Direction du Tourisme, France

these massive bilateral tourist movements are between countries with a common land border. Where they are not, they either require transit through a third country or, in one case (UK to France), demand a short sea crossing.

This analysis underlines some very important points about international tourism. First, in volume terms it is relatively highly concentrated between a small number of countries. Of the 240-odd sovereign territories in the world, the 15 largest tourism origin countries account for around 75% of all spending on international tourism and for seven in every ten trips. On the destination side of the equation, the top 15 destination countries receive almost 70% of all international tourism receipts. In arrivals terms, the 12 bilateral flows listed above account for almost 25% of all international arrivals worldwide.

We are accustomed to refer to and think of the international travel and tourism sector as a global economic activity. While that is true in one sense, the reality is that it is dominated by relatively few countries and could be quite accurately described as an activity open to an elite only – those at the top of the global income tree, living in relatively open, prosperous, stable and secure societies and generally travelling to similar societies either for leisure or business purposes. International travel is out of the reach of the great majority of the world's population. The 1998s arrivals of 635 million account for only around 11% of the world's population and obviously many within that 635 million make more than one international trip a year.

Regional issues

The great majority of international travel takes place within rather than between regions (although long-haul travel has shown some tendency to increase its overall share of the leisure market during the 1990s). Edwards and Graham (1997) estimate that 92% of trips from European countries are to European destinations, that 65% of North American trips are to North American destinations (including Mexico), and that 73% of Asia/Pacific trips are also intra-regional. Thus the recent downturn in travel within Asia which has accompanied the economic difficulties in the region cannot easily be replaced by traffic from extra-regional long-haul origin markets.

Europe is, as we have seen, the centre of international tourism and it is hard to see how it will ever be less than the regional leader, other than by changes in the definition of 'international' as already mentioned. *North America* is the next most dominant region, and together these two account for almost three in every four international arrivals, four in every five tourism dollars received and generate seven in every ten tourism dollars spent.

The *Asia–Pacific* region's explosive growth in international travel from the late 1980s until the onset of recession in the latter half of the 1990s in part reflected the immaturity of Asian origin markets – countries in which international travel had not previously featured in anything like the same degree as in Europe or North America. The leader in volume terms has been Japan. Elsewhere in the region, destinations such as China, Thailand, Australia, Hong Kong and Indonesia forged ahead during the 1990s. While some have been badly hit by economic and political upheavals in the past two years, others such as Australia and China still have great growth potential and can be expected to continue to expand their tourism sectors. China is, of course, also an increasingly important origin market.

The rest of the world as yet accounts for little volume in international tourism, either inbound or outbound. Africa, despite its above-average rate of growth in arrivals since 1990, remains tiny in its global tourism share, with less than 4% of arrivals and just over 2% of receipts. In the *Middle East* the key element in leisure tourism remains the issue of regional peace.

South America is perhaps the continent with the greatest potential to become a more important player on the international tourism scene. Although volumes remain small (Latin America – including the Central American republics, accounted for only 3.4% of global international arrivals in 1998 – a smaller share than that of Africa), the rate of growth in arrivals during the 1990s was the fastest in the world.

Finally in this rapid global tour, mention should be made of the *Caribbean*. Although the region receives less than 3% of global arrivals and accounts for a similar share of global tourism receipts, it is unique in its economic dependency on international tourism (individual countries such as the small islands of the Indian Ocean and the Pacific share similar features). Without tourism, the West Indian economy would be in serious trouble; no other region in the world is so dependent for its future on making the right policy decisions for the tourism sector.

Some broad conclusions

Of necessity this has been a whistle-stop tour of the subject against which issues can be examined in much greater detail. This chapter has avoided any mention of tourism forecasts since that is the province of other authors. None the less, some broad conclusions can be drawn before considering some of the issues that will determine the industry's future.

It has been shown that international tourism has yet to touch the lives of the majority of the world's population. While countries such as Austria and Switzerland have already achieved very high levels of travel intensity – defined as the number of foreign trips made per head of population, where both countries already make well in excess of two trips abroad per person per year – others have scarcely begun. The world's most valuable origin market, the USA, has a travel intensity of around 0.15. Europe's biggest origin market of Germany has achieved an intensity of around 1.3, the UK's figure is 0.85 and that of France is 0.68. Japan's travel intensity, for all its burgeoning growth during the late 1980s and early 1990s, has only reached 0.13. China, which offers perhaps the greatest potential and which has certainly shown rapid growth, has an international travel intensity of just 0.002.

To all intents and purposes international tourism is confined to a relatively small elite. A handful of countries account for the lion's share of the industry, both as origin markets and as destinations. To regard international tourism as a global activity in which every country has a major stake is misleading. Yet almost every country in the world, given peace with its neighbours and a rational approach to development, would like to see tourism play its part in their economies. This is mainly because tourism offers a ready source of employment, demands a wide range of skills, has the capacity to earn often scarce foreign currency, and the potential to fund conservation where few alternative sources of income exist.

While tourism, both domestic and international, is driven by many factors, the economic and environmental ones are of central importance. By the same token, examining the activity of tourism in the context of the behaviour of markets can help to focus attention on the determinants of demand and supply in future, and highlight some of the main issues involved.

Rising real incomes, expanding discretionary spending, increasing leisure time, faster and cheaper transport and the spread of global awareness through the printed and broadcast media and increasingly now through the Internet all fuel demand for travel. Most individuals in most countries, given the means and freedom to travel within their own countries and then to other countries would wish to take up the opportunity to do so.

At the same time, given the extreme inequalities in travel participation rates and travel opportunities, the potential for growth country-by-country is highly variable. In countries where travel intensities are already high, the scope for further growth is limited. This is not just a feature of the proportion of discretionary expenditure that individuals might wish to devote to travel, but is also affected by leisure time limitations. Travel is time-intensive, and there is growing evidence that leisure time ceilings have been reached in many of the industrialized countries – or even that available leisure time is shrinking. There are also other calls on leisure time and it cannot be taken for granted that travel will remain high on the priority list.

Another central influence on international travel demand has been the reduction in relative travel costs, especially in air transport. The progressive decline in seat-mile costs in air transport which has been achieved by step increases in the size, range and fuel efficiency of aircraft may be harder to maintain in the next 50 years of aircraft development than in the past 50. However, there are on the horizon some greater challenges to the maintenance of or further reduction in international travel costs.

Air transport and road transport infrastructure in the industrialized world, and especially in Europe, is showing signs of capacity constraints. While it may be possible to achieve the same level of flight intensity within Europe's air traffic control system as has already been achieved in the USA (and current limits are once again driving up average flight delays in Europe), the supply of airport facilities may prove much harder to expand. A free-market approach would show that, where there is a risk of excess demand, new supply will be introduced to meet it. Airport capacity, however, is driven by environmental and political concerns as well. If such concerns did not apply, Tokyo's Narita airport – an excellent example of unsatisfied demand for airport infrastructure – would have a second runway by now, and London's Heathrow might well have a third, but we all know that things are not that simple.

Ground transport is similarly under increasing threat of hitting capacity constraints. As well as influencing the airport debate directly, since ground access is integral to successful airport operations, rising congestion on the roads is reducing average speeds, raising average journey times and imposing additional time costs on travellers as a result. For the business traveller, these costs are relatively easily measurable and thus rational price-based solutions can be applied (such as the greater use of non-travel solutions like conference calls). For the leisure traveller these costs, although not so easily valued, manifest themselves in a willingness to travel to the chosen leisure destination, whether that is a seaside resort for a weekend, or an historic castle or a theme park for a day trip. Each individual will reach his or her own judgement on the point where the time costs involved in a given journey outweigh the benefits of the destination visit; at that point, behaviour will change and other, non-travel activities will be substituted.

The issue of congestion and excess demand may be thought to be a problem solely of the industrialized world, but this may not prove to be the case in tourism. For example, there are physical limits to the number of people who can have access to a given location at any one time – whether that is an ancient tomb, a natural beauty spot, a beach or an historic house. Left to market mechanisms, the solution is obvious – cause or allow the access price to rise to a point where excess demand is choked off. However, the proposition that access to desirable tourism destinations should be determined solely by the ability to pay might win few friends. Some kind of administrative limits would probably have to be imposed (countries such as New Zealand, for example, already limit access to national parks on a simple quantitative basis by setting annual visitation maxima).

The wider environmental issues implied by these problems might well turn out to be the most important influence on the future of international and domestic tourism in this new century. It is entirely conceivable that access to air transport, which has been so enormously widened in the past 30 years or so by a combination of rising wealth and falling relative prices, may soon go into reverse in some markets due to absolute limitations on transport infrastructure. While access to a national park on the sole basis of ability to pay may be unacceptable, access to international air transport on the same basis may be more acceptable, especially if seen in terms of meeting some of the costs of the negative externalities which are already part of the debate on road and private car pricing. There is much *a priori* evidence to suggest that relative travel costs may start to rise again in the coming years; if so, this would invalidate substantially some of the assumptions on which current travel forecasts are based. Continuing reductions in relative travel costs can no longer be taken for granted; it is possible that the same may apply in one form or another to access costs to leisure and tourism destinations.

The effect will be to invalidate today's tourism forecasts, and curtail tourism growth quite severely in certain regions – of which Europe is likely to be most affected. While there remains plenty of scope for vigorous tourism growth in some parts of the world – and South America seems to be the least constrained at present – in other parts the industry may well have to revise its objectives. In a nutshell, the emphasis will shift from counting numbers to assessing the net financial, economic and social benefits, including wider environmental considerations; from the business of accommodating and entertaining visitors from other countries to accommodating and entertaining visitors from and other regions of the same country.

This chapter will thus close with a few key questions to address:

- If physical and/or environmental capacity limits do arise in major destinations or in essential tourism infrastructure, how will tourism authorities deal with excess demand?
- What criteria should be applied to measure tourism's benefits?
- How can stakeholders in the tourism industry continue to produce growth?
- What policies should countries that depend on tourism for their livelihood adopt?
- Is it inevitable that international tourism will become more elitist, open in practice to a smaller percentage of the world's population than now?

References

Edwards, A. and Graham A. (1997) *International Tourism Forecasts to 2010*. London: Travel & Tourism Intelligence. (http://www.t-ti.com/publications. htm)

Peng, Li (1997) Opening address to Pacific Asia Travel Association Annual Conference, Beijing, China.

World Travel & Tourism Council (1998) *Progress & Priorities – Annual Report 1998*. London: WTTC.

World Tourism Organization On-line Statistical Database Service, World Tourism. WTO. (http://www.world-tourism.org/wtich.htm)

World Tourism Organization (1999) *Tourism Highlights 1999*, Revised preliminary estimates. Madrid: WTO.

2

The world of today and tomorrow: the global view

Marvin Cetron

During the past decade, the tourism and hospitality industry flourished, even as it struggled to cope with difficult challenges. This is a taste of things to come. In the years ahead, the global population will continue to grow and change, science and technology will tighten their hold on business and society, and the world will knit itself ever more tightly into a single market. As a result, both opportunities and trials will abound.

In general, I am optimistic about the next ten years. The global economy may be troubled, but it remains fundamentally sound. The recent economic union of Europe, evidence that Japan at last may be willing to address its financial troubles effectively, and many other indicators suggest that it will be even stronger in the future, and thus that the demand for tourism and hospitality will grow. Yet a number of issues are crucial to the world's future. Three stand out:

- Japan's economic crisis clearly is not over. A healthy Japan will spur global trade, while a crippled one could drag at the world's economy for years. It now appears that Japan has begun a solid recovery that dogged it for most of the 1990s. I believe that necessary reforms in banking and business practices will continue and that the current improvement will begin another long period of growth for Japan.
- Russia's economy is the second imponderable. Moscow must find some way to pay its military, to support its pensioners, and to pay the coal miners who keep the nation alive in the harsh Russian winter. And it must do so without creating money at a level that would trigger uncontrolled inflation. Thus far, it reels from one crisis to the next, staying on its feet only with the help of international lenders. Russia will be looking for no less than $50 billion over the next few years from the International Monetary Fund. I believe that this situation will improve only slowly, but I do believe that it will improve.
- Finally, Brazil must set its economic house in order. If Brazil can achieve slow, steady growth, the Latin market should provide a much-needed boost for world trade. If not, it could be the final straw for a troubled global economy. The International Monetary Fund is giving the government money to cover Brazil's $67 billion debt. Again, I believe this task of economic reform is well in hand.

Overall, I feel reasonably confident that these potential problems will be solved, and I have made my forecasts accordingly. However, the course of the next years depends heavily on how successfully Japan, Russia, and Brazil solve their current problems. Anyone with even a passing interest in the future must follow events in these lands closely.

With this caveat in mind, what follows is a summary of the most important forces I now see at work in the world. Whatever else happens, these trends will shape the environment in which the world's tourism and hospitality industry will prosper in the next 20 years.

Increasing affluence in the developed world

In the developed world for at least the next five years, widespread affluence, low interest rates, low inflation and low unemployment will be the norm. Real per capita income in the United States is rising at its strongest rate in decades. At the same time, wages and benefits have remained under control, consumer inflation was less than 2% in 1999, and as a result, long-term interest rates in the US are among the lowest since 1977.

GDP of the EU15 will continue to expand for the foreseeable future. National debts were brought under control throughout much of Europe when countries there prepared for monetary union. Establishment of a common currency among most EU member states will continue to stimulate trade within Europe. Relaxation of borders within the European Union should bring new mobility to the labour force and make for a more efficient business environment in Europe.

Japanese banks are finally writing off their bad debts and merging the nation's 800 banks into four banking groups. Thereafter, Japan should provide a much healthier trading partner for both the US and Europe. This will also shore up other beleaguered Asian economies, as Japan provides 50% of the money loaned to its neighbours. In all, 70% of the 'Asian flu' is related to Japan.

Many nations of the former Soviet Union are bringing order to their economies. As they do so, they are proving to be very viable markets for goods from Western Europe.

Implications for tourism and hospitality

Global travel will continue to grow rapidly for at least the next 20 years. Worldwide international arrivals are growing from 660 million in 1999 to an estimated 700 million in 2000, 1 billion by 2010 and 1.6 billion by 2020. Improving balance of trade means more business for European and Asian tourist destinations. Europe will remain the strongest magnet for tourism, with arrivals growth holding between 3% and 4% annually.

Low Asian currency values will continue to promote travel to the Far East, for so long as they last. Growth of the new middle and wealthy classes in Russia and other former Eastern bloc lands has created a profitable new market for vacation and business travel to the West. Demand from this quarter should grow for many years to come.

Technology dominates the economy and society

Discovery grows exponentially, as each new finding today opens the way to many more tomorrow. Thus the single greatest force for change in the 20th century can only grow more powerful in the 21st. The only factor slowing this process will be a shortage in trained, creative scientists, engineers and technicians to exploit all the opportunities available to us – and technologies such as computers and the Internet are reducing the impact of even that basic handicap. Advances such as more powerful computers, robotics and CAD/ CAM directly affect the way people live and work. Information appliances that combine a computer, fax, duplicator and telephone – with automatic language translation functions – with a large, flat screen will usher in the truly global economy.

The World Future Society identified ten technologies as most important for the next ten years: genetic mapping, super materials, high-density energy sources, digital high-definition television, miniaturization, smart manufacturing, anti-ageing products and services, medical treatments, hybrid-fuel vehicles, and 'edutainment'.

Robots will soon do mundane commercial and service jobs. Net connections, and soon satellite-based portable telephone systems, simplify relocation, speed new installations and ease communication with distant personnel.

Biotechnology offers the prospect of wholly new foods. Witness the 'quicken,' a transgenic hybrid of quail and chicken, high-protein trout, ultra-lean meats, and coffee beans 'naturally' low in caffeine, all proposed for future development by genetic engineers. Disease-resistant crops, crush-proof tomatoes and other such products already are making their way to market. 'Nutraceuticals', food products formulated or genetically engineered to combat stress, provide specific nutrition, or prevent or cure disease, will be the fastest growing new product area in the next 15 years.

Implications for tourism and hospitality

As technology knits the world into one electronic marketplace, business travel will not decline, but will grow rapidly. In a high-tech world, executives increasingly need the 'high-touch' (press the flesh) reassurance of personal relationships with their colleagues. The Internet changes the way consumers purchase goods and services. Cashless credit/debit systems of payment will continue to proliferate. Expect the use of 'smart cards' to provide detailed customer information for use in more efficient target marketing. Resorts, conference centres and other destinations are finding it increasingly easy to market themselves directly to consumers, rather than relying on intermediaries. So will air charter services and other transportation providers.

Travellers are also buying their airline seats and hotel rooms on the Internet, sometimes bidding for them through online auction services such as price-line.com. Over the next five years, this will sharply reduce the number of travel agencies required, as Generations X and .COM increasingly make their own reservations online. Tourism will benefit as video – and eventually Internet 'movies' – replace printed brochures in promoting vacation destinations. Programs include current, detailed information on accommodations, climate, culture, currency, language, immunization and passport requirements.

The Internet makes it possible for small businesses throughout the world to compete for market share on an even footing with industry leaders.

The population of the developed world is living longer

In the developed countries, healthier diets, more exercise, the decline of smoking in the United States and the trend toward preventive medicine are extending later life. Life expectancies in Japan are entering the nineties, and those in parts of Europe are not far behind. Medical advances could well help present-day middle-aged Baby Boomers to live far longer than can be predicted even today.

The elderly population is growing fastest throughout the developed world. In Europe, the United States and Japan the aged also form the wealthiest segment of society. These 21st century old folks are much healthier and more active than the elderly of previous generations. At the same time, nostalgia also is a strong influence on them. Many older people still want to indulge in the same activities and entertainment they enjoyed in their youth, and they now have more disposable income to spend on them.

Implications for tourism and hospitality

With above average wealth and relatively few demands on their time, the elderly will make up an ever-larger part of the tourist and hospitality market. This industry will prosper by catering to their needs for special facilities and services. More retirees will travel off-season, tending to equalize travel throughout the year and eliminate the cyclical peaks and valleys typical of the industry. Resorts that combine extra comforts for the elderly with an adventure-vacation theme will be in especially high demand.

Time is becoming the world's most precious commodity

Forecasters once imagined that computers would make it possible to cut the working week and give us more leisure. Instead, the opposite has happened. Companies have cut employee rosters, often dramatically, leaving more work to be done by fewer people. Rising costs and stagnant wages have driven former stay-at-homes into the labour force. Entrepreneurs, whose numbers are growing rapidly in the United States and have begun to expand elsewhere, work even longer hours than the rest of us. Time that once would have been spent shopping and taking care of household chores is now spent in factories and offices, and leisure is becoming ever more scarce. There is no sign that this trend will slow in the near future.

In the United States, workers spend about 10% more time at work than they did a decade ago. European executives and other non-unionized workers face the same trend. On average, two-thirds of European women from age 25 to 59 work outside the home. This sharply reduces the time available to them for cooking, cleaning and other household tasks. In this high-pressure environment, single workers and double-income couples are increasingly desperate for any product that offers to simplify their lives or grant them a taste of luxury.

Implications for tourism and hospitality

Brand names associated with high quality come to seem even more desirable, especially far from home. Two-earner households especially want and can afford the small satisfactions of buying what they perceive to be 'the best'. Small, affordable luxuries, such as hotel restaurant meals, increasingly are substituted for absent leisure.

Multiple, shorter vacations spread throughout the year will continue to replace the traditional two-week vacation. Demand for luxurious 'weekend getaways' will grow rapidly, especially in cultural centres and at destinations nearest large cities.

Values and lifestyles are changing

Technology brings new opportunities, but conflicts with tradition. Telecommunications bring news from around the globe. Western ideas infiltrate conservative cultures in Asia and the Middle East, often triggering a 'fundamentalist' backlash. These and many other pressures are eroding the values and lifestyles of previous generations. In their place, a new, opportunistic, technology-oriented eclecticism is beginning to appear throughout the developed world, among the intellectual and economic elites of some developing nations, and especially among the under-40 generations.

Consumer needs are changing under this pressure. For business and pleasure, international and intercontinental travel and tourism are becoming a normal part of life for most well-to-do workers and their families. Growing numbers of adults say their lives are too stressful, so convenience and a relaxing atmosphere will be the order of the day.

Implications for tourism and hospitality

The trend is toward ultra-high quality, authenticity and convenience—luxurious accommodations, fresh meals that seem like labours of love, and constant pampering of customers – all done at a price that will not make consumers feel guilty.

Two-income couples increasingly take several short, relatively luxurious weekend getaways rather than a single longer vacation.

Older, wealthier travellers also fly business class in preference to coach, but save money by travelling in off-peak periods and at odd hours. Unlike members of Generations X and .COM, who are relatively tolerant of impersonal service, however, they want to feel that they are recognized (especially if they are repeat customers) and respected. Xers could almost be addressed by their credit-card number; older patrons appreciate being addressed by name, as 'Mr' or 'Mrs'.

Life-long learning will become essential

Technology and communications are rapidly changing the way we live. New discoveries in science build at an exponential rate, while consumer products based upon them proliferate even more rapidly. Within a few years, new technologies create entire new industries, while the industries they replace wither and disappear. As a result, members of the generation now entering the labour force can expect to have an average of five entirely separate careers before their working days are over. At each new turning, our old skills become obsolete, and we are forced to learn anew. In the high-tech industries, this is already a fact of daily life: we work at one job while preparing for the next, which may be wholly unrelated to our previous experience. Over the next decade, this demand will affect everyone who hopes for a career of more than unskilled labour.

Implications for tourism and hospitality

New technology will greatly improve life-long learning. Video conferencing, probably based on the Internet and on corporate intranets, will make it possible to train and monitor workers at locations around the world. Large chains can use Net-based education to ensure product quality and uniformity by giving chefs and other personnel at the front and back of the house the same training around the world.

In the United States, corporations such as Motorola, IBM, Arthur Andersen and McDonald's have opened their own 'universities' to ensure that employees remain current with state-of-the-art technologies and business practices. Other industry leaders may wish to adopt this practice to help them remain competitive.

Concern for environmental issues continues to grow

As rain forests disappear and evidence of global warming builds, it is becoming ever more difficult to ignore our impact on nature – and its impact on us. At this point, the question is not whether we will change our industries and lifestyles to accommodate the environment, but how radically we must change, how quickly we must act, and how much it will cost us. This will not be an easy transition. As the United States continues to resist changes that could retard its economy and Third World countries assert their right to the same energy-consuming, polluting luxuries the West has long enjoyed, the controversy over environmental issues can only grow in the years to come.

Topics for attention include air pollution, acid rain, loss of forests, depletion of the ozone layer, waste disposal, toxic chemicals in our food and water, soil erosion, mass extinction of species and pollution of beaches, oceans, reservoirs and waterways.

Concern for the indoor environment will spread. New regulations will control the quality of indoor air, the effect of building materials, asbestos and radon gas.

Implications for tourism and hospitality

Demands for still more environmental controls are inevitable, especially in relatively pristine regions. 'Ecotourism' will continue to be one of the fastest growing areas of the tourism industry. The increasing dominance of high technology in our daily lives also promotes this trend. Rain forests, wilderness areas, the ocean, and other unpolluted regions provide a unique and necessary chance to escape from keyboards and cell phones.

Recycling, air quality, waste disposal, kitchen safety and other aspects of the workplace environment will be increasingly regulated and will require greater management attention and investment.

Generations X and '.COM' will have major effects in the future

There are approximately 50 million people in Europe between the ages of 15 and 24. Another 30 million are between 25 and 29. The under-30 cohort represents about 22% of the European population. They have grown up with computers, mass media and advanced telecommunications. As a result, their values often differ sharply from those of their Baby-Boom parents. They will present unique and difficult challenges for both marketers and employers in the years ahead.

The under-20 cohort is remaining in school longer and taking longer to enter the workforce than before. The age at which at least half of young Europeans either have a job or are seeking one rose from 18 in 1987 to 20 in 1995. EU-wide, 59% of all 18-year-olds in 1995 were exclusively in education or training. The number varied from 27% in the UK to 88% in Belgium.

Generation X should be renamed 'Generation E', for entrepreneurial. Throughout the world, they are starting new businesses at an unprecedented rate. Twice as many say they would prefer to own a business as opposed to being a top executive. Five times more would prefer to own a business rather than hold a key position in politics or government.

They have little or no loyalty to their employers, to their bosses, to established political parties, or even to branded products. They are extremely sceptical of all claims, and especially those of large institutions, whether in politics or in business. Compared with the Baby-Boom generation, they can be a marketer's nightmare. Perhaps as a result, they are extremely experimental, willing to try new products, foods, and attractions, but rarely patient enough to give a second chance to less-than-stellar offerings.

Implications for tourism and hospitality

Generations X and .COM will be major customers for tourism and hospitality services in the future and the industry will have to learn to market to them. This requires a light hand, with strong emphasis on information and quality. Brands credibly positioned as 'affordable luxury' will prosper.

They also will be the industry's future employees. This is both the good news and the bad. They are well equipped for work in an increasingly high-tech world, but have little interest in their employers' needs and no job loyalty at all. They also have a powerful urge to do things their way.

Institutions are undergoing a bimodal distribution

In one industry after another, the big get bigger, thanks to economies of scale. The small prospers by providing high levels of service in niche markets. The middle-sized, lacking either advantage, are either squeezed out or absorbed by larger competitors. This has been the single most powerful trend in business for the past 20 years, and the consolidation has yet to run its course. This trend is seen among hotels, retail stores, restaurants, private banks, hospitals, airlines and many other industries.

Implications for tourism and hospitality

Few companies, if any, are too large to be potential take-over targets. Hotel industry consolidation will be fastest in Europe, the Middle East and the Pacific Rim and Third World countries, where market-share leaders own less than 3%, 2% and 1% of rooms, respectively.

US corporations, blessed with record profits and easy access to capital, will be among the busiest players in the global acquisitions game.

Service, service, service replaces location, location, location

Competitive pressures are making it ever more difficult to distinguish one hotel or chain from the rest, especially at the level of the global chains. As soon as one offers a product or service that attracts customers, its competitors match it and try to improve upon it. The result is a generally high standard in basic products and services. Increasingly, what distinguishes one provider from another is attention to detail. This is the battleground on which hotels and restaurants will fight the competitive wars of the early 21st century.

Personal service and attention to detail set the best hotels, restaurants and resorts apart from the rest.

Implications for tourism and hospitality

Unique locations or facilities are the major exception to 'commoditization' in the tourism and hospitality industries. The only inn at a major ski resort has no effective competition. The alternative is for hotels to become destinations in themselves, known for luxurious surroundings, fine food, special amenities for repeat visitors, and the best possible service.

As customers grow more open to new experiences, unique facilities and attractions, cuisines offer a growing opportunity for hotels and tourist destinations to distinguish themselves from the competition.

3

The world of today and tomorrow: the European picture

Michael Willmott and Sarah Graham

Introduction: the travel industry in Europe

Europe's domestic and inbound travel and tourism industry is a vital and dynamic part of its economy. As an industry it is particularly responsive to cyclical economic change and consumer volatility, and is affected by the dual pincer effects of globalization. On the one hand, consumers have become increasingly sophisticated, with higher expectations. Lured by lower prices, they are increasingly looking to more exotic destinations. On the other, international players are taking advantage of liberalized markets and the lower transaction costs new technology has brought to move into Europe in order to escape their own mature, saturated markets. Less economically favoured regions are under particular threat, given their dependence on the sector.

ıle as an engine of growth for employment is not in question – the
y accounts directly and indirectly for 200 million jobs world-wide –
, 8% of total employment, with an additional 5.5 million jobs a year
st to be created until 2010[1] – but many jobs created are temporary,
seasonal and part-time. Women are disproportionately represented in employment in this sector, so collectively more at risk if it weakens.

Small and Medium Sized Enterprises (SMEs) are strongly represented
among travel and tourism companies in Europe, and contribute to the sector's
rich diversity – and fragmentation. They are frequently undercapitalized and
with a rudimentary or non-existent information technology infrastructure.

The travel industry and technology: current status

It used to be the case that for business and domestic purposes, Europe lagged
behind the United States both in penetration and sophistication of technology.
If we generalize greatly, it is tempting to say that Europe now only lags on
penetration – global distribution systems, for example, are as sophisticated the
world over – and that, even here, Europe is catching up. But this generalization
masks an unequal picture if we apply it to the tourism sector in Europe:

- There are technology 'haves' and 'have-nots' across the board – large and
  small companies, north and south.
- Larger companies tend to have more of their internal processes automated,
  while having uneven use of IT for their external communications.
- Micro businesses, when they embrace technology, do so with great zeal
  and often to great effect, recognizing that new technology can create a
  'level playing field' for the smaller company, providing an 'open all hours'
  professional interface at a low cost and offering access to a global marketplace.
- Many niche players reason that their current client bases are not in the
  consuming segments which use new technology in any case.

Travel and hospitality: drivers for change

To understand the drivers of change in the travel and tourism industry in the
future, we should first understand the changes in consumers' lives and
the changing ways in which they are prepared to do business. Consumers
are becoming more affluent and they are increasingly cosmopolitan in their
consumption and experience. (According to recent research by the Future
Foundation, in 1999 39% of respondents said they felt closer to people

of their own national background, as opposed to 60% in 1979.) With this in mind, in the following sections we concentrate on those wider changes in consumer behaviour and lifestyles which we think will most heavily impact the travel and hospitality industry in the years to come:

- Demographic shifts: an ageing population.
- Technology.
- Changes in working patterns.
- Time pressure.
- Changing modes of consumption in the travel and hospitality industry.

Demographic shifts: an ageing population

In Europe the population is increasing and ageing. By 2011 there will be an additional 2.8 million consumers in Britain, but the proportion of younger people has been steadily declining for years.

The travel industry will be obliged to take into account this structural shift in the population – not just with specialist services for the infirm elderly, since in the near future many of us will be hale and hearty well into our eighties and nineties. The whole area of travel motivation will shift – with increasing numbers of elderly travellers, the proportion of travel for visiting friends and relatives will grow. This shift will almost by definition increase the number of travellers who are flexible and who have the time and patience to seek out the best deals. It might well blunt the edges of seasonality, with travellers taking advantage of off-peak prices and milder weather conditions in many traditional sunshine resorts.

The travel industry customarily relies upon the services of young employees and as a sector will find itself impacted heavily by this demographic change. Already grappling with the implications of the minimum wage, it will have to face the challenge of taking on a larger number of older workers who may expect greater remuneration, and who may not be prepared to work unsocial shifts.

Technology

Technology penetration

Perhaps the single most important element in the future of the travel and tourism experience will be the impact of technology across the distribution

31

and delivery chain. Across the board, consumers' access to technology is increasing and as prices plummet, this trend will deepen. The Future Foundation forecasts that by 2010, 80% of UK households[2] will have access to interactive TV via PC or set-top box. This means that all but the most technologically excluded, including the very poorest in society, will have access to on-line booking and the means to search for cheap deals and consume advertising messages.

Consumers already venture onto the Net to purchase airline tickets in substantial numbers. Industry sources estimate that 11% of all world-wide transactions in 1998 were travel related, and that this will leap to 35% by 2002, with some 4 million Europeans shopping online by this year, creating a European travel market worth 6.4 billion Euros, up from 155 million (£99.7 million) in 1998.[3]

Willingness to use technology to conduct travel-related searches and transactions

The number of travel and tourism websites is booming and there are many on- and off-line information sources to help travellers navigate in real and cyber space. Consumers are in favour of a seamless automated process, which would enable them to obtain information about a holiday, and book tickets and accommodation at one go. The younger the consumer, the more enthusiastic they are about this possibility, with 74% of 15–24-year-olds agreeing they would find it interesting to be able to organize a complete trip on the Internet.[4]

The implications for travel agencies and other intermediaries

As Simon Calder says, 'The Internet does something much more profound than simply allowing me to book a ticket by pressing a few keys: it empowers me as a traveller by revealing many of the secrets of yield management'.[5]

The threat to the agency business – and any other intermediary – is very real. Travellers already clearly regard air tickets as a commodity purchase, involving an undervalued skill in seeking out the cheapest and most appropriate deals. But exhaustive web searches take time and patience and it is often only the most flexible travellers who can take advantage of the very cheapest seats.

In this area, as in many other industries, we imagine that we may see a more pronounced polarization of the offer, from the very cheapest 'no-frills' basic service provision to a more sophisticated selection process. Thus enabling consumers to take better-informed decisions at a price that takes account of the value of the service and information element. The trade-off between consumers' time – in seeking out offers and conducting negotiations – and money, in the form of the potential discounts obtainable, will nowhere be more transparent.

Business travellers on the Web

Corporate business travellers, whose itineraries are at the same time more complex and less flexible than those of leisure travellers, are less likely to switch wholesale to Internet searches on a regular basis, despite the potential savings. Toyota's travel purchasing manager, for example, has gone the direct route of negotiating discounts at source with the airlines, on the basis of an understanding of the company's travel patterns and needs, rather than seeking to save a few dollars here and there on each flight by dint of diligent *ad hoc* surfing.[6]

Business and leisure travel and 'remote' technology

We have seen that the advent of videoconferencing and other related technologies has not at a stroke decimated business travel – instead, they have forced a reappraisal of the reasons *why* we should travel instead of doing business remotely. E-mail and videoconferencing allow us to avoid some of the time-consuming trips we used to undertake in the past, while thrusting a greater resonance onto those trips we do continue to take. The advent of cheap webcams – now included free in some home PC packages – will allow us to see our friends and family via the Internet in real time for the cost of a local telephone call. At the same time we know that more and more travellers are taking trips abroad with the purpose of visiting friends and family, and we find it hard to imagine that these might be diminished by the technical capacity to see small, jerky images on a screen.

Just as the telephone failed to sound the death knell for the travel industry, but instead spurred an increase in travel by fostering personal and commercial networks, we feel that fears voiced about the possible adverse impact of new technology will prove to be largely unfounded. Indeed, increased 'remote' contact may well inspire more face-to-face trips. Casa Rovira,[7] a small family-run hotel in Tarragona, Spain, reports an interesting mixture of the effects of demographic change and the consumer technology revolution. An Internet listing enables potential visitors from around the world to consider a visit to Casa Rovira as a possibility when planning and booking forthcoming visits to Europe using the Internet. Many of these travellers were older than the usual customer base – but stayed longer, spent more and tended to arrive when the weather was milder, leading to a welcome extension of the normal working season by a month at each end.

Changes in working patterns

Self-employment and small firms

The proportion of people working as self-employed is set to increase over the next few years, with a forecast 4.25 million in the UK by 2005.[8] Recent research conducted by the Future Foundation suggests that this might be a conservative estimate. Substantial proportions of younger consumers say they would like to become self-employed or run their own business in the future, and of these nearly half say that they intend to do so within the next five years.[9] In parallel, the growth of the smallest firms has increased at the expense of medium-sized firms.

The self-employed, or those running small businesses, will have different travel requirements to those travellers working for a multinational. Their trips to gain new business will be speculative and therefore largely self-funded. The prestige conferred by high-grade travel when one is within a large organization and hierarchical niceties prevail will be undermined by the principle of having to justify costs from a personal budget. Few small businesses will be able to resist shifting a meeting by a few hours to qualify for a £100 saving for each of the staff members involved. The sharing of information with the customer empowers them to exploit systems that were previously concealed. Every business travel provider – whether offering rail, car rental or accommodation – ignores that at their peril.[10]

Self-employment offers the flexibility to take time away from work – in theory, at least, though we know that many of those in the first phase of establishing a business work longer hours. Once the business is established and has a management structure in place, there is no obstacle to taking extended periods of leave, or to combining work travel with a leisure element. The distinction between home and work is becoming increasingly blurred by taking work home and having access to the office via e-mail and the Internet, not to mention the mobile phone, 24 hours a day. We know that some 15% of consumers frequently work from home, accessing work systems via a modem, with over 50% agreeing that they sometimes work from home. In the same way, we think the distinction between work time and holiday time will increasingly become eroded.

Women workers

The proportion of women in the labour force has reached 48%, largely due to more women returning to work sooner after childbirth – if indeed they have children. This is a huge change in social terms, but only a limited number of hotel and travel companies have accounted for women's differential requirements when travelling abroad for business. We forecast a more widespread broadening of the offer, with specialized women's rooms *without* trouser presses, but with more appropriate facilities.

Time pressure

The desire to be transported

For many consumer groups – particularly working women – there is an acute sense of time pressure. The importance of 'time off' to individuals whose daily lives are full of routine, stress and obligation is easy to underestimate – and yet for many the process of booking and planning for a holiday is daunting and exhausting in itself.

We see an opportunity for travel service providers to offer a seamless, stress-free service, the objective of which is a totally relaxing experience. All potentially vexing decisions, such as destination, are taken out of the hands of the travellers, leaving them to concentrate instead on choosing their holiday reading list. While this may sound routine for the excessively wealthy and pampered, we feel that if such a service were offered at a price comparable to that of an activity holiday, there would be enthusiastic take-up.

Changing modes of consumption in the travel and hospitality industry

Further destinations, greater expectations, more specialization

We are travelling more often – and further afield, according to reviews of travel patterns. In recent years we have witnessed the 'democratization' of many

35

increasingly exotic destinations, whose price once rendered them out of reach of the mass market; this in turn has widened the gap between the experience of the independent traveller and the more 'passive' mainstream travel consumer. We expect to see this pattern deepening, with those determined to plough their own furrow turning to ever more exotic locations and ever more specialized pastimes in order to have an out-of-the-ordinary experience.

Specialization is the new watchword across the industry, too, with companies offering activities and accommodation to suit any demographic segment, pocket or inclination. There is a move towards holidays with an educational element – learning to cook in an Irish manor house, for instance, or in a Tuscan villa, improving one's creative writing on a Greek island. Motels for singles, for women travellers and for the older traveller are already commonplace, and we imagine that as ever more defined niche segments are able to identify kindred spirits via the Internet, then this in turn will create demand in the travel and hospitality sector.

Polarization of prices

As consumer affluence increases, we are seeing an interesting paradox emerging: that of the polarization of the offer between the most basic provision and the most extravagant. This is plainest in the hotel sector, as well as in the emerging war between low-cost airlines and their standard rivals. In late 1999, as British Airways conceded the damage done to its profits by Go, its low-cost subsidiary, and KLM recognized its inability to beat the low cost offers to Amsterdam and so decided it might as well join them, it was clear that the story was only just beginning. It is worth noting that while only 5% of passenger journeys are accounted for by low cost airlines in Europe, in the United States, where the phenomenon is more established, this figure is as high as 25%.

We have mentioned that the self-employed and those travelling under their own steam, for whom cost is an issue, have embraced the new offers with gratitude. But there are other motivations: consumers feel disgruntled at the prospect of full-price fares now that they have seen that it is possible for airlines to operate cheaply and well on much lower tariffs.

At the same time, airlines are struggling to justify their top fares with ever more luxurious and personal services to their highest-paying customers. When an economy class fare to Los Angeles from London Heathrow can cost as little as £200, the normal business class fare is twenty-five times that. Virgin Atlantic prides itself on its personal attention and indulgent services that it claims make their Upper Class travellers feel that the difference is worth it.

In the hotel sector, too, we have seen the same divergence: the Travelodge chain has burgeoned in the UK, with their no-frills, no extras policy. The Formule 1, Première Classe and Bonsai chains in France are a further example of this. With credit-card check-in, no mini bar or room telephone, and plain, decent, basic rooms, these hotels are finding a wide clientele among travellers who want a bed for the night but little more.

The paradoxical counterpoint to this is the boom in the luxury end of the market. Designer hotels, such as St Martin's in London and boutique hotels such as the Malmaison family in the north of the UK, flaunt their award-winning restaurants and seem set up to cater for the technological needs of any business traveller.

Conclusion

Consumers' expectations are increasingly soaring – and they often bring points of reference from other sectors, particularly in the area of information provision. For this reason it is vital to understand their choice mechanisms, as well as their behaviour in other areas of consumption – how responsive are they to direct communications? How strongly do they respond to brands in the travel and hospitality industry? Is there a concept of loyalty? What is the trade-off between time and money in their buying decisions?

It is worth bearing in mind, of course, that competition for consumers' travel spend will not come from within the travel and tourism industry alone. Potential travellers may defer a customary big annual holiday in order to pay off a chunk of their mortgage, assist their children through university or upgrade their home computer, for example. In years to come, the proportion of wages to be assigned to future pension and personal welfare provision might well be much greater or we might be obliged to remain in the workforce for very many more years, given the forecasts for greater longevity we have mentioned earlier. We will have longer lives to fill and fund, and a lengthening of the customary working life may well prove to be the solution. Both these changes would have a profound impact on the travel industry, as we know it.

Keeping changing consumer lives under constant review will be the key to understanding changing patterns of consumption in the travel industry in years to come – and to offering ever-more relevant and appetizing travel and hospitality propositions.

Notes

1 WTTC, *Key Statistics*, 1999. http://www.wttc.org/economic_research/keystats.htm

2 The Future Foundation nVision Service, *Changing Lives,* 1999.

3 Jupiter Strategic Planning Services.

4 *Eurobarometer* 46.1, 1997.

5 *The Independent*, Business Travel Section, 9 November 1999.

6 *FT Business Travel Analyst*, Issue 5, September 1999.

7 http://www.wp.com/vokes-spain/casa.html.1.

8 Office for National Statistics.

9 First Direct/The Future Foundation, *What's Next? Report,* 1999.

10 *The Independent*, Business Travel Section, 9 November 1999.

4

World population and standard of living: implications for international tourism

Douglas Frechtling

Introduction

In his comprehensive review of 85 international tourism forecasting studies, Crouch (1994b) noted, 'A reading of the past research leads one to conclude that income is the single most important determinant of demand for international tourism' (p. 12). The income of the residents of a nation can affect outbound travel in two ways. First, it provides the financial resources to fund this travel, especially for leisure purposes. Second, national income is an indicator of the business activity of a nation. If income is high and rising, it is quite likely that the business activity is growing and stimulating business travel to foreign markets.

Population has been a less popular explanatory variable in international tourism forecasting studies. Crouch (1994a) found that population was employed as an explanatory variable in only 15% of the 85 international tourism demand forecasting studies he reviewed (p. 50). However, population is an appealing instrument in the tourism demand forecaster's toolkit for at least two reasons. One is that it is people who do the travelling. And just as we usually deflate economic values stated in currency terms to remove inflation, we should deflate visitor volumes over time to remove that growth due simply to more people. This is common in studies of other national economic and social variables, such as income, automobile and telephone ownership, crime and disease stated on per resident ('per capita') bases.

Second, population for most countries has the distinction of being the socio-economic variable easiest to forecast with accuracy over the medium to long term: for 80% or more of all the people expected to be living a decade hence are already born. Demographers usually know a great deal about trends in birth rates and mortality rates by age, so that the number of people in each age cohort can be forecast ten years or so out with a relatively high degree of accuracy.

In this study, I investigate what past fluctuations in national income (represented by countries' real GDPs) and population sizes and structures can reveal about outbound travel from 20 countries. The intent is to discover relationships that can be used to forecast long-haul visitor volumes from these countries to 2010. These forecasts are necessarily long-term trends rather than annual point estimates. A host of other explanatory factors often push a country's outbound travel volumes off their long term trends for brief periods of time (e.g. Frechtling, 1996, p. 135).

Purpose and use

This chapter reports on efforts to discern the impact of population and income trends on outbound international travel over the past decade, in order to indicate trends in the first decade of the new millennium. Time series on outbound long-haul international travel from 20 countries, population trends by age grouping and real Gross Domestic Product (GDP) are analysed over the 1989–98 period to suggest major relationships among these variables. Projections of population by age group and real GDP for these countries are then used to project outbound international long-haul travel for these countries to 2010. Finally, some conclusions are drawn about the future of long-haul international travel.

To my knowledge, informed by extensive literature reviews by Crouch (1994a, 1994b) and Witt and Witt (unpublished paper, 1992, pp. 16–29), no published studies have investigated the change in individual age cohorts as an explanatory factor in international travel demand. The present study, then, is exploratory, providing the results of an initial investigation of these variables to aid understanding of international travel demand.

This study should be of interest to marketers planning where to devote their resources to develop visitor markets from an array of origin countries. The findings herein could be used in a two-stage model of inbound visitor forecasting suggested by Smeral (1998). In the first stage, the total volume of outbound visitors or visitor spending is estimated for major originating countries. In the second stage, the distribution of this outbound tourism among destination countries is estimated, based on marketing expenditures, relative prices, air fares, exchange rates, etc.

Finally, this study should provide additional intelligence on a tourism generating factor largely ignored in tourism demand literature: the age structure of national populations. The world's rate of population growth is declining, and the inhabitants of this planet are collectively growing older. The volume of residents of some countries has already begun to decline, with more countries projected to enter these ranks in the decade ahead.

Definitions and base data

I employ here the definitions of international travel adopted by the United Nations Statistical Commission in 1993 in response to the World Tourism Organization's (WTO) report on tourism statistics (UN/WTO, 1994, p. v) In this system of classification, the central statistical unit is the 'visitor'. 'International visitor' is defined as 'any person who travels to a country other than that in which he/she has his/her usual residence but outside his/her usual environment for a period not exceeding 12 months and whose main purpose of visit is other than the exercise of an activity remunerated from within the country visited' (UN/WTO, 1994, p. 29). By extension, the terms 'international trip' or 'international visit' describe any travel to a place outside the country in which the visitor resides (UN/WTO, 1994, p. 42).

This report focuses on the 'outbound' visitors a country generates, that is, the number of trips recorded by residents of the country under study to all other countries of the world (UN/WTO, 1994, p. 11). Outbound travel is further classified by the spatial extent of the international trip. 'Long-haul' is used to indicate that an outbound visitor has travelled to one or more countries outside the multi-country region in which the visitor lives as defined by the World Tourism Organization (Travel Industry Association of America,

1999, p. 47). Complementarily, 'short-haul' indicates outbound travel by the residents of a country to other countries within the same region, as defined by the WTO. 'Total outbound' travel is the sum of long-haul outbound travel and short-haul outbound travel from a country (1999, p. 47).

All estimates of long-haul visitors for each of 20 generating countries used in this study were derived from the most recent Travel Industry Association of America report (1999), covering the years 1989–98. Note that these visitors/trips are computed as the residences reported by visitors to each receiving country as compiled by the WTO. Since a given international visitor may visit two or more countries on a single trip, the total outbound estimates for individual generating countries used in this study are likely to exceed the estimates of outbound visitors or trips reported by the countries of visitors' residences. The aggregate of outbound trips by residents of these 20 countries comprised over 62% of total world arrivals in 1998.

'Gross Domestic Product' (GDP) is defined as 'equal to the total gross expenditure on the final uses of the domestic supply of goods and services valued at purchasers' values less imports of goods and services valued c.i.f.' (Organisation for Economic Co-operation and Development, 1999, p. 7). It is thus a standard measure of the net output of goods and services within the political borders of a country. This study employs annual estimates of 'real' GDP for the 20 countries analysed published by the OECD at 1990 prices and exchange rates (Organisation for Economic Co-operation and Development, 1999, p. 138) for the years 1989 through 1997. The 1997 GDP estimates were updated to 1998 for each country by the figures provided to the author by the WEFA Group. GDP represents national income herein, since it is also the sum of incomes to all factors of production residing within the country's borders.

Estimates of each country's total population and population by three major age groups were collected from the US Bureau of the Census International Data Base as listed on the Internet at http://www.census.gov/ggi-bin. The data for Canada were incomplete, so the author obtained these population estimates from Statistics Canada at www.statcan.ca/datawarehouse/cansim/cansim.cgi.

The WTO database published by TIA includes data on the 20 countries listed in Table 4.1 with their WTO regions. The only exception to this convention is that while Israel is included by WTO in the Europe region, in this study, long-haul trips comprise those visits to countries outside WTO's Middle East region. The 'economic status' of the country is as provided by the World Tourism Organization's Compendium of Tourism Statistics (WTO, 1999).

Table 4.1 Countries included in the present study by WTO region and economic status

Generating country	WTO region	Economic status
Argentina	South America	Developing
Australia	East Asia/Pacific	Industrialized
Belgium	Europe	Industrialized
Brazil	South America	Developing
Canada	North America	Industrialized
France	Europe	Industrialized
Germany	Europe	Industrialized
Israel	Middle East	Industrialized
Italy	Europe	Industrialized
Japan	East Asia/Pacific	Industrialized
Korea, Republic of	East Asia/Pacific	Developing
Mexico	North America	Developing
Netherlands	Europe	Industrialized
Spain	Europe	Industrialized
Sweden	Europe	Industrialized
Switzerland	Europe	Industrialized
Taiwan	East Asia/Pacific	Developing
United Kingdom	Europe	Industrialized
United States	North America	Industrialized
Venezuela	South America	Developing

Sources: Travel Industry Association, 1999; World Tourism Organization, 1997a, pp. 256–7

The present

Figure 4.1 presents the 1998 estimates of outbound visitors for each of the 20 generating countries.

The United States leads all countries of the world by far in current outbound long-haul visitors, supplying one-third of the total for all 20 countries. Japan and the United Kingdom form a second tier of long-haul generating countries, with Germany and France following.

As Figure 4.2 indicates, generally, outbound long-haul travel varies with the population size of the countries. However, Mexico and Brazil produce considerably fewer long-haul visitors than their populations would indicate, suggesting the impact of relatively low income and/or an extremely unequal distribution of income among residents are among factors dampening this demand. Japan, on the other hand, is producing considerably more long-haul

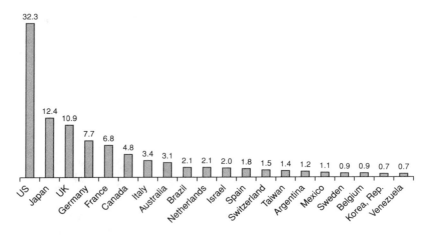

Figure 4.1 Long-haul visitors from selected countries, 1998 (millions). (*Source:* WTO)

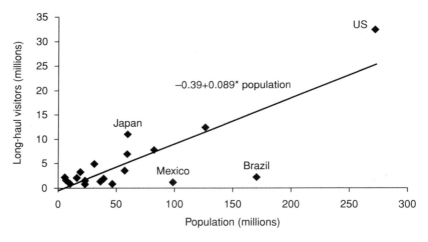

Figure 4.2 Long-haul visitors and population of selected countries, 1998. (*Source:* WTO and US Census Bureau)

visitors than its population size, suggests the effects of an island nation with a large economy and a government encouraging outbound travel. For all 20 countries in 1998, population size accounted for about 64% of the variance in long-haul visitors generated.

Figure 4.3 shows the relatively close relationship between real GDP in 1998 and volume of long-haul outbound trips. Among the countries, the United Kingdom stands out as producing considerably more long-haul visi-

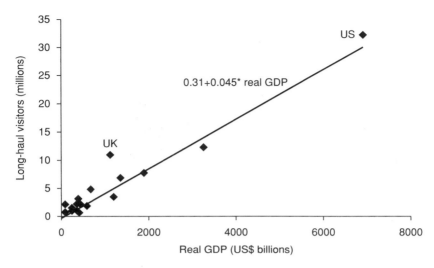

Figure 4.3 Long-haul visitors and real GDP of selected countries, 1998 (millions). (*Source:* WTO and US Census Bureau)

tors than expected given its population size. All other countries fall relatively closely to the regression line, indicating that each US$ one billion addition to a country's real GDP generated 4.5 thousand more outbound long-haul visitors during 1998. The relatively good fit reinforces the close relationship between a country's income and its outbound travel found in Crouch's study and others. Real GDP accounts for 95% of the variance on long-haul visitors generated across these 20 countries in 1998.

Of course, outbound travel among nations may vary only because resident populations differ: a large population country could be expected to produce more outbound visitors annually than a country with a small population. This relationship could obscure other factors explaining outbound visitor volumes.

Figure 4.4 ranks the 20 countries on the basis of outbound travel intensity, that is, the average number of visitors generated per resident of the country. This shows a considerably different ranking from that in Figure 4.1. Israel surpasses all other countries by far, with the industrialized nations of Switzerland, United Kingdom, Australia and Canada forming a second tier. Most of the developing nations fall at the end of this scale.

Long-haul visits per resident is a useful measure for tourism demand forecasting. It indicates how active the individual resident is in travelling abroad. Although not conclusive, the measure suggests how widespread international travel is among the population. We could expect that a larger percentage of

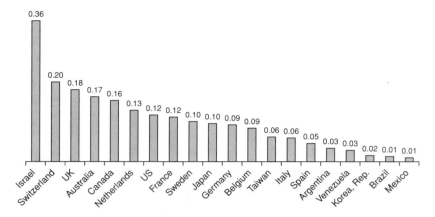

Figure 4.4 Long-haul visitors per resident for selected countries, 1998 (millions). (*Source:* WTO, US Census Bureau, author's estimates)

Israel's population travels abroad in a year than of the United States' population, for example. Destination marketers attempting to access the most productive outbound markets could expect greater success promoting to Israeli residents than to US residents as a whole.

In addition, this measure of travel intensity helps us avoid problems of multicollinearity, which plague attempts to forecast international travel (Witt and Witt, unpublished, 1992, p. 17). In regression analysis, when two or more explanatory variables are highly correlated with one another (i.e., are multicollinear), regression analysis has difficulty assigning coefficients to them, and these estimates become highly unstable, i.e., have high standard errors (Frechtling, 1996, p. 242). Population by itself is likely to be multicollinear with several other socio-economic variables of interest to the forecaster (e.g., Frechtling, 1996, p. 143). Adjusting outbound visitor volumes over space and time by population removes one source of multicollinearity in this demand forecasting. Moreover, little correlation was found between these countries' absolute long-haul visitor volumes and their intensities of this travel for 1998, indicating that the latter is a new variable that may shed light on important income and population relationships to this travel.

Figure 4.5 indicates that there is no discernible relationship between countries' population sizes and intensities of long-haul travel generated. For example, regardless of population size, the developing nations in the sample produce low long-haul travel intensities. The relatively small country of Israel produces an intensity three times that of the large USA.

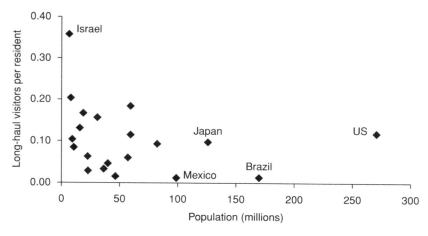

Figure 4.5 Long-haul visitor intensity and population of selected countries, 1998. (*Source:* WTO and US Census Bureau, author's estimates)

There is a weak relationship between long-haul travel intensity and real income per capita (Figure 4.6). The regression line for these 20 countries explains only about 22% of the variance in long-haul visitors per resident in 1998. The six developing countries in the sample all produced lower outbound long-haul intensities than the average for the group.

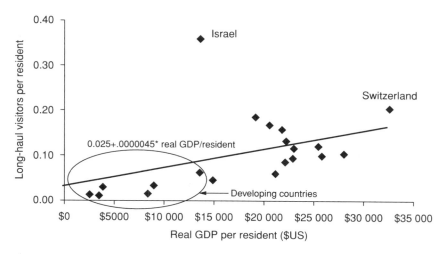

Figure 4.6 Long-haul visitors per resident and real GDP per resident for selected countries, 1998. (*Source:* WTO, US Census Bureau, author's estimates)

Age cohorts

Figure 4.7 ranks the selected countries by population size and shows the volume of residents by three age cohorts: 19 years of age and under, 20–64 years of age and 65 and older. These roughly conform to youth, working age and retired populations, respectively. The cohorts vary widely in absolute size among the nations profiled.

Figure 4.8 more clearly distinguishes the age structures of these populations by proportion, beginning with Italy with less than one-fifth of its population in the youth category, to Venezuela and Mexico, each with more than one-third. Investigations of possible relationships between the age cohorts and intensity of long-haul travel by regression analysis produced no significant relationships for these countries for 1998.

Conclusions on the present

For 1998, the following conclusions can be drawn regarding outbound long-haul travel for these 20 countries:

■ The volume of long-haul outbound visitors varies considerably, with developing nations tending to produce the smallest absolute numbers.

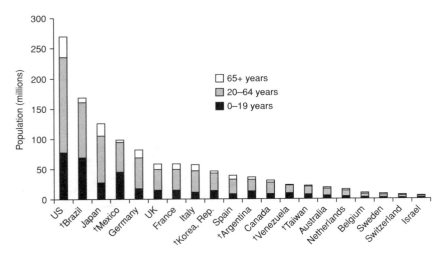

Figure 4.7 Age cohorts of resident population of selected countries, 1998: † denotes developing country. (*Source:* US Census Bureau)

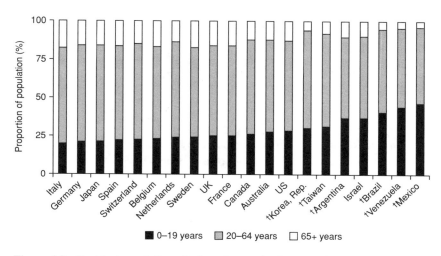

Figure 4.8 Resident population of selected countries by age cohort, 1998: † denotes developing country. (*Source:* US Census Bureau)

- There is a moderate relationship between population and number of long-haul visitors generated by a country, with developing nations tending to fall below the average for their population sizes.
- There is a stronger relationship evident between the absolute size of real income and volume of outbound long-haul visitors.
- There appears to be little relationship between the volume of long-haul visitors generated and the growth in this activity over the previous decade.
- The intensity of outbound long-haul travel generated does not vary systematically with population size, with developing countries falling below the averages for their population sizes.
- There is a weak relationship between long-haul travel intensity for the generating countries and real income per resident, with developing countries falling below the averages for their per-capita incomes.
- The relative sizes of young, middle and upper age groups vary considerably among the countries, with developing countries tending to show the highest proportions for the youngest age cohort.
- There is no discernible relationship between the age structure of a country's population and long-haul travel intensity.

These conclusions relate only to 1998. The next section analyses the changes over the past decade in these magnitudes.

The past

Trends over the past decade can further inform us of the relationships between population and national income on the one hand, and changes in outbound long-haul visitor volumes for the selected countries.

Figure 4.9 shows the growth in outbound long-haul visitors by country for the 1989–98 decade. Taiwan is the major outlier, but the developing countries of the Republic of Korea, Argentina and Venezuela also lead the sample with growth rates of 100% or more over this period. Switzerland, Australia, Sweden, Mexico and Canada lag the rest with growth rates below 50%.

There is no statistical relationship between population growth over the past ten years and growth in long-haul travel for these countries (Figure 4.10). Five of the six developing countries show faster rates of growth than their population increases would suggest. Italy's population count did not change over the 1989–98 period, yet this country still managed to double its outbound long-haul visitor volume. Clearly, something more than total population growth drove the long-haul travel increases.

Income growth is one of these driving factors. The regression trend line in Figure 4.11 explains about one-third of the variance in long-haul visitor growth over the past decade. Taiwan again dominates, even though its real GDP grew more slowly than Argentina's. Except for Taiwan, the developing countries selected followed the sample in relating long-haul travel growth to rising income.

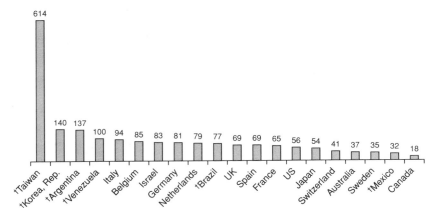

Figure 4.9 Long-haul visitor growth (%) for selected countries, 1989–98: † denotes developing country. (*Source:* WTO and author's estimates)

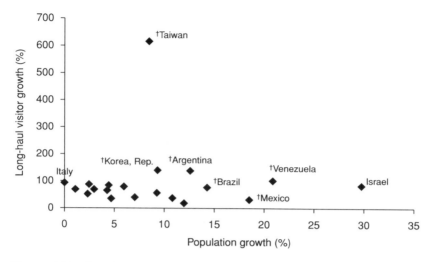

Figure 4.10 Growth in long-haul visitors and population of selected countries, 1989–98: † denotes developing country. (*Source:* WTO, US Census Bureau, author's estimates)

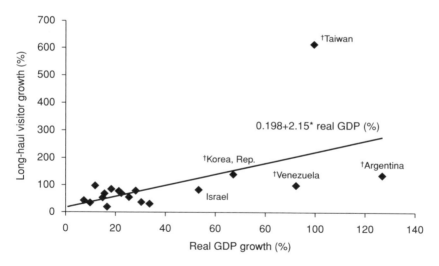

Figure 4.11 Growth in long-haul visitors and real GDP of selected countries, 1989–98: † denotes developing country. (*Source:* WTO, OECD and author's estimates)

If Taiwan is removed from the sample, the trend line accounts for nearly one-half of the variance of the 19 countries' long-haul visitor growth, but it also shifts downward to show a more moderate relationship between income growth and long-haul visitors generated (trend line becomes 0.472 + 0.724* real GDP %).

As per capita incomes rise in a country, we could expect the per capita incidence of long-haul travel to rise as well. The population is better off financially, and this should translate into additional spending on luxuries such as long-haul travel. Figure 4.12 indicates this is the case for the countries under analysis here. The regression line slopes upward and explains about one-quarter of the variance in real income per resident growth rates. In this case removing Taiwan does not appreciably increase the regression's explanatory power. Except for Venezuela and Argentina, the developing countries produced long-haul visitor growth equal or exceeding what would be expected from their income growth rates.

Population estimates by age cohort are available for the entire decade for 16 of the countries, as shown in Table 4.2. It is evident that the proportion of the total comprised by the youth cohort has fallen for most countries, and substantially for several of the underdeveloped countries and Japan. On the other hand, the proportion comprised by the retired age cohort has risen significantly for all nations but the United States, Sweden and the United Kingdom show declines.

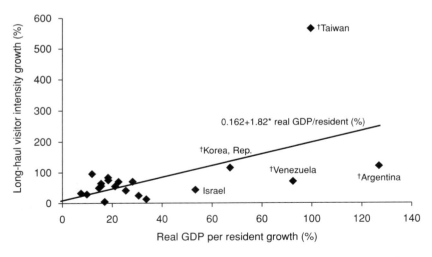

Figure 4.12 Growth in long-haul visitor intensity and real GDP per resident, 1989–98: † denotes developing country. (*Source:* WTO, OECD and author's estimates)

Table 4.2   Change in incidence of total population of three age cohorts for selected countries, 1989–98

	0–19 years (%)	20–64 years (%)	65+ years (%)
Argentina*	−4	1	11
Australia	−8	2	12
Belgium	−6	−1	14
Brazil*	−11	9	25
Canada	−5	0	13
France	−8	1	13
Israel	−9	6	7
Japan	−21	2	37
Korea, Rep. of*	−17	8	33
Mexico*	−10	11	11
Netherlands	−7	2	6
Sweden	0	1	−2
Taiwan*	−14	5	41
United Kingdom	0	0	−1
United States	−1	0	2
Venezuela*	−8	7	12

*Developing country.
Source: US Bureau of the Census

Investigation of the statistical relationships between the age cohort changes and the intensity of outbound long-haul travel for these 16 countries shows that the retired age group accounts for more than one-third of the variance in long-haul travel intensity changes over the decade. Figure 4.13 indicates the relationships. The developing nations in the sample show about the same sensitivity to the retired cohort's growth as do the rest of the selected countries.

Conclusions on the past

The analysis of changes in population, income and outbound long-haul travel over the past decade suggests the following:

■ Developing nations tended to lead the growth rates of long-haul travel.

Total population growth does not provide a very satisfactory explanation for this travel growth among the nations studied over the past decade, but developing nations produced greater growth rates in outbound long-haul visitors than their population growth rates would indicate.

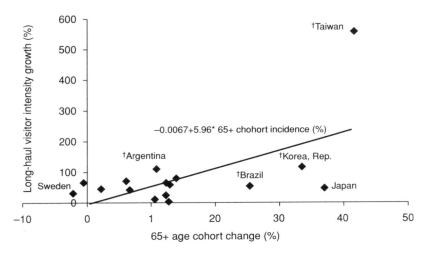

Figure 4.13 Change in long-haul visitor intensity and incidence of 65+ age cohort for selected countries, 1989–98: † denotes developing country. (*Source:* WTO, US Census Bureau and author's estimates)

- Growth in real national incomes was much more powerful in explaining long-haul visitor growth over the past decade than population growth; developing nations shared this relationship with the industrialized nations in the sample.
- The elasticity of long-haul visitor growth to income growth was about two for both absolute visitors and the intensity of long-haul travel generated by the sample.
- Two of the three age cohorts for which data are available over the past decade show no relationship to the growth in outbound long-haul travel, but the 65 and over age group did demonstrate a significant relationship.

The future

Based on these findings, various regression equations were tested to find the one that best explained the course of outbound long-haul visitors per resident for each country over the 1989–98 period. 'Best explained' was defined as the equation producing the largest coefficient of determination (R-squared) adjusted for degrees of freedom where independent variable coefficients were significantly different from zero at the 95% confidence level, and the coefficients showed reasonable signs. The last condition required ignoring equations where the relationship of long-haul travel intensity to the incidence of an age cohort in the population was negative, or where the relationship to real GDP per resident was negative.

The incidence of each of the three age cohorts in the population and real GDP per resident comprised the explanatory variables tested for each country. The impact of the Gulf War was also tested for the 1991 period and was found to be significant (at the 90% confidence level) for eight of the countries. Israel's generation of outbound long-haul travel was found to be significant for 1991 and 1992.

Table 4.3 indicates population changes over the past decade and projected to 2010 for the selected countries. Compound annual rates of change are employed for this comparison since the two time periods differ in length.

Table 4.3 Populations and rates of change for selected countries, 1989–2010

Generating country	2010 forecast (millions)	1998–10 CARC (%)	1989–98 CARC (%)
Argentina*	42.0	1.2	1.3
Australia	20.4	0.8	1.2
Belgium	10.1	−0.1	0.3
Brazil*	191.0	1.0	1.5
Canada	34.3	0.9	1.3
France	59.7	0.1	0.5
Germany	81.0	−0.1	0.5
Israel	6.7	1.4	3.0
Italy	55.3	−0.2	0.0
Japan	127.1	0.1	0.3
Korea, Rep. of*	51.2	0.8	1.0
Mexico*	118.8	1.6	1.9
Netherlands	16.2	0.3	0.6
Spain	39.2	0.0	0.1
Sweden	9.1	0.2	0.5
Switzerland	7.4	0.1	0.8
Taiwan*	24.2	0.8	0.9
United Kingdom	60.0	0.1	0.3
United States	298.0	0.8	1.0
Venezuela*	27.3	1.5	2.1
Total	1,279.0	0.6%	0.9%

CARC = compound annual rate of change.
*Developing country.
Source: US Bureau of the Census

Whereas Italy was alone in posting no increase in population in the past decade, Italy, Belgium, Germany and Spain are projected to show no growth or decline to 2010. Indeed, no country is expected to increase its resident population in the future as fast as it did in 1989–98. Even the developing countries will post significantly lower population gains in the next decade or so. Overall, population for the group will grow only two-thirds as fast as it did in the past decade.

Compound annual rates of change (CARC) in outbound long-haul visitors forecast for 1998 to 2010 are shown in Figure 4.14. The developing countries of the Republic of Korea and Taiwan are projected to lead all others in the rate that they generate these outbound trips, with Germany close behind. At the other end of the scale, Switzerland is projected to produce only negligible rises in this outbound travel over the next 12 years.

Table 4.4 summarizes the projected growth of outbound long-haul travel for each of the 20 countries selected for this study, along with comparisons of growth rates over the ensuing 12 years compared to the historical period. Compound annual rates of change are employed for this comparison since the two time periods differ in length.

For these 20 countries in aggregate, long-haul outbound travel is projected to grow to 2010 only two-thirds as fast as over the 1989–98 period. Argentina, Belgium, France, Italy, Sweden, Switzerland, Taiwan, the United States and

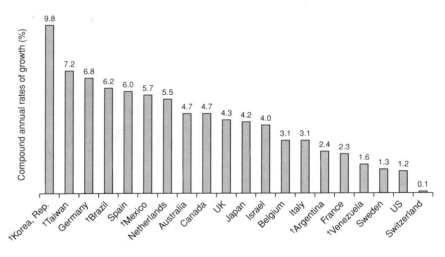

Figure 4.14   Long-haul visitors forecast rates of growth, 1998–2010: † denotes developing country. (*Source:* author's estimates)

Table 4.4   Long-haul visitors and rates of change for selected countries, 1989–2010

Generating country	2010 forecast (000)	1998–2010 CARC (%)	1989–98 CARC (%)
Argentina*	1 639	2.4	10.1
Australia	5 391	4.7	3.6
Belgium	1 249	3.1	7.1
Brazil*	4 324	6.2	6.6
Canada	8 300	4.7	1.8
France	8 874	2.3	5.7
Germany	16 933	6.8	6.8
Israel	3 229	4.0	7.0
Italy	4 925	3.1	7.7
Japan	20 138	4.2	4.9
Korea, Rep. of*	2 262	9.8	10.2
Mexico*	2 063	5.7	3.2
Netherlands	3 923	5.5	6.7
Spain	3 637	6.0	6.0
Sweden	1 076	1.3	3.4
Switzerland	1 500	0.1	3.9
Taiwan*	3 158	7.2	24.4
United Kingdom	18 002	4.3	6.0
United States	37 391	1.2	5.1
Venezuela*	814	1.6	8.0
Total	148 828	3.6%	5.5%

CARC = compound annual rate of change.
*Developing country.
Source: WTO and author

Venezuela are projected to grow at less than half their previous rates in generating long-haul visitors.

On the other hand, Australia, Canada and Mexico are forecast to grow at a faster pace than in the past, and Germany and Spain will maintain their previous rates of outbound long-haul travel growth.

It should be emphasized that these are long-term trend projections based upon the most powerful population and income explanatory variables investigated. The actual long-haul visitor totals may differ from these in 2010 due to the impact of political, economic, socio-cultural and technological variables not considered here.

No correlation was found between the projected rates of outbound long-haul visitor growth to 2010 and total population growth or absolute size of these visitors in 1998 for the 20 countries studied. However, these rates of growth are somewhat related to projected growth in real GDP for these countries, as projected by the WEFA Group. This relationship is presented in Figure 4.15 for the 16 countries for which WEFA provided estimates (missing are the developing countries of Argentina, Brazil, Republic of Korea and Venezuela). The regression line shown accounts for somewhat more than one-third of the variance of the visitor estimates.

Conclusions on the future

This forecasting exercise suggests the following about the future of long-haul visitor generation over the next 12 years:

- The volume of outbound long-haul visitors will continue to grow over the initial decade of the 21st century for all countries, even though populations will increase at slower rates for all countries studied, and decline for a few.
- The rate of long-haul visitor growth will slow for most countries, developing and industrialized alike, to 2010.
- Projected age cohorts and real incomes in some countries, however, are expected to boost rates of growth in long-haul visitors generated over the next decade from their rates over the past ten years.

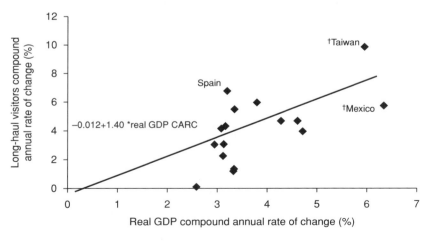

Figure 4.15 Forecast growth rates for real GDP and long-haul visitors, 1998–2010: † denotes developing country. (*Source:* WEFA Group and author's estimates)

- The rates of growth forecast are not related to current long-haul visitor volumes, rates of growth over the past decade, or population projections for the next.

The rates of growth forecast appear to be related to projected growth in real GDP for most countries to 2010.

Implications

Other data, such as the US Department of Commerce's In-flight Survey of International Air Travelers, indicate that long-haul travellers are especially lucrative sources of spending for destinations and international transport modes. They tend to stay longer at the destinations they visit than the average visitor, and often spend more per day. Consequently, the following overall conclusions should be of particular interest to destinations and business firms seeking to attract this lucrative market:

- Long-haul travel generated by the Republic of Korea, Taiwan, Germany, Brazil, and Spain will be especially robust in the first decade of the 21st century, offering good prospects for destination and international transportation marketers.
- The United States will remain by far the largest source of such travel, with Japan, the UK and France in the second tier.
- Despite rapid growth rates, developing countries will remain relatively small generating markets for long-haul travel.
- The retired market is a large and growing segment generating long-haul travel.

The author expresses his special thanks to the World Tourism Organization and the Travel Industry Association of America for providing historical data on international travel essential to this chapter. He also appreciates the generosity of the WEFA Group of Eddystone, PA 19022, USA for providing forecasts of GDP for selected countries.

References

Crouch, Geoffrey I. (1994a) A study of international tourism demand: a survey of practice, *Journal of Travel Research*, XXXII (4): 41–55.
Crouch, Geoffrey I. (1994b) A study of international tourism demand: a review of findings, *Journal of Travel Research*, XXXIII (1): 12–23.

Frechtling, Douglas C. (1996) *Practical Tourism Forecasting*. Oxford: Butterworth-Heinemann.

Organisation for Economic Co-operation and Development (1999) *National Accounts, Main Aggregates 1960–1997*, Volume 1, Washington, DC: OECD.

Smeral, Egon (1998) Tourism demand, economic theory and econometrics: an integrated approach, *Journal of Travel Research*, XXVI (4): 38–43.

Travel Industry Association of America (1999) Travel Industry Association of America's Market Share IndicatorSM. Washington, DC: Travel Industry Association of America.

UN/WTO (United Nations and World Tourism Organization) (1994) *Recommendations on Tourism Statistics*. New York: United Nations.

World Tourism Organization (1997a) *Compendium of Tourism Statistics, 1991–1995*, 17th edn. Madrid: WTO.

World Tourism Organization (1997b) *Tourism Economic Report*. Madrid: WTO.

World Tourism Organization (1999) *Compendium of Tourism Statistics, 1993–1997*, 19th edn. Madrid: WTO.

5

Tourism and hospitality into the 21st century

Hansruedi Müller

Experience has taught us that the future is usually not what we would have expected from extrapolating past developments, but rather what we make of it. Jacques de Bourbon-Busset once wrote: 'What we want is not to guess at the probable future, but to prepare one that is desirable and perhaps even to go that bit further and try to make the desirable future the probable one.' To do so, we have to focus on the future, something that seems appropriate at the dawn of a new millennium.

The challenges of our time

A backward glance reveals that tourism development has always fluctuated, though since the Second World War this fluctuation has been very slight, with trends pointing steadily upwards. What is more, all forecasts indicate tremendous growth in international tourism.

Numerous, particularly turbulent changes are currently taking place in the immediate and wider context of leisure and travel. Not only has the new consumer gone into top gear, society as a whole has become ever more fragmented. Political boundaries are being abolished to be replaced by others. In contrast, as the result of worldwide globalization mechanisms, our planet is turning into a 'global village' with a uniform, commercialized culture. And lastly, what was regarded as ecological stability appears to be becoming increasingly unstable. Although we know more and more about our world, travel it extensively, study and investigate it, interrelations are becoming more and more complex and less comprehensible. To put it in a nutshell, we face tremendous challenges.

The challenge of globalization

Dealing with world-wide globalization trends is new to all of us. Everything is in a state of flux: demand, labour, know-how and capital are all flowing to where the biggest hopes for the future lie, with the resultant standardization of production technologies, business strategies, marketing plans and management styles. Although tourist production is tied to local conditions, the tourism industry cannot avoid being affected by globalization. Tourist products, and even whole destinations, are becoming interchangeable; continental and inter-continental transport networks determine the direction and speed of development; distribution channels and/or reservation systems are increasingly a decisive factor in success.

Worldwide excess capacity in all departments of tourism – carriers, accommodation, adventure and leisure parks, sports facilities, cultural events, etc. – is a key driving force in globalization. Drops in tourism figures in highly differentiated national economies (Austria, Switzerland, Germany, etc.) are largely due to the fact that almost all national economies worldwide have discovered tourism as a development-promoting factor and been drawn into the globalization maelstrom through the competitive situation.

The challenge of the changing climate

The environmental discussion is hotting up from two sides. On the one hand, many places are already virtually at their ecological limits, and the consequences will become increasingly visible and tangible over the next few years. On the other, the process of environmental awareness is continuing among broad segments of the population. Holidaymakers too are becoming more and more environment conscious, but in an opportunistic fashion: they are particularly sensitive to environmental damage when it threatens to spoil their holiday pleasure.

The consequences of the changing climate are crucial for tourism. Not only the rising snow line or higher sea levels, but also the increasingly capricious weather with a greater tendency towards natural disasters, changes in the permafrost areas, adjustments by flora and fauna as well as the melting glaciers represent major challenges for mountain and coastal regions.

Thus, the dilemma facing tourism is particularly great because tourism, with its high transport energy consumption, generates a large proportion of greenhouse gases (especially CO_2) and because the distances travelled are growing longer and longer while stays are becoming progressively shorter.

The challenge of an ageing population

Setting aside the fact that the populations of highly industrialized countries may be considerably influenced by influxes of refugees, the assumption can (or must) be that the population of the industrialized countries is stagnating. On the other hand, the population's demographic composition will change radically. While the proportion of young people will fall drastically in the coming years, the percentage of senior citizens will increase by up to 1% per year. With the contraceptive pill we started an experiment that is unique in human history and whose consequences will leave their mark on the 21st century. There will be fewer and fewer young people and more and more active 'younger senior citizens' with time and money on their hands who will set the tone in the leisure and travel market.

The challenge of changing values

The process of changing values is equally turbulent. It is characterized by a basically hedonist attitude (desire, enjoyment, living out one's dreams) which, however, goes hand in hand with a certain pessimism about the future. The system of shared basic values that makes for social cohesion has now virtually disappeared. Our live-for-the-moment society is characterized not only by individualism but also by many sub-groups with their own value patterns, each of them claiming to represent society. Cultural identity seems to be increasingly reduced to leisure behaviour, and travel with its utopian, ritual and mythical nature is steadily becoming the last common identity area (Thiem, 1994). The so-called 'mega generation' makes itself heard loud and clear, and its values are mainly as follows:

- substantial material demands;
- little willingness to do anything special to merit these;
- call for more freedom in all areas of life;
- growing escapism;
- growing unwillingness to take orders from others;
- fewer inhibitions;
- individualization of the masses.

In mega-generation 'scenes', it is becoming ever more difficult to choose between burn out (exhaustion) and drop out (exclusion). The division between 'the knows' and 'the don't-knows' is obvious. Signs of these behavioural patterns can be detected in the alpine snowboard scene, for instance, or at the beach with Ballermann.

Matthias Horx (1995, p. 43) has detected a mega-trend which could be essential for tourism, namely 'soft individualism'. He describes the basic shift in values of our time as follows:

- the 'economic miracle' phase with the values of fulfilment, duty, discipline, family, loyalty and piety has been replaced by
- the 'ego era' with the values of adventure, performance, desire, 'number one', eros, materialism and fun, which is followed by
- the 'soft individualism' phase with the values of experience, commitment, calm, friendship, honesty, spirituality and responsibility.

Basing one's argument on Horx, it could be said that whenever everything becomes commercialized, materialized, rationalized and technical, people more and more come to long for 'spirituality'.

The challenge of mobility

The fact that a growing number of people can drive combined with the individualization of society is leading to greater motorization in all Western European countries, despite intensive debates about the ecological aspects. The willingness to be mobile, and hence the need for greater mobility during leisure time, will also continue to increase. For instance, leisure-time mobility in Switzerland rose from approximately 35% in the 1960s to over 50% at the end of the 20th century.

With little probability of major adjustments to transport infrastructure and in view of the poor coordination of school holiday arrangements in Europe, this will involuntarily but inevitably result in even greater traffic problems and in total traffic chaos, particularly when it comes to holiday traffic. Nevertheless, little change in mobility patterns can be expected from the majority of people. Holiday traffic jams have established themselves as part of the vacation ritual. The percentage of people suffering from 'mobility exhaustion' will rise more and more.

The challenge of mass leisure

On the whole, people in employment will have more leisure time, in particular through additional free days and as the result of longer (unpaid) breaks among young people. It appears that in addition to its mass prosperity, mass mobility and mass tourism, a kind of mass leisure is the hallmark of our society.

For more and more people, using their leisure time is becoming a problem. This time is increasingly used for media addiction, further consumption based on the 'shopping, cinema, eating outside' formula, frenzied activity or mobility addiction. Only few people manage to interpret leisure time as social time, culture and education time or 'time really for themselves'. In other words, yesterday's working society runs the risk of becoming tomorrow's mass leisure society with media, consumption, activity and mobility time as its salient features. Leisure time – even during holidays – should be upgraded to social, cultural, educational and personal time.

Two contrasting social development patterns

Against the background of the emerging challenges of the 1990s, various social development patterns – on the lines of scenarios – are conceivable. The following remarks describe two opposing pictures of societal development developed as presented in an experts' report submitted to the Swiss Federal Council (BFK, 1991, p. 28 et seq.).

The 'totally mobile singles society'

The trend towards individualism further intensifies, moving towards a society of people interested solely in their own welfare and 'self-fulfilment'. They are in love with themselves, tolerant in the sense of indifferent, consumption-oriented and live by the motto 'Everything has its price', even social services delegated to the state and private suppliers. Political commitment is confined to 'involvement democracy'.

This 'totally mobile singles society' is not tied to one place, so it relates little to local communities, requires a lot of living space and travels longer and longer distances. A majority of economically competitive people stand over and against a growing minority of less well-trained people, the elderly and disabled who, while they receive financial support, are relegated to the fringes of society. The growing number of people in need of care are 'professionally' looked after. The question of what social expenditure is to be borne by which social groups becomes the main political conflict.

The 'partnership with commitment'

The tendency towards 'going it alone' is triggering growing unease, thus reinforcing counter-trends on the lines of upgrading partnerships with commitments. Individuals are increasingly prepared to take on social responsibility. Partnerships on traditional or less conventional lines are gaining in importance. However, in parallel with this collective sense of responsibility, social control and intolerance of 'incorrect' behaviour are also intensifying, for instance in the field of ecology.

The non-material components in quality of life are becoming increasingly significant, and with them the willingness to become involved in social and political issues. On the scale of values that is emerging, political and social services constitute an essential part of a person's 'life's work'. Both sexes are moving towards a holistic approach to life in which professional and social work complement each other. This strong link to residential environment and neighbourhood encourages new forms of ownership promotion, with a decrease in mobility and a shift to public transport. The immediate residential area becomes the main point of reference, both politically and socially, encouraging the development of small networks spanning the generations and the related social services.

Changing travel habits

Upheavals in the immediate and less immediate environment of leisure-conscious persons also affect their travel and holiday habits. Horst W. Opaschowski (1995, p. 22) described the holiday of the future as follows:

- Attractive natural setting and clean landscapes are automatically expected.
- People will continue to seek sun, beaches and the sea.
- Artificial holiday paradises will become tomorrow's standard holiday venues.
- Holiday hopping ('here today – there tomorrow') will spread.

- Vacations will become the ultimate adventure.
- The holiday world of the future must be as exotic as possible.
- More and more young families will discover indoor luxury bathing complexes.
- Culture and study trips will develop into a stable market segment.
- Holiday clubs will lose their attraction as something out of the ordinary.

This description of the tourism of the future highlights the fact that some conflicts are bound to become more acute, in particular:

- growing pressure on the remaining nature reserves;
- the distances travelled are becoming longer and longer, consuming more and more energy, with serious consequences;
- the growing risk that holiday destinations will be downgraded to the fast-food articles of the throw-away society;
- the continuing trend towards 'exoticism' with its cultural and health risks for travellers and host populations.

The ongoing long-haul travel boom was summed up in figures in a Delphi study entitled 'Fernreisen 2005' conducted in Germany, Austria and Switzerland. At approximately 5%, the annual growth rates for long-haul tourism are far higher than those for domestic tourism (0.5–1%).

In addition to these changes in respect of future holiday models, there are also signs of changes in booking and travel habits:

- *Trend towards adventure-oriented holiday behaviour:* seeking a more intensive leisure experience.
- *Trend towards going it alone:* seeking even more independent holidays in line with personal ideas, with a preference for more flexible holiday products.
- *Trend towards more sophisticated travel products:* seeking trips that offer culture and education, as well as variety; both passive recreation and hyperactive sport are 'out'.
- *Trend towards more wellness during holidays:* seeking forms of travel that offer overwrought modern man holistic relaxation, with a healthy diet, gentle exercise, beauty and body care and a wide variety of therapies as the keywords.
- *Trend towards 'second homes':* seeking cosy holiday accommodation as home-like refuges with a high degree of comfort.
- *Trend towards sunny travel destinations:* seeking holiday destinations with guaranteed sunshine – above all during cold, wet winters.

- *Trend towards cheaper travel:* seeking (cheap) products that represent value for money: holidays at rock-bottom prices and growing market transparency thanks to the Worldwide Web encourage this tendency.
- *Trend towards more frequent, shorter trips:* seeking products that offer occasional variety.
- *Trend towards spontaneous travel decisions:* seeking offers that can be booked at the last minute (or even at the last second) and which are not only cheap but also comprise an element of surprise.
- *Trend towards more mobile travel patterns:* seeking products with frequent changes of location, with travelling as the major attraction.

This spotlight-like future analysis leaves considerable scope for interpretation about the future openings for tourism. Making the most of these trends calls for visionary innovation, targeted cooperation, clear marketing strategies and careful nurture of existing core attractions.

New lines of thrust in tourism development

Trends point to changes and determine the future. In order to prepare a desirable future, we should not only analyse trends but also find a joint approach. That is why I should like to conclude with a few requirements to serve as guidelines for tourism professionals and policy designers in making the desirable future the probable one.

Tourism must become more efficient

Although tourism has achieved a high degree of development in our part of the world, structures in many destinations are still inefficient. Desperate efforts are made to create profiles for far too many brands in order to survive in a keenly competitive environment. In so doing, people overlook the fact that guests are not very interested in structures, which have grown up over the years. What they are looking for is a comprehensive, well-coordinated service package. Consequently, joint regional and interest-focused tourism ventures or even mergers should be encouraged. Individual places and tourism associations should be persuaded to combine as destinations proper in the sense of strategic business areas.

Tourism must improve its quality

People have long been talking about developing quality in tourism. What is required, however, is the implementation of comprehensive quality management at operational and destination level. For today's increasingly demanding guests, it is important for the quality of the total local package to be coordinated. In Total Quality Management (TQM), guest satisfaction, employee expectations, the outcome for the environment and society as well as economic success are the focus of efforts, calling for intelligent process control and a high standard of leadership.

Tourism must become more environmentally aware

The sources of ecological danger in tourism development have long been identified, so all that remains is to take them seriously and undertake preventive action so as to side-step environmental problems. The aids developed in recent years such as environmental compatibility reports, environment management systems, environmental audits or environment officers should be used to disclose conflicts and seek sustainable solutions. The discrepancy between knowledge and action should be constantly reduced.

Tourism must allow greater participation

In tourism, there are not only 'winners' but also many people negatively affected by external effects. In highly developed tourism areas, a kind of 'tourism weariness' is spreading, with people talking of inadequate tourism awareness. To prevent the resultant defensive attitudes, those affected must be given an active role. This presupposes greater participation in tourism development, particularly at destination – but also at operational level.

Tourism needs to be slowed down

Tourism requires mobility. 'The more transport is available, the more tourism there will be' was – and still is – the branch motto. But in time, transport has become a key problem, undermining the attractiveness of tourism. Tourism's own threat to itself has taken on a new dimension. However, there is only one key to the mobility issue – namely deceleration – because in the long term, speed is the only variable in the mobility system. If there were speed limits like 400 km/h for planes, 200 km/h for trains, 100 km/h for cars, 30 km/h in built-up areas and in holiday resorts, areas where pedestrians can stroll around, the CO_2 goals could be easily reached.

Tourism must be made more authentic

For many years, many tourism destinations were famous for their situational pioneering; unique natural and cultural characteristics were skilfully turned to best advantage. But these 'organic' values are increasingly being cast overboard. Under pressure from globalization, products are becoming standardized and unique characteristics levelled out. In the new century, potential guests will be on the lookout for the natural, organic, unmistakable and authentic.

Tourism must become more human

Pressure to make profits and competitive outlooks have left their mark on many of us. Supported by methods such as lean management or re-engineering, many people have become hard-hearted, strategy-conscious tourism professionals focused on rational action. However, sustainable tourism development is based on human qualities such as emotions, empathy, cordiality or intuition. In a branch that attaches maximum importance to emotional values, human warmth and situational empathy, such qualities should be encouraged and nurtured more.

If visionary design skills are combined with sensitive responsibility, tourism can look forward to a hopeful future in this new century.

References

BFK (Bundesamt für Konjunkturfragen) (1991) *Schweiz morgen: vier Szenarien zur schweizerischen Zukunft: Bericht der Eidgenössischen Expertenkommision an den Bundesrat.* Berne: Bundesamt für Konjunkturfragen: Vertrieb: Eidg. Drucksachen- und Materialzentrale.

Horx, Matthias (1995) *Megatrends für die späten neunziger Jahre.* Düsseldorf: ECON-Verlag.

Opaschowski, Horst W. (1999) *Tourismus und Freizeit 2000 – Wohin die Reise geht.* Address given at the 'Tourism and Leisure' economic event organized by the Industrie und Handelskammer Schwarzwald on 24 April 1999 in Bad Dürrheim.

Opaschowski, Horst W. (1995) *Tourismus mit Zukunft.* Urlaub 94/95, Hrsg.: BAT-Freizeit-Forschungsinstitut, Hamburg.

Thiem, Marion (1994) Tourismus und kulturelle Identität, *Berner Studien zu Freizeit und Tourismus,* No. 30.

6

The future of leisure time

Colin Clark

Introduction: post-industrial society

Seeing the title of this chapter, some of you may remember seminars back in the 1970s that looked forward to an age of leisure for all, supported by information technology and robotics. As we all know it has not worked out like that. Here, I shall try, based on some recent work for the World Tourism Organization (WTO), to outline what is happening to leisure time, why, how it affects tourism and finally take a look at prospects for the future.

Post-industrial society was first discussed in the United States in the 1950s. The golden age of post-war prosperity inspired the hope that a good life for all could be built, in a great society, which would abolish poverty, and be increasingly egalitarian. (Patterson, 1998). That dream now seems remote, and the phrase has subsequently been used more modestly to suggest that we have become a post-industrial society simply in the sense that, in the case of Britain, less than one-sixth of employees still earn their living in manual jobs (Roberts, 1999). Balancing that decline has been the dramatic rise in professional and managerial employment, which, in the case of the United States, is now 60% of the workforce.

Underlying these radical changes in employment, which have been accompanied by rising levels of education and income, the Harvard economist Juliet Schor identifies the emergence of 'post materialists' who are less concerned with getting and spending, and more interested in quality of life and leisure. Perhaps, in these workaholic times, some of them have in mind Oscar Wilde's comment that work is the refuge of those with nothing better to do.

Background

Be that as it may, in tourism we have generally assumed that as incomes rise people will increasingly buy experiences, such as travel, rather than goods and that the leisure time available to do this is increasing. But is it?

To find out WTO commissioned us to study the prospects for leisure time. WTO noted that in recent years the attention of governments and industry around the world has been on responding to globalization by improving competitiveness, rather than on improving the conditions of employment, such as paid holiday entitlements. The WTO wanted to know whether as a result the growth in leisure time has been cancelled or at least deferred and if so how the industry should respond. To answer those questions we gathered information on leisure time and tourism in 18 of the world's most important tourism-generating countries. Those countries are – Americas: Brazil, Canada and the United States; Asia Pacific: Australia, China, Japan, Korean Republic, Malaysia, Singapore; Europe and Africa: Austria, France, Germany, Italy, Netherlands, Sweden, Switzerland, UK and South Africa. They include today's leading tourism generators – Western Europe, America and Japan – and some major generating countries of the future and represent about three-quarters of world tourism spend.

In most of these countries leisure time is shaped by laws defining working hours, public holidays and paid holidays and often, within that framework, by agreements between employers and employees. But globalization is creating new pressures on leisure time, particularly through reduced staffing levels, the intensification of work and more flexible working practices. To explore the implications for tourism we consulted governments, the travel industry, employers' organizations, trade unions and a number of international bodies.

The tourism growth of the past 40 years reflected rising incomes, cheaper travel and increasing leisure time. The working week became shorter. Holiday entitlements grew. Working life tended to start later and finish earlier. But in recent years for many people reductions in working time slowed or reversed. The world economy has become fiercely competitive and employment less secure. The working hours, particularly of many full-time, skilled employees, have risen.

Youth tourism

But what about the years before we face the challenges of working life? The leisure of the more fortunate young in prosperous countries is constrained by limited income rather than time. Twenty per cent of travellers are students. Many take the opportunity to travel before or after as well as during their years at university. They may well see travel as a necessary preparation for a high-flying career. Once embarked on their careers the changing pattern of employment, with less emphasis on lifetime careers, encourages them to take further breaks between periods of work. There are also indications that the young are determined to achieve a better balance between work and leisure than their parents do.

On the other hand, young people are entering a much more competitive employment market, and are often in debt at the end of their studies. So they are likely to take earning a living more seriously than earlier generations. In addition they are told they must maintain their employability and begin saving immediately for a long retirement.

Despite this, the youth travel market is buoyant, well developed in terms of products and targeted marketing, and will grow in the years ahead, mainly because of the rising proportion of young people entering tertiary education.

The years of employment

Once people enter employment, their leisure comes as either paid leave, public holidays or weekends. These vary around the world but countries fall into three broad categories. Those with paid holidays as a legal entitlement include all Western European countries. Among countries where paid holiday depends on individual employment contracts, with no statutory rights, the United States is the most important, possibly the only country in this category. Countries with strong traditions of public holidays but where legal entitlement to paid holiday is relatively new include many Asian Pacific countries. So holiday taking during working life differs widely. Let us look at the position in some of the 18 countries.

The United States of America

The United States is the world's largest economy but paid annual leave is typically some 10 days. American productivity has tripled since the 1950s but Americans have largely taken this in pay rather than more free time. In a long hours culture it is difficult to trade income for more leisure and a dramatically increased standard of living has been bought at the cost of a very demanding lifestyle.

Over a 20-year period there has been a reduction in leisure time of 140 hours per year for the average employee. Many opinion surveys suggest that some Americans would sacrifice an element of income if they could have more leisure. The countervailing factor is the commercial pressure on employers to minimize employee numbers and all related costs, including employment related taxes, and holiday and pension benefits.

Juliet Schor argues that there is a failure in the employment market, which creates a structural bias towards spending and against free time. An alternative equilibrium is blocked off by the large career sacrifices an individual must make to get shorter hours. In addition she argues that many Americans are more concerned to purchase goods than experience (Schor, 1998).

These factors, together with a rigorously liberal economic policy and the weakness of trade unions, help explain why American leisure time lags behind European. Nevertheless, in response to the pressure for more leisure time some employers enable employees to work extra hours above the normal schedule to build up an occasional three-day weekend. Others make no distinction between sick leave and vacation, giving employees an overall total to use as they wish.

Yet even taking 2 weeks leave together may be seen as lacking commitment and research by Hilton showed that one-third of Americans took only 50 per cent or less of their vacation. Despite continuing debate on the need for a better work–leisure balance it seems likely that the American travel industry will continue to offer tourism products to meet the needs of a time pressed market, which takes multiple short trips with high daily spend. Until retirement, lack of time will continue to bolster the enormous domestic tourism market and inhibit overseas travel. However, incentive trips, the ultimate reward in a time-squeezed culture, will surely continue to flourish.

Japan and the Asian tigers

In Japan, the world's second largest economy, average statutory holiday entitlement is 17 days: 9.5 days are taken. A regular two-day weekend is still only enjoyed by some 50% of employees. The 14 public holidays continue to be the central focus of Japanese leisure, recently reinforced by reallocating two of them to create two more Happy Mondays – three-day weekends.

At present recession and job insecurity have led to gloom and, in the words of the Japan Travel Bureau, a general disinclination to travel abroad. Nevertheless a view is emerging, championed by the Japanese Association of Travel Agents that, in the longer term, a more relaxed attitude towards taking holidays must be encouraged, perhaps by new legislation, to ensure that employees take their holiday entitlements. But rising unemployment and anxiety about pensions make any increase in spending on leisure travel unlikely until economic conditions improve.

Before the 1998 crash, the Korean Republic, Singapore and Malaysia were building up strong outbound markets, albeit on the basis of limited holiday entitlements. That growth received a substantial setback and recovery is likely to be slow.

Western Europe

Western Europeans enjoy some 24 days annual paid leave, generous public holidays and a five-day working week. The EU Working Time Directive 1993 gives all employees a minimum of 4 weeks paid holiday and Europeans are, of course, the world's biggest outbound market.

But there is another side to the European position. The chairman of Lufthansa has commented that it cannot be right for employees to have some 8 weeks holiday, more than anywhere else in the world. There is anxiety about the international competitiveness of an economy that supports such generous employment related benefits.

In Europe – as in America – work pressure and job insecurity, which make people reluctant to be away from work too long, encourage shorter breaks. The new statutory holiday rights in the EU cannot be exchanged for money. But, as in America, some employers are now offering flexible employee benefits. So, above the statutory minimum, individuals may have to choose between, for example, more holiday or an enhanced pension contribution or childcare vouchers. The demands of work can be so intense that people simply opt not take their leave. In the Netherlands, in response to this, employees have won a right to sell some holiday back to their employers.

In the United Kingdom, 25 per cent of employees do not take their full holiday. The main reason given is pressure of work. The Institute of Personnel

Development recent report *Living to Work?* highlighted the health and family life consequences of the excessive hours worked by many management employees.

Today European trade unions rather than seeking more paid holiday want more family-friendly working hours to ease the strains on family life and make flexible working a two-way street. They are also interested in sabbaticals, as a means of bringing more reality to the idea of lifelong learning. So future discussions on leisure time are likely to be very broadly based and to reflect some of the changes in the relationship between work and leisure.

Only in France, with the introduction of the 35-hour week, is an attempt being made to reduce working hours. The objective is to create more jobs but it is not clear whether this will be achieved. The scheme is strongly opposed by French employers. Nevertheless it is being used to increase flexibility by annualizing working time and therefore will often result in extra days off rather than simply shorter hours each week. We should watch the new French policy closely. If it does succeed, further raising France's high levels of productivity and increasing leisure time, as well as creating some employment, it will certainly influence policy elsewhere.

Paid leave and public holidays

Table 6.1 summarizes paid leave and public holidays in all 18 countries. The Japanese and Americans have significantly less holidays available than Europeans.

Retirement

For the retired, leisure time is abundant. The better off retired have become the key tourism growth market. All 18 countries have an increasing proportion of people over 60 years old and in many they are retiring earlier, fitter and with wide leisure interests. But whilst this market will go on growing and is largely free of time constraints there are some clouds on the horizon.

Governments are reducing pensions, raising the retirement age, requiring increased pension contributions and encouraging people to save more towards their retirement. The American Commission on Retirement Policy has proposed raising the retirement age from 65 to 70. Last year the British National Association of Pension Funds suggested that the retirement age for state pensions in Europe should be 70. Similar changes are happening elsewhere. They

Table 6.1   Paid leave and public holiday entitlement in 18 selected countries

	Paid leave	Public holidays
Austria	30	13
Italy	30	12
Korean Republic	22	18
Sweden	25	11
France	22	11
Germany	24	11
Brazil	24	10
Netherlands	25	8
Japan	17	14
UK	23	8
Australia	20	8
Switzerland	20	8
South Africa	14	12
Canada	15	11
Korean Republic (actual)	7	18
Malaysia	12	13
Japan (actual)	10	14
Singapore	10	11
United States	10	9
China	10	7

will take effect slowly but are already influencing behaviour, as younger age groups, for example Baby Boomers, begin to save more for their old age. In Singapore, the retirement age is also being raised and the important point is made that this will be good for tourism because older people may have less time but will have more money to spend on travel.

The prospects for leisure

So, competition in the world economy is putting a brake on increases in leisure time. Employees are more worried about security of employment and income than long holidays. Increasing life expectancy and control of public expenditure are leading governments to reduce and defer pensions, making the retired ever more value conscious. What then are the prospects for leisure time?

Globalization seems set to continue. Economic policies around the world are increasingly liberal, including policies within the European Union, where the social market approach has enshrined high levels of leisure time in statutory rights. In these circumstances governments will go on sharpening economic performance. Businesses will continue to minimize employee numbers and all benefit costs. The pressure on employees' time, especially the time of more senior staff will continue. These employees are not normally paid overtime and are usually outside the protection of working hours legislation. Their leisure time can be squeezed at no cost to their employer. How are these pressures reflected in lifestyles?

In the UK the number of non-working hours in a week has reduced substantially over a four-year period – by 100 hours a year. Yet there are increasing demands on that reduced leisure time. The rise in the number of women working and in the number of families dependent on dual incomes greatly reduces family leisure time. It also complicates holiday planning. Husband and wife must co-ordinate their holidays and for parents school holidays are a further complication. Increasingly, flexible working hours, including the substantial rise in those working at weekends, are changing the rhythm of leisure time. The working and leisure time of individuals through the week and through the year is increasingly variable, more fragmented, less predictable. Working hours are being annualized to fit work peaks and troughs more closely. More people are employed on fixed term contracts and simply take time off between work commitments.

Time for holidays?

What do these changes in leisure time mean for tourism? Overall, the response is a move towards shorter, more frequent and more intensive holidays, spread more evenly through the year. Shorter because people cannot or do not wish to be away from work too long. More frequent because holidays are needed to get away from it all and to recover. More intensive because the more their leisure time is squeezed the more people value it and the more they want to get out of it. In addition, many have more to spend. So there are lots of opportunities. Demand is more constant, less peaked. Higher-spend, shorter-stay visitors means a better return on investment.

But there are also challenges for tourism. Holidays need a lot of time so the time squeeze strengthens competition from in the home and near to home attractions. The leisure windows in consumers' lives are targeted from every angle.

The blurring of leisure boundaries

There is a blurring of leisure boundaries while leisure options continue to expand. This widening range of leisure time activities – increasingly active, stimulating and varied – is interlinked. There is a boom in fitness centres and fitness enthusiasts are prime prospects for activity holidays. Cultural interests developed at home stimulate the market for an ever-widening range of cultural tourism products.

There are many opportunities to develop relationship marketing by analysing clients' holiday purchases and then presenting them with tempting future holidays. Products can be offered which reinforce travel as an essential element of their personal lifestyle – for which time must be found.

Strengthening the motivation for tourism is important because people feel short of time, many are already well travelled, and because leisure industry investors in the tourism-generating countries are creating a wide range of leisure facilities near to home. Examples include the many new combinations of shopping complexes with other leisure facilities and theme parks close to conurbations. These add to the range of day trip possibilities, offer lots of enjoyment and encourage a high spend in a short time. Then there are the substitutes for international travel – like Center Parcs in Europe and the safari park – Animal Kingdom – in Florida, based on Serengeti. So much more convenient, so much less time-consuming and, it may be argued, ecologically preferable to forcing tourists onto possibly reluctant local communities.

Segmenting the holiday market

In a market increasingly segmented by time as well as money we have the time-poor, money-rich interested in a wide range of shorter breaks – upmarket cultural packages, being pampered, the exotic, the fashionable. Their time is more valuable to them than their money. They expect excellent products, which can be tailored to tight schedules and will maximize the value of their precious leisure time.

The money- and time-rich, open to enjoying several holidays each year, also have many home-based interests competing for their time.

Then there are those with less money who seek a wide range of affordable holidays. Many also have work pressures and take opportunities to get away when those pressures permit.

Finally, those free of time constraints, but with limited income, will be interested in extended but inexpensive trips.

Behind this analysis, in addition to changes in leisure time, the other factor accelerating the segmentation of the market is the increasing polarization of incomes, those with the highest income often having the least time.

Travel hassles

The squeeze on leisure time adds to the importance of efficient services for selecting and purchasing holidays on ever-shorter lead times. This presents many opportunities for creative marketing, including modular packages and e-commerce, tailoring products to individual requirements.

The time squeeze adds to the value placed upon hassle-free, efficient journeys. There are many opportunities here for nearby destinations, exploiting same country, region, or time zone advantages. The time-pressed do not want avoidable jet lag, slow ground services or accommodation with poor communications links. Many are never truly off duty. Even on holiday they must keep in touch with work, reachable and ready for action.

For governments it will be important to facilitate travel (for example, visa complications do not attract the time-pressed) and to respond to the premium on time efficiency by improving transport, in particular the quality of airport and related surface infrastructure. This is a challenge indeed, particularly in the United States, Europe and Japan.

Conclusions

In contrast to the leisure oriented society so widely forecast we find a leisure squeeze for many, arising from work pressure and changes in family structures and lifestyle. At the same time there are debates in the United States, Europe and Japan on the economic issues involved in improving the balance between work and leisure and growing recognition that high standards of living are not necessarily accompanied by a high quality of life.

Better information is certainly needed about what is happening to leisure at a time of rapid economic change. Happily Eurostat has recently settled a blueprint for time use surveys which will provide much better information on holiday nights spent away from home in the European Union countries. There are plans for similar work by the Federal Government in America.

Looking to the future, the prospects for leisure time depend on whether strongly deregulatory economic policies continue to dominate the global economy as we move into the new century or are challenged. Such a challenge might come from Western Europe where there is scepticism about whether economic growth measured in terms of GDP, especially when accompanied by congestion, pollution and the postponement of leisure is an accurate measure of the growth of welfare and an improved quality of life.

Certainly the European Union seems to be searching for a model of social and economic development which combines economic dynamism with a humane working time regime. The World Trade Organization's embarrassment at Seattle suggests that there is now wide recognition of the need for globalization to have a human face and, in the words of the United Nation's Human Development Report of 1999, to be seen to improve the quality of life.

Looking to the future, the leisure industries should participate in these broader debates, focusing particularly on how to ensure that economic growth, as well as raising incomes also enables people to achieve a sensible balance between work and leisure. Meanwhile, the more immediate challenge is to meet the needs of markets, which are increasingly segmented by available time as well as by income.

References

Bell, D. (1999) *The Coming of Post-Industrial Society*. New York: Basic Books.

Haworth, J. (1997) *Work, Leisure and Well-being*. London: Routledge.

Martin, W. and Mason, S. (1998) *Transforming the Future: Rethinking Free Time and Work*. Sudbury: Leisure Consultants.

Patterson, J. (1998) *The Oxford History of the Twentieth Century*. Oxford: Oxford University Press.

Rifkin, J. (1995) *The End of Work*. London: Tarder Putnam.

Roberts, K. (1999) *Leisure in Contemporary Society*. Wallingford, Oxfordshire: CABI Publishing.

Schor, J. (1991) *The Overworked American, The Unexpected Decline of Leisure*. New York: Basic Books.

Schor, J. (1998) *The Overspent American*. New York: Basic Books.

Schor, J. (1999) *A Sustainable Economy for the 21st Century*. New York: Seven Stories Press.

World Tourism Organization (1999) *Changes in Leisure Time: The Impact on Tourism*. Madrid: WTO.

7

Tourism research and theories: a review

Betty Weiler

Introduction

This chapter sets out to review 20th century tourism research and theories and to consider their relevance, including new directions, for the tourism industry in the 21st century. The chapter is mostly concerned with the latter, directions for the future, and it comes in the form of five observations about tourism research, together with a series of lessons for research doers, or *producers*, and research users, or *consumers*, which correspond with these five observations. But before these observations and lessons for the 21st century, I provide a brief overview of the growth of research in tourism.

The following data are taken largely from the work of Professor Chuck Goeldner, the well-known and respected editor-in-chief of *Journal of Travel Research* (*JTR*). In a keynote paper presented in late 1999 at an international tourism conference in Hong Kong, Goeldner (1999) gave the following as indicators of the explosion of tourism research since the early 1960s.

The first scholarly research journal in tourism was *The Tourist Review*, the official publication of the Association Internationale d'Experts Scientifiques du Tourisme (AIEST), in its 55th year of publication by the year 2000. This was followed by *JTR*, which commenced publication in 1972, and was joined by *Annals of Tourism Research*, which started publication in 1973. The next several years saw just a handful of other new research journals in tourism. The explosion in new tourism research journals came in the late 1980s and in the 1990s, coinciding with the growth of tourism courses and academics teaching and researching in tourism at universities. In 1999, there were some 50 refereed journals being published globally which focused on hospitality, tourism and leisure research. If we assume an average of four issues per journal per year, this represents some 200 journal issues. Of course, additional studies with a tourism focus are also published in the research journals of disciplines such as marketing, consumer behaviour, economics, psychology, sociology, anthropology, geography and transportation studies.

Then there are the tourism research conferences. As Goeldner (1999) points out, there are several international and national research conferences held around the world every year, as well as tourism 'sessions' run at disciplinary conferences such as geography, sociology and marketing. The proceedings of these conferences, together with the publications of university and other research centres, government departments and now web-sites make up the so-called grey literature of tourism research, which is probably even more vast than the published research literature.

An annotated bibliography of tourism research was published in the mid 1960s, and was 371 pages long (Goeldner, 1999: 34). Even if it were possible to produce a bibliography of all the tourism research now being published, the sheer diversity of studies suggests that no one individual could possibly have the expertise to conduct a fair and objective critical evaluation. Consider, for example, the kinds of knowledge required to analyse research on tourism forecasting, consumer behaviour, cost–benefit analyses, advertising images and environmental impacts of tourism.

Eight years ago, Professor Jafar Jafari, the editor-in-chief of the international journal *Annals of Tourism Research*, set out to document the state of tourism research and scholarship with a colleague (Graburn and Jafari, 1991). However, he very wisely recognized that a comprehensive and critical review of all tourism research was beyond the scope of any single human being, indeed, even beyond the capacities of the long-term editor of a very prestigious journal in the early 1990s when there were far fewer academics active in tourism research.

What Jafari did is produce a special issue of *Annals* in which he invited 20 eminent scholars to review the research in their respective disciplines, identify the best tourism research in their discipline and critically evaluate their contribution. Anyone who is serious about gaining even a basic awareness of the scope of research and its contribution to our understanding of tourism phenomena should read Graburn and Jafari's introductory paper and the ten papers in that issue of *Annals* (Vol. 18, No. 1) as well as the 25th anniversary issue of *Annals* (Vol. 27, No. 1), in which a number of authors endeavour to provide a status report on tourism research to 2000.

Both Goeldner and Graburn and Jafari offer valuable insights into how tourism research has matured, and what direction tourism research might take in the next few years. In this chapter I address one issue that I believe has been largely neglected: the gap that still exists between tourism research producers and research consumers. I believe this gap has widened in recent years due to the trends I have just outlined. The number of specialist tourism research publications, specialist tourism research conferences, and the vast number of academics who now work in university departments of tourism, has led to a great reduction in cross-fertilization both with academics in other disciplines and with industry. The 'new' generation of tourism academics is much more likely to have an undergraduate and postgraduate tourism qualification, rather than grounding in another discipline. They are less likely to have an industry background or work experience in the tourism industry, and are therefore less comfortable with interacting with those in the 'real world' of tourism.

I present my analysis of this gap between tourism research producers and tourism consumers as a series of observations, together with what I believe are some salient lessons for each of the 'research partners'. I believe partnership is the essence of what is needed in order to enhance tourism research in the 21st century. I know this view is shared by many of my research colleagues. To advance tourism research in the 21st century, research consumers and research producers need to make more of an effort *to dance together*. And just as dancing partners must move in response in one another's rhythm, so must research partners respond to the reality of each other's tendencies. As my observations will indicate, research producers and research consumers need to make an effort to dance together, and this includes learning each other's favourite music and steps.

Observation 1

Tourism research has exploded globally, and this growth of qualified researchers and research centres focused on tourism has increased the psychological and even physical distance between research producers and research consumers.

Why? Tourism research is no longer atheoretical (Jafari, 1990), but with theory and academic legitimacy comes a price: alienation by industry. There are now regular tourism research conferences, which are attended largely by academic staff and students, while those in the tourism industry attend separate conferences, with very few academics in attendance. The volume and sophistication of research publications means that people in industry find it increasingly difficult to keep apace with research methods and findings.

Then there are the government and business persons who believe that theoretical ideas are just 'excess baggage' (Lynch and Brown, 1999: 74), of little value to the practical realities of tourism management.

The reactions of my research colleagues and peers, those who do research, to the explosion of tourism research output is to narrow their focus and lay claim to an area of specialization in which they feel confident to undertake and critically evaluate research. Unfortunately, in many cases this has tended to result in a distancing from the real and increasingly complex realities of the tourism industry. Like their counterparts in industry and government, researchers fear the unknown, and unless forced to do so, will often stay within their comfort zone of the ivory tower and specialist tourism research conferences and events.

Lessons for research consumers

■ Respect tourism research for what it is – a field of specialization every bit as complex as managing a hotel or a major international event – and appreciate the fact that there is good research and there is poor research, just as there are tourist facilities and attractions and events that are managed well and there are those that are managed badly.
■ Respect the fact that there are specializations in tourism research – just as a tour operator is not in a position to judge how well a particular hotel is being managed, an individual researcher with expertise in the environmental impacts of tourism may not be able to evaluate the reliability of forecasts of visitation in the next century.

85

- Respect does not mean 'avoid' – stretch your comfort zone, talk to tourism researchers, find out what they do, invite them to your parties, dance with them!
- Be open to what research may have to offer and be willing to change as a result of it.

Lessons for research producers

- Respect your professional colleagues in industry, and let them know when you think they are doing a good job, and why; support industry award schemes.
- Learn their language and read industry publications; talk about your research in ways that relate to their immediate work environments.
- Respect does not mean 'avoid' – stretch your comfort zone, talk to people in industry, invite them to classes and university events, participate in industry events, give them opportunities to get involved in joint research activities; dance with them!
- Believe in the practical benefits of theoretically informed research and work at demonstrating these benefits to industry players.

Observation 2

Despite the growth in research output, tourism research consumers still feel that research is not meeting their needs.

Why? The major obstacle lying between them is the difference in the reward systems within which they work. Private industry relies on indicators of profit and growth, and in both the private and public sectors job security depends on quality service to key constituencies or customers. For academics, job security depends on research output, usually in the form of refereed publications. 'Research publications are the path to travel, financial rewards, promotion, prestige, and job offers. These are powerful incentives to produce quality research' (Goeldner, 1999: 41). Increasingly, however, there is recognition and reward for applied research that provides benefits to industry, and where these reward systems exist, there are researchers willing and able to do industry-relevant research.

Another difference between the two parties is the timelines within which they work. Research grants often have application-and-decision lead times of several months, and the final output from research projects may take years. Governments and industry work on different financial years, and accountability for research funds may require answers to research questions and research publications within very short timelines and usually less than a year.

Lessons for research consumers

- Find out what expertise and resources providers have (e.g. qualified and student researcher time and enthusiasm, computer hardware/software, communication and publication outlets) and target those that have what you need.
- Partner with research providers and communicate often and regularly what your research needs are (e.g. lists of potential student projects; short-term and long-term research priorities).
- Actively seek opportunities to serve on university advisory boards related to your research needs. Tell these people that you want to be involved. They will welcome you with open arms, and they will ask for your financial support to conduct research for you. But with that support comes control, including control over the questions the research addresses and control over your publication needs. Dance not only with researchers, but also with university administrators, deputy-vice chancellors and university presidents.
- Build short-term research outputs into projects in order to meet your needs, but do not hamstring researchers by ignoring or rejecting their need also to publish in academic journals in the longer-term. They must do that regularly or you won't have them around for very long.

Lessons for research producers

- Provide information about your expertise and capacity (including student researcher capacity) in various and accessible forms (e.g. web-sites) and keep your communications up-to-date.
- Consolidate by collaborating with other research providers and select areas of specialization in order to eliminate duplication within and between universities. Make use of expertise and resources in non-tourism departments such as economics, business/management, cultural and environmental studies, etc. – in other words, dance not only with industry, but also with colleagues in other departments and at other universities!
- Select industry partners who can benefit from your particular areas of expertise and who can provide in-kind support.

- Build in short- and long-term research outcomes that allow for student participation and that meet the immediate needs of industry, while facilitating your long-term research goals.
- Actively and aggressively seek feedback from industry about the use and relevance of your research and learn from it.
- Give industry partners some control in exchange for their support. Engage them not only in funding, but conceptualization and evaluation of your research. Their control will improve your research, not hinder it.

Observation 3

The rapid growth in tourism researchers and publication outlets may lead to excess quantity and a compromise in quality, which has the potential to widen the gap between research producers and consumers.

Why? Because journals need research manuscripts in order to survive, and because the headlong rush to produce academics who can teach in the ever-increasing number of university tourism programmes may have encouraged less-than-rigorous research training at the postgraduate level. Moreover, the days of one-on-one apprenticeship-style mentoring of a postgraduate student are gone, due to academic staff carrying much heavier workloads – more classes, larger classes, more postgraduate students to supervise, more administration – together with increasing pressure to bring in research and consultancy funds to their universities.

Some organizations such as the Council for Australian University Tourism and Hospitality Education (CAUTHE) have worked very hard at improving communications between industry and academia and between tourism academics and their counterparts in the more traditional disciplines, and maintaining high research standards. Some of the lessons for research producers below are outcomes of a workshop organized by CAUTHE (Bushell *et al.*, 1997).

Lessons for research consumers

- Learn where research is published and how to identify quality publication outlets.
- Learn how to read and critically evaluate research; in other words, take dancing lessons.
- Employ people who already know the dancing steps, i.e. who can review

and provide bureaucrat-friendly reports on published research results and pay them to do this on a regular basis.

Lessons for research producers

- Teach students of all levels (future industry personnel) to be able to read, critically evaluate and apply research findings.
- Uphold the peer-review process, educate students and industry about its purpose and continue to be rigorous in setting and maintaining standards for publication in refereed outlets.
- Invite chairs of funding organizations and grant programmes to your dances, to address tourism research conferences. Invite critical review and use it to improve quality.

Observation 4

A growing body of relevant and useful research findings exists but is rarely tapped, because too often academics use media, formats and writing styles that are alienating to industry.

Why? In academia and professional research circles, the name of the game is publication in refereed journals. Researchers are rarely rewarded for anything else. In refereed journals and at research conferences, academics are taught and evaluated to communicate with *each other*, not with applied practitioners. One hundred plain-language reports to industry count for virtually nothing as compared to even a single article in a respected scholarly journal. This is not the researcher's choice. As it is for the applied side of industry, it is simply the way real human beings must perform in order to keep their jobs.

However, in some countries this is changing: if current proposals become Commonwealth government policy in Australia, then universities will be required to demonstrate that their research is collaborative with and relevant to industry as part of their funding conditions.

Lessons for research consumers

- Require that industry-sponsored research (i.e. research you pay for in cash or in-kind) be reported in media and formats and language that meet your needs.

- Provide incentives and opportunities for researchers to present findings at industry-based events and in industry publications (e.g. waive registration fees if presenting at industry conferences; pay researchers to publish in industry magazines and newsletters).
- Learn to use the new dance steps, electronic literature searches and research databases, to search quickly for subjects/topics. Better yet, develop partnerships with universities that require them to provide this type of training to your employees.

Lessons for research producers

- Learn to present research in non-technical ways and give research students the skills to do this. There is a whole literature just on this topic and you have a responsibility to concern yourself with it. David Attenborough and Carl Sagan are archetypes of eminent scientists who have changed the world by making esoteric science approachable and understandable – and thereby important – to non-scientists. There should be a little of David and Carl in each of us I believe.
- Use multiple outlets and media (e.g. verbal, written, web-based).
- Budget time and money for each research project for wide dissemination including industry events and to various sectors of the industry and various levels of government.
- Show research benefits to industry, decision-makers and policy-makers often and regularly, e.g. media releases.
- Provide incentives for researchers to publish in trade journals and other publication outlets appropriate for practitioners. Build these incentives into annual performance evaluations and promotion reviews.
- Give dance lessons: organize workshops for industry and government personnel that teach how to access, read and use research.

Observation 5

Gaps remain in our understanding of tourism phenomena and a need for more research, particularly at the community and regional levels and in developing countries.

Why? I mentioned earlier the enormous number of refereed journals and other publication outlets for tourism research. Yet gaps remain in our understanding of tourism phenomena, and a return for a closer look at the 50 tourism, hospitality and leisure research journals provides evidence of one very real weakness. The publishers, editors and authors of tourism research are largely from developed countries. For example, 40% of the 50 research journals are published in the United States, 26% in the UK, 20% in Canada and Australia, 8% in Europe, and only 6% in the developing world. Although there have been an increasing number of published studies about tourism in less-developed countries, the vast majority of the authors and editorial board members of these journals are from the developed world. TRINET, the major international electronic list used by active researchers in tourism, is made up of researchers largely from the developed world; there are still many research producers and consumers in developing countries who do not have regular access to e-mail. In keeping with my first four observations, there is a need for more collaborative research with both industry and with academics in these countries, particularly at the community and regional levels.

Also, it should be noted that much of the scholarly interaction, both written and verbal, is in English, with little evidence that researchers from predominantly English speaking countries are attempting to communicate their findings to the non-English speaking world.

Research knowledge is growing laterally, but depth is still in short supply. Replicating somebody else's research (and even our own) is sometimes seen as mundane and un-insightful. This stems from the incorrect assumption both on the part of consumers and researchers that a single study provides definitive evidence. It does not.

Lessons for research consumers

- Provide opportunities and in-kind support for the kind of research you need and want, e.g. access to databases, employee time, access to visitors and visitor data, feedback/input into research focus and outcomes, accommodation and transportation assistance.
- Provide incentives to producers to collaborate with local universities and NGOs (e.g. student scholarships, prizes, awards, etc.) to undertake research that will directly benefit your region. Give prizes for the best dance teams. And don't forget that your direct financial support for research puts you in the driver's seat!
- Budget for cash support: e.g. data collection costs (travel, mail surveys, wages for research assistants).
- Capitalize on non-tourism grant programmes and organizations in your region that can help you meet your needs.
- Do not assume that research findings produced for another organization will apply to your situation. Support and advocate the replication of research.

Lessons for research producers

- Encourage and provide incentives for replicative and case study research by staff and postgraduate students.
- Provide incentives for students to do industry-relevant research (e.g. build it into assessment criteria) and showcase their results; have a competition for the best dancers.
- Provide incentives for academic staff to collaborate with partners in developing countries and to undertake industry-relevant research (e.g. build into performance appraisal, promotion criteria, criteria for study leave, etc.).
- Learn to adapt your dance steps to local conditions, adopt new styles of doing research, and find ways to communicate your findings to non-English speaking users.

Conclusions

This chapter has attempted to demonstrate that those who do tourism research and those who use research have grown further apart in recent years, and thus 'partnership' is an indispensable ingredient for research in the new millenium. Partnership between academia and industry requires a shift in thinking and approach by both tourism research consumers and research producers. Research consumers cannot sit back and wait for researchers to come to them, *i.e. to invite them to dance.* They must provide incentives and rewards for collaborative and industry-relevant research, they must be prepared to adapt to the timelines and reward systems of academia, attend their conferences, step onto their campuses, and generally work with academics and research students in all aspects and stages of the research process. As in other more mature industries, production of research knowledge must become a part of the culture of tourism businesses and government agencies (Lynch and Brown, 1999).

By the same token, research producers in all disciplines, even in prestigious well-funded research centres such as the Smithsonian Tropical Research Institute or Australia's Commonwealth Scientific and Industrial Research Organisation (CSIRO) are actively developing strategies to better disseminate their research findings to a range of target audiences. Tourism research producers need to *take dance lessons* from these other industries. They need to step out of their comfort zone, learn the language of industry, attend and present at industry conferences and events, and above all respect the reward systems of the private sector and their need to stay competitive in order to survive. *In short, they must become better dance partners for their counterparts in industry.*

The challenge for researchers is to meet the needs of research consumers, without loss of theoretical integrity and methodological rigour and therefore publishability (Lynch and Brown, 1999). Over time, the best research will be research that is theoretically informed and stands up to replication and practical application in the 'real world'. And the best researchers will be those who get personal satisfaction from making a difference in the real world of tourism business, not those who are content to be alone with their lofty ideas, disconnected from the things that improve the human condition. *Dancing well requires grace and rhythm, but it also requires learning, practice and adaptation to the needs and tendencies of a willing partner.* To the extent that research producers and research consumers work at adapting to one another's needs and tendencies in the next millennium, the contribution of research to advancing global tourism will reach unprecedented proportions. *Keep dancing.*

References

Bushell, R., Faulkner, B. and Jafari, J. (eds) (1997) ARC *Report Tourism Research in Australia: A Strategy to Mobilise National Research Capabilities.* Occasional Paper, Bureau of Tourism Research, Canberra.

Goeldner, C.R. (1999) Directions and trends in tourism research: past, present and future, in V.C.S. Heung, J. App and K.F. Wong (eds), *Proceedings of Asia Pacific Tourism Association Fifth Annual Conference*, Hong Kong, pp. 33–43.

Graburn, N.H.H. and Jafari, J. (1991) Introduction: tourism social science, *Annals of Tourism Research,* 18 (1): 1–11.

Jafari, J. (1990) Research and scholarship: the basis of tourism education. *Journal of Tourism Studies,* 1 (1): 33–41.

Lynch, R. and Brown, P. (1999) Utility of large-scale leisure research agendas, *Managing Leisure,* 4: 63–77.

8

Hospitality research and theories: a review

Michael Olsen

Introduction

This chapter is about research in the field of hospitality management over the 20th century. It is a limited view of the epistemology of a relatively young field of study. As in any emerging discipline, scholars have tried to achieve credibility in their work as they pursued the opportunity to add to the body of literature. And, as in any new endeavour with little foundation, it is full of exploration, self-questioning and doubt. This has been driven in part by the need to serve two very powerful masters. On the one hand, researchers have had to measure up to the demands of scholars in general who, in many cases, had decades, even centuries, of prior research experience. On the other, the users of this research are very practical people who demand relevance and immediacy to the solutions of their problems.

These dual demands have had enormous influence on how scholars are developed and the work that they pursue. As we enter this new millennium, scholars and practitioners are beginning to realize that forthcoming research will be needed and is important to all stakeholders in the industry. It is even safe to say that there is emerging a common view or set of expectations about what research is important and relevant. It is indeed, a new dawn for a maturing field of endeavour.

The objective of this chapter is to provide a generalist view of the evolution of hospitality research, the researchers and the value of their work, the status and future of the body of knowledge, research methods and the future of scholarly work. It is not an attempt to provide a comprehensive review of the research over the 20th century because that has been amply done in such works as Brotherton (1999), *VNR's Encyclopedia of Hospitality and Tourism* (Khan *et al.,* 1993) or in recent special editions of journals, including *the International Journal of Hospitality Management* Vol. 17, No. 2. It is instead a commentary on where we started from in the early part of the 20th century and where we may be going now. It is also meant to be provocative and challenging.

Getting under way – a chronology

Webster's *New World Dictionary* (of the American Language) defines epistemology as 'the study or theory of the origin, nature, methods, and limits of knowledge'. Figure 8.1 helps to convey this graphically as it summarizes the nature of hospitality research from its earliest stages to the present. In looking at the origins of hospitality research, one can go back to the 1940s, when early interest in research in the hospitality industry was complemented with the development of formal education in the field. At that time, research was very contextual. It was designed around the basic and applied needs of the industry. The focus was simply trying to describe practices and procedures that would assist in improving the performance of hospitality enterprises. This early work may be best characterized as descriptive with attempts to capture the best practices at the time.

In these early stages, numbers drove the core research agenda. The numbers were accounting-related and thus research was somewhat influenced by the work undertaken in the accounting profession. Additionally, food and its quality preparation represented the other area where scholars and practitioners attempted to develop a body of knowledge. Great chefs endeavoured to share their secrets of how best to do things, although somewhat reluctantly. In general, all this work could best be described as *'how to'*.

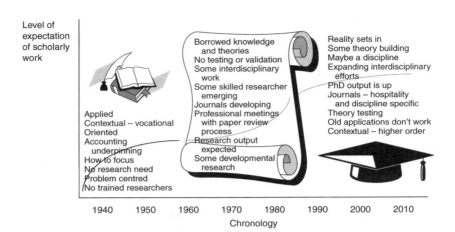

Figure 8.1 The evolution of hospitality research

This inauspicious origin of hospitality research, with a focus on practicality and 'how to', provided the underpinnings for the next phase of work. While no clear threshold marked the beginnings of a more ambitious phase, nevertheless, attempts began to emerge that would move away from the earlier pragmatic efforts. Still, it appeared that no attempt had been made at this time to address the question of whether or not there was a need to follow a more scientific approach to building a body of literature. Research appeared to be driven more by serendipity than by strategy. It may be that the prevailing view was 'anything was better than nothing at all'.

Perhaps this next phase can best be characterized as imitation and borrowing. With only a haphazard array of information to build on, hospitality researchers looked to other fields for foundation and literature. Work that was occurring in the fields of business, engineering and the social sciences served as points of reference and departure for a newly emerging group of hospitality researchers clustered mainly in colleges and universities that offered curricula in hospitality management.[1] This wholesale borrowing often did not really include any serious attempt to validate the application of these theories in the context of the hospitality industry.

During the period from the early 1950s to the late 1960s, scholarly journals began to develop. While they did not come close to approximating the quality of the scientific journals in other disciplines, an organized method of sharing information beyond the typical trade journal had begun. Little effort was given to disciplined scholarly review processes with editorial content being determined by a relatively few academics. Actual manuscript submissions to journals were few as faculty were not encouraged to do much research in this period and emphasis was placed more on knowledge exchange and sharing.

The textbooks that were developed had matured from the pure best practice orientation to attempts to include theoretical underpinnings, although borrowed and applied without serious validation of this application. Writers began to reference scholarly works from a wider array of other fields. It was also during this time that research expectations began to be recognized as important to academics. Professional societies developed which gave scholars opportunities to share their thinking and work. In this case however, what was shared was primarily introspective looks at how educators where doing things.

Reality began to set in in the 1970s and beyond. Academics were being pressured into publishing and the work was beginning to be looked upon more carefully to see if real contributions to knowledge were occurring. The number of journals in the field began to grow along with quality. Serious review procedures were emerging. Scholars were required to develop a research focus and produce a stream of research that actually did contribute new knowledge. While at present this is still sparse, the expectations have been set.

During this contemporary period output of PhDs began to occur, which suggested that hospitality was becoming a more serious endeavour, maybe even becoming a discipline. However, according to some, the hospitality field of study had still not matured in the eyes of those that must sit in judgement of the quality of research effort under way. Hospitality academics often talk to each other and do not benchmark the standard measures of research effort and quality outside of their own field. The work and evaluation remains insular. This dangerous approach has left research in still a rather primitive state. While new young scholars who have come from outside the field are now beginning to change the ethos, they are fighting an uphill battle as those who now sit in judgement of their work developed their scholarly habits in the free-wheeling days just referred to above. This tends to suppress the quest for excellence in research, which is badly needed if the field of hospitality is to mature to the next level.

Researchers and the value of their work

Looking back over the past 100 years, researchers can be grouped into four categories of professionals based upon their employment affiliations of academics, consultants, government and trade organizations. Any discussion that

I may put forward as to the perceived value of their work is likely to draw controversy from those who will be compelled to defend their efforts. Nonetheless, a discussion of the value of the research should be undertaken, if for no other reason than to stimulate discussion and substantive evaluation of quality and relevancy. The main problem is how to conduct such an evaluation and what metrics to use? In this chapter I will try to present a two-dimensional view of hospitality research and its value. Figure 8.2 contains the graphic designed for this purpose.

The first metric chosen focuses on the complexity of the industry problem or research question at hand. Since hospitality is a complex social phenomenon, it does not lend itself to simple research questions, designs, methods and generalizability. However, given the epistemology just outlined, researchers have tried to simplify this complexity. Nevertheless, we must recognize that there are so many cause and effect relationships affecting the success of hospitality enterprises that trying to offer simple solutions to these challenges is perhaps not possible. Therefore, complexity in this case refers to the number of constructs shaping the relationships, which affect the success of hospitality enterprises.

The value of research is of course a relative issue. Thus, it cannot properly be defined, measured, or judged by any single set of criteria or individuals. Given this dilemma and at the risk of significant and welcomed challenge, I try to use the criterion of relevancy as the second metric. By this I mean, is this research actually read and used by anybody? For academics, this can

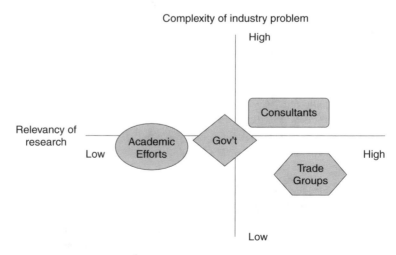

Figure 8.2 The researchers and the value of their work

be measured using a standard citation analysis to see how often a work is quoted or used. The danger in relying on this measure alone is the afore-mentioned insular nature of the field. The better measure is how are those for whom it was intended using the work. In the hospitality field that would be the industry itself. Thus, relevancy is expanded to mean how much of the scholars' research has penetrated and benefited the industry. This is more difficult to measure but may be put simply as the question: is this research and the researcher in demand by the industry?

Using these assumptions, the reader is now given the opportunity to argue for or against the placement of the research of the four categories of scholars in Figure 8.2. As can be seen, scholarly work has not been viewed very highly in this framework. This is not to say that it is of no value, it perhaps is just not perceived by the end user to be or has not been communicated in such a way as to convince others of its value.

Given the current status of the hospitality industry it is not surprising that the research of consultants and trade groups is perceived to have greater value. Perhaps it has to do with the fact that the end user pays for this work which suggests that they need and want it and therefore will value it higher if they had to pay large sums for it. Or perhaps, it is just more relevant to today's needs. Government work is valued but generally the industry is suspicious of anything government does. This work also tends to be more quantitative and underpinned in economic theory.

Sharing the body of knowledge

Scientific advancement is based upon research that contributes to a body of knowledge in a specific discipline. Any doctoral student preparing for a pre-liminary examination knows the pressure related to being responsible for knowing that body of knowledge. In some areas the body of knowledge is very narrow and specific, in others it is eclectic. The latter is the case in the hospi-tality industry. It can cover a complete range from food science to human behaviour. The nightmares of doctoral candidates in this field can be many.

The body of knowledge is advanced when researchers pass manuscripts through a review process and share their findings with the rest of the field. This is usually accomplished through scientific journals that have rigorous refereeing processes. In addition, knowledge is spread through popular publi-cations, conferences, government publications, textbooks and trade groups. It is no different in the hospitality industry. There are four main sources of academic/scholarly journals including textbooks, consultants' reports, government reports, and trade and industry publications, including conferences, seminars etc.

One way to judge if a body of knowledge is advancing is to review the media by which this knowledge is shared to determine whether it is being built upon prior knowledge or just repackaging what is already there. From a very personal perspective, I would have to say that the hospitality industry does a lot of repackaging. A casual meta-analysis of the body of knowledge across specific subject matter areas reveals a tremendous amount of contextual and replicative work. This is especially so in research regarding pedagogy.

There are perhaps several possibilities that exist for this phenomenon. First, possibly scholars have not explored the body of knowledge so as to build upon it rather than repackage it. Secondly, those who referee work may themselves not be familiar with or value the prior body of knowledge. Thirdly, it may be that those who are seeking it do not value the traditional sources of new knowledge such as scientific journals. Fourthly, there may be a limited number of researchers who are engaged in serious theory building across the multi-disciplinary field of hospitality. Fifthly, a well-developed research agenda from a community of leading industrialists and scholars has yet to be developed to provide direction and need. There are no doubt other reasons behind this observation.

Figure 8.3 attempts to capture the relationships among the media by which the body of knowledge is shared, the extent to which the information in these

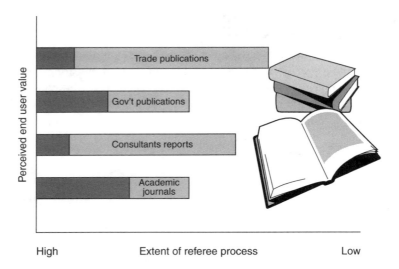

Figure 8.3 Sharing the body of knowledge

channels is refereed and the perceived value of each to the end user. Using this framework it can be seen that trade and industry publications are the primary means of spreading knowledge. The collective readership in the public domain of this source of information is the largest. However, the extent to which this material is reviewed in a scholarly refereed sense is minimum compared to the other medias.

The next most valued source of information in the public domain is government publications and here the review process is more extensive. Consultants' reports are not usually part of the public domain, except for the generic reports that serve as marketing pieces for many firms. It is assumed that these reports are refereed internally but this is not always guaranteed. Academic journals, while probably having the most extensive review process appear to be the least valued source among all four. As stated earlier, the approach taken in this analysis of research is to use the standard of relevancy to industry needs. As Figure 8.3 indicates, the scholarly research in this field has not yet been perceived as having met this subjective standard.

Methods used

There is an old rule of thumb that is followed in research. It suggests that the methods used should be matched to the problem under investigation. This presumes that the problem defines the methods and not vice versa. In reviewing research over the past 100 years, the methods have generally fallen into four categories: case study techniques, multivariate techniques, conceptual and survey tools. Figure 8.4 contains a graphic look at the specific methods employed within each category and provides a rough assessment of the volume of published work in each. Additionally, it points out the relative

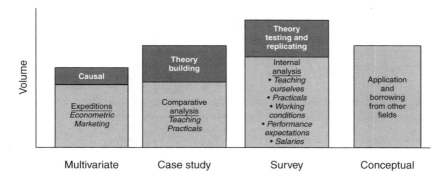

Figure 8.4 Research methods

proportion of work that has focused upon theory testing, building and causal relationship analysis. As can be seen, most of the work is descriptive as indicated by the light grey in the bar charts.

The majority of work has relied upon survey research methods. In this case, a relatively small proportion of the work has been in the area of theory testing which includes replication studies. This makes sense in the context of the earlier discussion, suggesting that scholars have borrowed theory from other disciplines and applied it directly to the hospitality context. Therefore, their work has been focused primarily upon testing theories of others or trying to replicate earlier work in this industry context. The largest proportion of the survey research work has been highly focused upon inclusive types of studies. We have tended to look a lot at ourselves, assessing teaching methods and techniques. Additionally, we have investigated how hospitality programmes have handled the practicals or field experiences. Researchers have also looked into working conditions, and performance expectations within the industry. And hospitality educators have always been concerned about salaries, so efforts have been made to capture this type of information on a regular basis.

Case study research has been employed but less so than survey methods. In this category of research method, a small amount of effort has gone towards theory building. The probable reasons for this are many. Chief among them may be the reliance upon theory from other disciplines, the contemporary ethos of the hospitality researcher, the lack of interest in developing theory, the apparent lack of need for this by practitioners and perhaps a lack of competency in this area. The bulk of case work has been focused upon comparative analysis and also has been inclusive to the hospitality field. Much of the comparative work has been among educators and educational institutions comparing and looking at each other and how they do things.

In the multivariate methods category, the bulk of work has been in the econometric area along with marketing investigations into consumer-related problems. In a few instances, causal analysis has occurred where researchers have recently begun to tackle large multivariate problems in the hopes of building theory. This is encouraging work but for the most part is still in the replicative and theory testing arena. However, the collective ability of newly trained researchers suggests that this is a positive sign.

The conceptual approach has supported research development in the field and probably served as important underpinnings for the other methods. This type of work is important but it cannot be confused with what I call the Sunday afternoon manuscript, which characterized much of the early published work. The allusion is that many authors went to the library on Friday afternoon, checked out a lot of books on a topic, reviewed the material and then sat down to write an article on Sunday. This is reminiscent of term paper writing. There were many instances no doubt when a conceptual piece was not researched or validated in the industry context.

Tomorrow

I have tried here to share my perception of the epistemology of hospitality research. In trying to step back and take a broad look I have come to some personal disappointing conclusions. For a field that has been a viable academic pursuit for almost a complete century, the body of knowledge is nowhere near defined. There appears to be no common understanding of what should be in this body of knowledge and almost no work that has addressed this problem. Scholars seem to be content in replicating the work of others or continually looking inwardly.

The journals, which now include more than 30 titles, seem to have very mixed review processes. The reviews are often handled within institutions, seriously inhibiting the need to broaden the scope of work and diversity of view. Many reviewers appear to approach the process in a casual fashion. Authors appear reluctant to make changes recommended by reviewers or even fail to see the problems identified in their work. The quality of work, from basic writing and simple methodological flaws to large-scale mismatches of methods and problems suggests we have much work to do. In many instances authors have tried to brow-beat editors into publishing their work despite serious concerns. This assessment is not meant to ignore those who attempt to achieve high standards here. They are, however, in the minority at this time.

Similarly, conference programmes that have an official call for papers have refereeing processes that fall short of the rigours one would find in other fields. In many cases papers are sent to reviewers who have absolutely no competency in the body of knowledge in the area. In fact, many efforts in this regard are quite cavalier, with presenters not even beginning to do the research until they have heard whether or not their paper has been accepted. Here again the standards seem to be very low for a field trying to establish itself as more than just another vocational enterprise.

At the start of this new millennium, it is now time to reassess this current state and address the most pressing needs going forward. The first is actually to begin the massive effort to define a body of knowledge, or more appropriately, all the bodies of knowledge that contribute to this diverse and complex field of endeavour. Educational, research and trade associations and societies must accept this as the first step in moving the field forward. This will no doubt be a decade-long effort that will involve hundreds if not thousands of scholars. If future researchers are to contribute in a significant way to the entire spectrum of knowledge, they must know from where to begin.

Secondly, a new ethos of researcher must enter the scene. If we are to become a field with our own bodies of knowledge, then we must limit the theory testing and replicative work in favour of substantive attempts to build theories that are relevant. The key word here is relevance. Recently, after completing an analysis of the abstracts of more than 400 doctoral dissertations, it became quite clear that many failed to answer a very simple 'so what' question. The relevance issue will haunt scholars unless they make serious attempts at determining the long-term research needs of an industry, which is longing for applications of new knowledge. This must become the second most important objective for the new millennium. If we don't achieve relevance, we will simply exist in an esoteric setting that will grow to have less value for all concerned.

Leadership is the third issue. It must begin with the objective of identifying industry needs, not just at present but also well into the future. Once this is accomplished, leadership is required to establish and push a research agenda forward. Leadership is also needed in raising the standards for the research itself, the review and refereeing process associated with publication, and with the journals and other mediums of dissemination. There is some evidence today that suggests that there is a realization of the need for higher standards across the academic and industry worlds but it will be necessary for research oriented institutions to take up the leadership challenge.

As with any developing field, it must pass through phases of growth and development. Hospitality is no different. However, because it is so diverse and applied, it will demand visionaries from across the spectrum of industry and academic stakeholders who are capable of taking it to the next level. All scholars must address and question their comfort levels with the current state of research and begin to shape theories that are relevant to this heterogeneous hospitality community going forward into the future.

As we move to a knowledge-based world where educational institutions have lost their monopoly on knowledge, it must be accepted that scholars will no longer come from the traditional institutions of higher learning. New knowledge will be created by whoever is in a position to do so and wherever it is needed and valued. If current researchers do not recognize this important trend, they will find themselves forever wondering why no one seems interested in their work. Let the new millennium serve as the catalyst for the metamorphosis of hospitality into a serious scholarly pursuit.

Note

1   Hospitality management is a term that emerged in the latter two decades of the 20th century but is used throughout to maintain consistency.

References

Brotherton, B. (ed.) (1999) *The Handbook of Contemporary Hospitality Research.* Chichester: John Wiley and Sons.

Jones, P. (ed.) (1998) Special Issue: Hospitality Research: The State of the Art. *International Journal of Hospitality Management,* 17 (2).

Khan, M., Olsen, M.D. and Var, T. (1993) *VNR's Encyclopedia of Hospitality and Tourism.* New York: Van Nostrand Reinhold.

9

Forecasting future tourism flows

Stephen Witt and Haiyan Song

Introduction

Accurate forecasts of tourism demand are essential for efficient planning by the various sectors of the tourism industry. Forecast accuracy is particularly important in the tourism context, as the tourism product is perishable. Empty airline, ferry, bus and restaurant seats, and unused hire cars, hotel rooms, rental apartments, cruise ship rooms, holiday tour packages and tourist entertainment facilities cannot be stockpiled – once the potential sale is lost it is lost forever.

The purpose of this chapter is to review and evaluate the existing empirical literature on tourism demand forecasting in order to draw out any principles that appear to have been established, where principles are defined as empirically supported guidelines.

With regard to tourism demand forecasting, various time horizons are relevant to decision-making; for example, short-term forecasts are required for scheduling and staffing, medium-term forecasts for planning tour operator brochures, and long-term forecasts for investment in aircraft, hotels and infrastructure. However, the bulk of published forecasting studies on tourism demand concentrates on the short to medium term, and hence the principles also relate to these forecast horizons.

Various levels of aggregation are also relevant to decision-making; for example, governments are interested in total international inbound and outbound tourist expenditures at a country level, hotels in tourism demand by city or region, and airlines in tourism demand by route. However, the great majority of published studies on tourism demand focus on highly aggregated (i.e. country to country) forecasts. The principles therefore also relate to this level of aggregation.

International tourism demand is usually measured in terms of the number of tourist visits from an origin country to a foreign destination country. Less frequently it is measured in terms of tourist expenditure by visitors from the origin country in the destination country; and considerably less frequently by the number of tourist nights spent by visitors from the origin country in the destination country.

Tourism forecasting techniques

A comprehensive review of the tourism forecasting literature indicates that the majority of tourism demand forecasting papers involve econometric studies. Although it is often pointed out in such studies that the econometric models developed may be used for forecasting purposes, the models are often *not* used to generate outside sample forecasts that are then evaluated. Other quantitative forecasting techniques that have been used in tourism situations include spatial models (particularly gravity models) and time series models. Empirical research on qualitative forecasting in tourism has centred on Delphi studies and scenarios.

As the purpose of this study is to investigate whether any forecasting principles have been established, attention will centre on those techniques for which forecast evaluations exist. Therefore, spatial models, Delphi studies and scenarios are not included in our discussion. The focus is on econometric forecasting (in which the factors that influence tourism demand are taken into account in order to generate the forecasts) and time series forecasting (in which past history on tourism demand is extrapolated without reference to the influencing factors).

Econometric forecasting

Explanatory variables

The determinants of tourism demand depend on the purpose of visit. Approximately 70% of international tourist trips take place for holiday purposes, 15% for business purposes, 10% in order to visit friends and relatives and 5% for other purposes (where 'other' includes pilgrimages, and sports and health reasons). The emphasis in empirical research on tourism demand modelling has therefore been very much on holiday tourism, with only a few studies being concerned with business tourism. We shall therefore also concentrate on the demand for foreign holidays. Substantial agreement exists about the explanatory variables that are important in the case of international holiday tourism (Witt and Witt, 1992, 1995).

Population   The level of foreign tourism from a given origin is expected to depend upon the origin population, an increase in population resulting in an increase in demand. Sometimes population features as a separate explanatory variable, but generally modifying the dependent variable to become international tourism demand per capita accommodates the effect of population.

Income   The appropriate income variable is personal disposable income or private consumption expenditure in the origin country (in constant price terms), and is expected to have a positive influence on tourism demand. Income commonly enters the demand function in per capita form, corresponding to the specification of demand in per capita terms.

Own price   There are two price components – the cost of travel to the destination, and the cost of living for tourists in the destination (both in constant price terms) – and these are expected to have negative influences on demand. The cost of travel is often measured by the economy airfare. Usually the consumer price index in a destination country is taken to be a proxy for the cost of tourism in that country on account of lack of more suitable data, and Martin and Witt (1987) have shown this to be a reasonable approximation. The consumer price index is then adjusted by the exchange rate between the origin and destination currencies. If data relating to the price of the tourist's basket of goods/services are available these would be more appropriate, but usually such data do not exist.

Exchange rates are also sometimes used separately to represent tourists' living costs, possibly in addition to the exchange-rate-adjusted consumer price index. The justification is that consumers are more aware of exchange rates than destination costs of living for tourists, and hence are driven to use exchange rate as a proxy variable. Clearly, however, the use of exchange rate alone can be misleading because even though the exchange rate in a destination may become more favourable, this could be counterbalanced by a relatively high inflation rate.

Substitute prices The prices of substitutes may be important determinants of tourism demand, and are expected to have a positive influence. For example, an increase in holiday prices to Spain is likely to increase the demand for holidays to Portugal. The impact of competing destinations may be allowed for by specifying the tourists' cost of living variable as destination cost relative to a weighted average value, calculated for a set of alternative destinations, and by specifying the travel cost variable as travel cost from origin to destination relative to a weighted average value calculated for travel from the origin to competing destinations. The weights are generally based on previous market shares and are often allowed to vary over time.

Marketing National tourist organizations engage in sales-promotion activities specifically to attempt to persuade potential tourists to visit the country, and these activities may take various forms including media advertising and public relations. Hence, promotional expenditure (in constant price terms) is expected to play a positive role in determining the level of international tourism demand. Much tourism-related marketing activity is not, however, specific to a particular destination (e.g. general travel agent and tour operator advertising) and therefore is likely to have little impact on the demand for tourism to that destination. The promotional activities of national tourist organizations are destination-specific and are therefore more likely to influence tourist flows to the destination concerned.

Lagged dependent variable A lagged dependent variable, that is an autoregressive term, can be justified on the grounds of habit persistence. Once people have been on holiday to a particular country and liked it, they tend to return to that destination. There is much less uncertainty associated with holidaying again in that country compared with travelling to a previously unvisited foreign country. Furthermore, knowledge about the destination spreads as people talk about their holidays and show photographs, thereby reducing uncertainty for potential visitors to that country. In fact, this 'word of mouth' recommendation may well play a more important role in destination selection than does commercial advertising. A type of learning process is in operation and as people are, in general, risk-averse, the number of people choosing a given alternative in any year depends (positively) on the numbers who chose it in previous years.

A second justification for the inclusion of a lagged dependent variable in tourism demand functions comes from the supply side. Supply constraints may take the form of shortages of hotel accommodation, passenger transportation capacity and trained staff, and these often cannot be increased rapidly. Time is also required to build up contacts among tour operators, hotels, airlines and travel agencies. Similarly, once the tourist industry in a country has become highly developed it is unlikely to dwindle rapidly. If a partial adjustment mechanism is postulated to allow for rigidities in supply, this results in the presence of a lagged dependent variable in the tourism demand function, with the parameter lying between zero and unity (Witt, 1980).

Qualitative effects Dummy variables are often included in international tourism demand functions to allow for the impact of 'one-off' events. For example, the imposition by governments of foreign currency restrictions on their residents is likely to reduce the level of international tourism, as are threats of terrorism (for example, after the United States bombing of Libya in 1986), and threats of war or wars (for example, the threat after the Iraqi invasion of Kuwait in 1990, followed by the Gulf War in 1991). Similarly, various events are likely to stimulate international tourism, such as hosting the Olympic Games and other major attractions. Witt and Martin (1987) discuss a range of one-off events, which have been accommodated in international tourism demand functions by dummy variables.

Problems with traditional econometric demand models

Most of the published studies on causal tourism demand models before the 1990s were classical regressions with ordinary least squares (OLS) as the main estimation procedure. The functional form of most of these models was single-equation in either linear or power form. Normally, the simple-to-general modelling approach was followed. This approach starts by constructing a simple model that is consistent with demand theory, and the model is then estimated and tested for statistical significance. The estimated model is expected to have a high explanatory power (R^2), and the coefficients are expected to be both 'correctly' signed and statistically significant. In addition, the residuals from the estimated model are assumed to be a white noise process. However, if the estimated model is unsatisfactory, the model is then re-estimated by either introducing new explanatory variables, and/or using a different functional form, and/or selecting a different estimation method. This procedure is repeated until the final model is both statistically and theoretically acceptable. The specific-to-general modelling approach is often criticized for its excessive data mining, since researchers normally only publish their final models, with the intermediate modelling process omitted. Different researchers equipped with the same data set and statistical tools can end up with totally different models.

In addition, the data used in estimating tourism demand models based on the simple-to-general approach are mainly time series, and most of these time series, such as tourist expenditure, tourist arrivals, income, tourists' living costs and transport prices are trended (non-stationary). The estimated tourism demand models have tended to have high R^2 values due to these common trends in the data. Statistical tests based on regression models with non-stationary variables are unreliable and misleading, and therefore any inferences drawn from these models are suspect. Moreover, tourism demand models with non-stationary variables tend to cause the estimated residuals to be autocorrelated, and this invalidates OLS. The problem of autocorrelation in tourism demand models has normally been dealt with by employing the Cochrane–Orcutt iterative estimation procedure. However, this diverts attention from searching for the correctly specified model (autocorrelation is normally indicative of model mis-specification).

General-to-specific modelling approach

Recent advances in econometrics, specifically the use of general-to-specific approaches to modelling, enable us to overcome the problems associated with the traditional modelling procedure discussed above. The general-to-specific modelling methodology was initiated by Sargan (1964), and subsequently developed by Davidson *et al.* (1978), Hendry and von Ungern-Sternberg (1981), and Mizon and Richard (1986). In contrast to the specific-to-general modelling procedure, the general-to-specific approach starts with a general model, which contains as many variables as possible suggested by economic theory. According to this framework, if a dependent variable is determined by k explanatory variables, the data generating process (DGP) may be written as an autoregressive distributed lag model (ADLM) of the form:

$$y_t = \alpha + \sum_{j=1}^{k}\sum_{i=0}^{p} \beta_{ji} x_{jt-i} + \sum_{i=1}^{p} \phi_i y_{t-i} + \varepsilon_t \tag{1}$$

where p is the lag length, which is determined by the type of data used. As a general guide, $p = 1$ for annual data, $p = 4$ for quarterly data, $p = 6$

for bimonthly data and $p = 12$ for monthly data. However, the lag lengths of the time series may vary, and they are normally decided by experimentation. In Equation (1) ε_t is the error term which is assumed to be normally distributed with zero mean and constant variance, σ^2, i.e., $\varepsilon_t \sim N(0, \sigma^2)$. With certain restrictions imposed on the parameters in Equation (1), a number of econometric models, such as the static, growth rate, leading indicator, finite distributed lag, partial adjustment and error correction models, may be derived. A detailed explanation is given in Song and Witt (2000), but here we only briefly describe the steps and criteria used.

The general-to-specific modelling approach involves the following steps. First, a general demand model that has a large number of explanatory variables, including the lagged dependent and lagged explanatory variables, is constructed in the form of Equation (1). Economic theory suggests the possible variables to be included, and the nature of the data suggests the lag length. Secondly, the t, F and Wald (or LR or LM as appropriate) statistics are used to test various restrictions in order to achieve a simple but statistically significant specification. Thirdly, the normal diagnostic tests, such as those for autocorrelation, heteroscedasticity, functional form and structural instability, are carried out to examine whether or not the final model is statistically acceptable. Fourthly, the final model can be used for policy evaluation or forecasting.

Thomas (1997) has summarized the various criteria for model selection within the framework of general-to-specific modelling. These criteria include consistency with economic theory, data coherency, parsimony, encompassing parameter constancy and exogeneity. The first criterion for model selection is that the final model should be consistent with economic theory. This is very important; for example, in general we cannot use a demand model for policy evaluation and forecasting if the model has negative income elasticity. Although such a model may be acceptable according to the diagnostic statistics, it should still be rejected because it invalidates a law of economics. The data coherency criterion ensures that economic data also have a role to play in the determination of the structure of the final model. It implies that the preferred model should have been subject to rigorous diagnostic checking for mis-specification. The parsimony criterion states that simple specifications are preferred to complex ones. In the case of modelling tourism demand, if two equations have similar powers in terms of explaining the variation in the dependent variable, but one has six explanatory variables while the other has only two, the latter should be chosen as the final model. This is because we gain very little by including more variables in the model, and moreover large numbers of explanatory variables tend to result in inadequate degrees of freedom and imprecise estimation. The encompassing principle (Mizon and Richard, 1986) requires that the preferred model should be able to encompass all, or at least most, of the models developed by previous researchers in the same field. The encompassing criterion does not necessarily conflict with that of parsimony; the preferred model may be structurally simpler than other models, but still encompass them. The parameter constancy criterion is particularly important when we use econometric models to forecast. In order to generate accurate forecasts, the parameters of the model should be constant over time. The final criterion for selecting a model is that the explanatory variables should be exogenous, that is they should not be contemporaneously correlated with the error term in the regression.

In modelling tourism demand, the final preferred model should ideally satisfy all of the above criteria. However, this can sometimes be very difficult on account of various reasons, such as data limitations, errors in variables and insufficient knowledge of the demand system. Any of these may result in the above criteria not being satisfied. Even if we find a demand model that satisfies all the criteria, it should be borne in mind that the model can still only serve as an approximation to the complex behaviour of tourists, and it is possible that the decision-making process of tourists will change due to changes in expectations, tastes and economic regimes. Therefore, we should be always prepared to revise our model to take account of such changes.

Time varying parameter approach

One of the recurrent features of causal tourism demand forecasting models when compared with simple time series models, such as the no change model, has been predictive failure. Predictive failure is normally associated with model structure instability, i.e. the parameters of the demand model vary over time, and structural instability is mainly related to important social, political and economic policy changes. The appropriate way of dealing with the problem is to choose an alternative approach, e.g. the time varying parameter (TVP) regression, to model structural changes. The tourism industry has evolved from a supply-led industry to a demand-driven one since the 1970s. Political, economic and social shocks such as the two 'oil crises' in the 1970s, terrorism attacks in the 1980s and the Gulf War in the early 1990s have also had sustained impacts on the demand for international tourism. Although the dummy variable approach could be used to attempt to capture structural changes due to the above-mentioned shocks, the use of the TVP methodology is probably a more realistic alternative. The TVP approach is capable of simulating different types of shocks that may influence the relationship between the dependent and explanatory variables, and the model is also unique in incorporating structural changes into the forecasting process.

Vector autoregressive (VAR) modelling approach

The above models are single-equation tourism demand models in which an endogenous tourism demand variable is related to a number of exogenous variables. The single-equation approach depends heavily on the assumption that the explanatory variables are exogenous. If this assumption is invalid, the estimated parameters of the single-equation demand model are likely to be biased and inconsistent. Sims (1980) argues that the exogeneity assumption imposed by the single-equation approach is unlikely to be credible, and that the VAR specification is more appropriate when we are not sure about the exogeneity of the explanatory variables. For example, Equation (1) specifies that tourism demand is influenced by the price of the tourism product, but the converse could be true also.

The VAR model is a system equation in which all variables are treated as endogenous. The VAR specification suggests that the current values of the variables should be regressed against lagged values of all the variables in the system. Each equation in the system is individually estimated by OLS.

Principles

What does the empirical evidence suggest about the accuracy of different forecasting methods in the tourism context: econometrics versus time series; different econometric models; and different time series models?

Various principles appear to have been established, but with varying levels of evidence – strong, medium and weak – based on the number of studies and the number of cases examined in the studies. Only those principles for which at least medium evidence exists are reported. In the following, 'short-term' forecasts denote a forecast horizon of up to one year ahead and 'medium-term' forecasts denote a forecast horizon greater than one year and up to two years ahead.

Causal modelling

1   It is not possible to build a single model that is appropriate for all origin-destination pairs. Certain explanatory variables appear to influence

international tourism demand for some origin-destination pairs but not others. Furthermore, the estimated coefficients, as expected, vary widely across tourist flows. *(strong)*

Examples of evidence: Martin and Witt (1989); Song and Witt (2000); Kulendran and Witt (2001).

Forecasting

General

1   No single forecasting method performs consistently best across different situations (origin-destination country pairs, forecasting horizons, accuracy measures). *(strong)*

Examples of evidence: Martin and Witt (1989); Witt and Witt (1991); Song and Witt (2000).

2   The relative performance of different tourism forecasting techniques is highly dependent on the choice of accuracy measure, so the tourism forecasting requirement must be considered carefully before deciding on a forecasting method. *(strong)*

For example, for some decisions it may be more important to minimize the size of forecast error while for others it may be more important to forecast correctly the direction of movement of tourism demand.

Examples of evidence: Witt and Witt (1989); Witt and Witt (1991).

When forecasting accuracy is measured in terms of error magnitude

1   The no change model generates more accurate short-term tourism forecasts than simple univariate time series and traditional econometric models. *(strong)*

Examples of evidence: Martin and Witt (1989); Sheldon (1993).

2   The autoregressive model generates more accurate medium-term tourism forecasts than the no change, other simple univariate time series and traditional econometric models. *(strong)*

Examples of evidence: Martin and Witt (1989); Witt, Witt and Wilson (1994).

115

3 The TVP model often generates the most accurate short-term tourism forecasts, outperforming both univariate time series models and other causal models (including the ECM). *(medium)*

Examples of evidence: Song, Witt and Jensen (1999); Song and Witt (2000).

4 The univariate ARIMA model generates more accurate short-term tourism forecasts than the ECM. *(medium)*

Examples of evidence: González and Moral (1995); Kulendran and King (1997).

5 The neural network model generates more accurate short-term tourism forecasts than simple univariate time series models. *(medium)*

Examples of evidence: Pattie and Snyder (1996); Law and Au (1999).

6 The no change model generates more accurate short- and medium-term forecasts than the VAR model. *(medium)*

Examples of evidence: Song, Witt and Jensen (1999); Song and Witt (2000).

When forecasting accuracy is measured in terms of direction of change error

1 Traditional econometric models generate more accurate short-term tourism forecasts than the no change and simple univariate time series models. *(medium)*

Examples of evidence: Witt and Witt (1989); Witt and Witt (1991).

Some of the evidence regarding the accuracy of recent forecasting approaches is mixed. For example, González and Moral (1996) found that the basic structural model outperforms the ARIMA model, whereas Kulendran and King (1997) discovered the converse to be true. Song, Witt and Jensen (1999) and Kulendran and Witt (2001) found that the error correction model is outperformed by the no change model, while Kim and Song (1998) and Song, Romilly and Liu (2000) found that the error correction model generates more accurate tourism forecasts than the no change model. Clearly further research is required to establish the relative accuracy of some of the more recent forecasting approaches in the context of international tourism demand.

References

Davidson, J., Hendry, D.F., Saba, F. and Yeo, S. (1978) Econometric modelling of the aggregate time series relationships between consumers' expenditure and income in the United Kingdom. *Economic Journal*, 88: 661–92.

González, P. and Moral, P. (1995) An analysis of the international tourism demand in Spain. *International Journal of Forecasting*, 11: 233–51.

González, P. and Moral, P. (1996) Analysis of tourism trends in Spain. *Annals of Tourism Research*, 23: 739–54.

Hendry, D.F. and von Ungern-Sternberg, T. (1981) Liquidity and inflation effects on consumers' expenditure, in A.S. Deaton (ed.), *Essays in the Theory and Measurement of Consumer Behaviour.* Cambridge: Cambridge University Press, pp. 237–60.

Kim, S. and Song, H. (1998) An empirical analysis of demand for Korean tourism: a cointegration and error correction approach. *Tourism Analysis*, 3: 25–41.

Kulendran, N. and King, M.L. (1997) Forecasting international quarterly tourist flows using error correction and time series models. *International Journal of Forecasting*, 13: 319–27.

Kulendran, N. and Witt, S.F. (2001) Cointegration versus least squares regression. *Annals of Tourism Research*, 28 (forthcoming).

Law, R. and Au, N. (1999) A neural network model to forecast Japanese demand for travel to Hong Kong. *Tourism Management*, 20: 89–97.

Martin, C.A. and Witt, S.F. (1987) Tourism demand forecasting models: choice of appropriate variable to represent tourists' cost of living. *Tourism Management*, 8: 233–46.

Martin, C.A. and Witt, S.F. (1989) Forecasting tourism demand: a comparison of the accuracy of several quantitative methods. *International Journal of Forecasting*, 5: 1–13.

Mizon, G.E. and Richard, J.F. (1986) The encompassing principle and its application to testing non-nested hypotheses. *Econometrica*, 54: 657–78.

Pattie, D.C. and Snyder, J. (1996) Using a neural network to forecast visitor behaviour. *Annals of Tourism Research*, 23: 151–64.

Sargan, J.D. (1964) Wages and prices in the United Kingdom, in P.E. Hart, G. Mills and J.K. Whittaker (eds), *Econometric Analysis of National Economic Planning.* London: Butterworths, pp. 25–64.

Sheldon, P. (1993) Forecasting tourism: expenditures versus arrivals. *Journal of Travel Research*, XXXII (1): 13–20.

Sims, C. (1980) Macroeconomics and reality. *Econometrica*, 48, 1–48.

Song, H. and Witt, S.F. (2000) *Tourism Demand Modelling and Forecasting: Modern Econometric Approaches.* Oxford: Elsevier.

Song, H., Romilly, P. and Liu, X. (2000) An empirical study of UK outbound tourism demand. *Applied Economics*, 32 (5): 611–24.

Song, H., Witt, S.F. and Jensen, T. (1999) Forecasting performance of tourism demand models: the case of Denmark. Paper presented at the Nineteenth International Symposium on Forecasting, Washington, DC.

Thomas, R.L. (1997) *Modern Econometrics: An Introduction.* Harlow: Addison–Wesley.

Witt, S.F. (1980) An abstract mode – abstract (destination) node model of foreign holiday demand. *Applied Economics*, 12: 163–80.

Witt, S.F. and Martin, C.A. (1987) Measuring the impacts of mega-events on tourism flows, in AIEST (ed.), *The Role and Impact of Mega-Events and Attractions on Regional and National Tourism Development.* St Gallen: AIEST, pp. 213–21.

Witt, C.A. and Witt, S.F. (1989) Measures of forecasting accuracy: turning point error v. size of error. *Tourism Management*, 10: 255–60.

Witt, S.F. and Witt, C.A. (1991) Tourism forecasting: error magnitude, direction of change error and trend change error. *Journal of Travel Research*, XXX (2): 26–33.

Witt, S.F. and Witt, C.A. (1992) *Modelling and Forecasting Demand in Tourism.* London: Academic Press.

Witt, S.F. and Witt, C.A. (1995) Forecasting tourism demand: a review of empirical research. *International Journal of Forecasting*, 11: 447–75.

Witt, C.A., Witt, S.F. and Wilson, N. (1994) Forecasting international tourist flows. *Annals of Tourism Research*, 21: 612–28.

Part

II

Global Regions' Futures

10

Africa

Victor Teye

Introduction

With its land mass of about 11.7 million square miles and comprised of more than 50 countries, the continent of Africa has an enormous potential for tourism development. This potential is based on an assembly of diverse physical and cultural resources that have been well-documented (Teye, 1987; Ankomah and Crompton, 1990). Despite this potential, a viable tourism industry has not emerged in the majority of the countries in Africa.

Africa has made a number of concerted efforts to diversify its economies in order to provide sustainable economic opportunities to improve the quality of life for its citizens. Within this context, tourism development has been highlighted but has actually played a marginal role in the continent's overall economic development. One such concerted effort at regional economic development began in 1980 when the Organization of African Unity (OAU) adopted the Lagos Plan Action (LPA) which eventually became the bedrock of Africa's economic development strategy (OAU, 1981; UN, 1986). The economic reasons included the urgent need to reverse the economic decline that has characterized the continent since the early 1970s, leading to the label 'the lost decade'. The political arguments for a new strategy for economic development were traced to the consequences of the 'Scramble for Africa' and the 'Partitioning of Africa' which occurred in the latter half of the 19ᵗʰ century. It has been argued that the consequent economic and political realities presented Africa with immense challenges, including fragile national borders, limited effective domestic markets, narrow resource base, and susceptibility to external market shocks (Dieke, 1998). Regrettably, these conditions exist today and pose even greater challenges to African development than they did when the LPA was first adopted. One main reason is that Africa's population has almost doubled to about 700 million during the period, thereby placing tremendous stress on all aspects of economic, social, cultural, environmental, as well as political development. In this context, it is important to note the elevated status of tourism by the United Nations (UN) Economic Commission for Africa (ECA) which clearly recognized the potential role of tourism in the economic and social development of Africa (ECA/WTO, 1984, Sako, 1990).

The discussion in this chapter is limited to sub-Saharan Africa (Africa south of the Sahara), and the term 'tourism' is used to include travel, tourism, hospitality and directly related industries. The focus of the discussion will be on international tourism since data on domestic tourism in Africa are almost non-existent. In general, domestic tourism tends to account for as much as 90% of the total for the industry (both domestic and international) in industrialized countries. As such, it should play a significant role in Africa's economic development as living standards improve, disposable incomes expand, the industry is developed, and residents are encouraged to participate in domestic tourism activities.

A review of the global and regional dimensions of the international tourism industry indicates that while Africa experienced a modest annual growth rate of 6.8% in international tourist arrivals between 1989 and 1999, the region on the whole accounted for a mere 4.0% of world arrivals and an even smaller 2.2% of receipts. Furthermore, the industry is concentrated in a handful of countries, while the majority of the countries on the continent have marginal tourism industries, well below their potential. A question arising from this review is this: What were some of the main obstacles to tourism development in the past, and how can they be overcome in the future? Implicit in this question is the fact that most African countries have, to differing extents, made attempts during the recent past to develop a tourism industry. During this period, the debate over the role of tourism development in developing countries in general was also played out on the African continent.

Table 10.1   Top 20 tourism destinations in Africa, 1998 (international tourist arrivals)

Rank	Country	No. arrivals (000)	% of total
1	South Africa	5898	23.6
2	Tunisia	4718	18.9
3	Morocco	3242	13.0
4	Zimbabwe	2090	8.4
5	Kenya	857	3.4
6	Botswana	740	3.0
7	Nigeria	739	3.0
8	Algeria	678	2.7
9	Namibia	560	2.2
10	Mauritius	558	2.2
11	Tanzania	450	1.8
12	Reunion	391	1.6
13	Zambia	362	1.4
14	Senegal	352	1.4
15	Ghana	335	1.3
16	Swaziland	319	1.3
17	Cote D'Ivoire	301	1.2
18	Uganda	238	1.0
19	Eritrea	188	0.8
20	Malawi	178	0.7
	Total	**23 194**	**92.7**
	Total Africa	**25 023**	**100.0**

Source: World Tourism Organization

Given the fact that the issues centred on the debate are even more relevant today, it is important to examine them, particularly, since they will have to be addressed in the future.

The tourism development debate

This section of the discussion begins to introduce the challenges facing tourism development in Africa in the future within the context of the post-independence period. It attempts to synthesize some of the main arguments advanced in the 1970s and 1980s in support of tourism development on the continent. For the most part, these were the same arguments, mostly economic in nature, that were advanced for developing countries in general (de Kadt,

Table 10.2   Top 20 tourism earners in Africa, 1998 (international tourism receipts, excluding transport)

Rank	Country	US$ mn	% of total
1	South Africa	2738	27.3
2	Morocco	1675	16.7
3	Tunisia	1557	15.6
4	Tanzania	570	5.7
5	Mauritius	503	5.0
6	Namibia	288	2.9
7	Ghana	274	2.7
8	Reunion	265	2.6
9	Kenya	233	2.3
10	Senegal	178	1.8
11	Zimbabwe	177	1.8
12	Botswana	175	1.7
13	Nigeria	142	1.4
14	Uganda	142	1.4
15	Seychelles	111	1.1
16	Cote D'Ivoire	108	1.1
17	Madagascar	91	0.9
18	Eritrea	75	0.7
19	Zambia	75	0.7
20	Sierra Leone	57	0.6
	Total	**9434**	**94.0**
	Total Africa	**10 011**	**100.0**

Source: WTO, 1999

1979; Lea, 1988). However, some of the arguments took into consideration specific African conditions and concerns.

First, it was argued that most African governments see their responsibility as including the provision of an adequate supply of foreign exchange for the payment of imports of capital and consumer products. Tourism was seen as a means to diversify Africa's mono-cultural economies, since the economic fortunes of most countries were highly dependent upon the export of a few unprocessed agricultural and mineral products. For example, by the mid-1980s, 25 out of 46 sub-Saharan African countries were totally dependent on agricultural exports, and 17 countries derived over 80% of their export earnings from less than four commodities.

Second, and closely related to the foreign exchange arguments, was assertion that tourism could assist in preventing and alleviating widespread and persistent unemployment in African countries. This argument was even more appealing to development experts since it identified tourism as being labour-intensive, requiring a significant proportion of unskilled labour, and stressed the existence of a hospitable African population to deliver hospitality-based services. Those who held traditional views that pointed to the fact that the service sector (including tourism) is the third phase in the process of economic development, progressing from agriculture and industrialization, were strongly met with research and statistical evidence to the contrary. For example, Lee (1987) referred to studies carried out by the United Nations Conference on Trade and Development (UNCTAD) and concluded that: 'the development of a whole range of services is a necessary precondition to stimulate growth in other sectors and the services industry finds itself in a key position at the heart of the national economic fabric' (Lee, 1987: 87). Summary (1987) provided further evidence from Kenya, where a 70% increase in tourist expenditure between 1971 and 1976 was estimated to have increased output in the agricultural sector by as much as 262%, and enhanced productivity in the food preparation sector by 720%. For the proponents of tourism development, this was further evidence that the industry can promote inter-sectoral linkages.

Third, it was argued that tourism supports policies that pursue spatially comprehensive regional development activities. In this regard, a Zimbabwe minister for tourism stated that the tourism industry 'provides jobs and economic growth points in areas that would remain undeveloped because they are not fit for either agriculture or resettlement purposes. The gains of tourism are ploughed back to the development areas where they are generated' (Novicki, 1983: 53).

In addition to the economic arguments in favour of tourism development, environmental and social benefits were also cited. According to Bell (1987), by the mid-1980s the number of national parks and reserves had more than doubled since the early 1960s, thereby facilitating the conservation of ecological systems that provide the basis for ecotourism in general, and wildlife tourism in particular. The social and cultural benefits that were articulated in support of tourism development in Africa are illustrated by the following statement made by the late President Nyerere of Tanzania: 'To have visitors is a special honour, and to treat a visitor well and hospitably is an act of good manners. A visitor [who] comes to Tanzania, stays for a while, and leaves praising this country, is a good ambassador of us abroad, and he is an ambassador who costs us nothing' (Adelson, 1976: 45). Besides the facilitation of international understanding, goodwill and contributing to peace, the educational benefits to both residents and visitors provided claims of additional benefits. For example, the Zimbabwe Tourist Board attempted to establish cultural centres close to major tourist attractions so that visitors could meet with locals and be afforded the opportunity to learn the history and culture of the area. (Novicki, 1983).

It must be emphasized that African countries were presented with not only the positive side of the tourism development debate, but the negative arguments as well. While the issues that emerged from the debate are too diverse and complex to be adequately examined here, suffice it to say that they have been extensively covered elsewhere with respect to developing countries (de Kadt, 1979; Britton, 1982; Erbes, 1973; Lea, 1988; Go and Jenkins, 1997) and about Africa (ECA, 1986; Teye, 1991, Dieke, 1993). Briefly, the counter-arguments against tourism development include the possibility of enclave development, leakage of foreign exchange; state subsidized development for the benefit of foreign investors; seasonal unemployment; exacerbating rural to urban migration; destruction of social patterns; reinforcement of neo-colonialist relationships of exploitation, dependency and servitude; inflationary pressure and land speculation; commercialization of cultural assets; westernization of society, particularly Africa's youth; increase in crime; and threats to the moral fibre of society. After considering both sides of the argument, Tanzania, for example, denounced tourism development in the late 1960s as inconsistent with the country's political philosophy. Despite his initial more positive stance on tourism, the late President Nyerere went on to label tourism as a 'necessary evil' and suggested that tourists must be isolated from the general population (Nyerere, 1969). There are other examples of concerns about the potential adverse impact of tourism development in Africa. In the early 1970s, a national debate that involved the head of state focused on the impact of foreigners on Ghanaian culture through the social demonstration effect. One contribution to the debate pointed out that: 'Without mincing words, the youth of Ghana today have come to accept anything British, American, and for that matter foreign as the all-in-all. Anything African and Ghanaian is second rate . . . No decent society will sit down aloof to see its youth copy useless foreign cultures at the detriment of the nation . . . Africans nations cannot allow the nation-wrecking Western permissive society to corrode our society' (Ayi, 1974: 5). Cultural activities such as festivals and special events also generated concerns such as: 'The Americans brought out the curse of traditional ceremonies in West Africa – the European or Black American with a camera. Possession of this device, they appear to think, entitles them to roam the area at will, obstructing the view of other people and generally reducing the whole sacred ceremony to a second class circus. . . . The rule had better be firmly established before all the German tourists arrive' (Williams, 1974: 10–11). The Gambia, with its small population of less than half a million, also had its share of social problems back in the

1970s whereby: 'Swedes have sometimes offended Gambian morals by appearing naked on the beaches or scantily clad in the towns. As a result, the authorities have insisted on proper dress . . . and have been known to expel overland tourists who do not conform to the Gambian concept of well-dressed Westerners' (Uweche, 1975: 73).

Critical issues

The economic, social and environmental issues embedded in tourism development constitute greater challenges for the African region in the future for a number of reasons. First, the majority of African countries are economically worse off than they were at or shortly after independence in the 1960s. The World Bank (1996) estimated that sub-Saharan Africa's gross domestic product (GDP) grew by only 1.45% during the period 1991 to 1994. The Bank went on to say that: 'In most of the continent, growth is not nearly sufficient to make a dent in poverty reduction, and despite recent improvements, Africa's GDP and export growth rates, savings and investment levels, and social indicators remain below those of other regions' (World Bank, 1996: 71). Even countries such as Botswana, Ghana and Uganda, which were recently regarded as economic success stories by the World Bank and its affiliate institutions, are currently experiencing serious problems. The situation in Ghana illustrates the nature and persistence of old economic problems at the close of this century; specifically, foreign exchange constraints due to dependence on a few mineral and agricultural exports. The price of cocoa, the country's leading agricultural export, which was $1711 per tonne during the 1997/98 season, had declined to $1040 by September 1999. Similarly, the country's principal export, gold, which was $288 an ounce in December 1998 had declined to $260 per ounce. To complicate the economic situation – and placing enormous pressure on foreign exchange reserves – the price of imported crude oil was $10.21 in December 1998 but had more than doubled to about $23 at the end of September 1999. While the short-term solution appears to lie in the implementation of several austerity measures, the long-term economic diversification strategy includes the comprehensive development of the tourism sector. For example, Ghana established a Ministry of Tourism in 1993 and has a 15-year tourism Master Plan for the period 1996 to 2010. This appears to be the trend in several African countries which are pursuing planned tourism development projects, with the assistance of such agencies as the United Nations Development Program (UNDP), WTO and regional organizations such as the Southern Africa Development Community (SADC).

Second, the environmental challenges in Africa are even more diverse, complex and critical today, mainly due to such factors as the rapid population growth, expanded land-use and congested urban areas. While many African countries have established environmental protection agencies and ministries for the environment, several are turning to tourism-related activities in order to protect the ecosystem. For example, the Upper Guinea Forest Ecosystem in West Africa which extends from Ghana through the Ivory Coast, Liberia, Guinea and Sierra Leone, originally occupied about 728 000 square kilometres but currently all that remains is only about 13% (92 797 km²). This reduction has been attributed to human activity over a long period of time but most intensely in the past 20 years. Classified as one of the world's priority conservation areas because of what is regarded as its high endemism, Conservation International (CI) has been working with the governments of Ghana and the Ivory Coast to establish National Parks and reserves with tourism components such as attractions and visitors' centres. Similar projects directed at conserving the environment and its habitat with potential for ecotourism development can be found in such countries as Madagascar and Botswana (the Okavango Delta).

Finally, cultural tourism and in particular, the ethnic tourism component has provided several African countries with the opportunity to begin to preserve and restore cultural attractions, including several World Heritage Sites. However, in addition to the old issues that were discussed earlier in this chapter, new challenges are beginning to emerge. For example, the restoration of the slave forts and castles in Senegal (Gore Island) and Ghana (Elmina and Cape Coast) have evoked emotional responses from Africans in the diaspora, mostly from the United States and the Caribbean (Bruner, 1996). The Slave Route Project currently being proposed by the United Nations Educational, Scientific and Cultural Organization (UNESCO) in partnership with the WTO is bound to add tremendous resources to Africa's cultural tourism inventory, but will certainly raise many complex issues. The diverse economic, social, cultural and environmental issues related to tourism development will have to be addressed at country, region and local levels as well at the intra-African regional level. In the broader context, however, several factors constitute impediments to tourism development. These will have to be addressed by African countries if they are to succeed individually or collectively in their tourism development efforts.

Obstacles to tourism development

A myriad of obstacles has been identified in the literature as hindering tourism development in Africa (Ankomah and Crompton, 1990). A few of them are summarized below.

Political instability

These include civil wars, *coups d'état*, dictatorships, terrorist activities and other forms of political unrest. These can adversely affect the flow of visitors as well as investment into Africa, and impact the delivery of existing tourism goods and services (Teye, 1986, 1988). Events associated with political instability usually include human misery and tragedy which, when relayed through the print and electronic media, reinforce the negative images that are incompatible with the safe and relaxing destinations desired by the majority of leisure visitors. Some studies published in the tourism literature have documented the fact that international leisure and business travellers use beliefs and ideas about Africa to construct it socially as 'dangerous and to be avoided' (Carter, 1998: 349). There are still many areas of political conflicts such as Angola, the Democratic Republic of Congo, Rwanda, Sierra Leone, Somalia and the Sudan. Even countries that appear to be relatively stable have fragile political conditions, which threaten safety and security of visitors as well as residents. Recent examples from Egypt, Nigeria, Kenya, South Africa, Tanzania and Uganda illustrate this point. Furthermore, there is a tendency on the part of potential visitors from the long-haul points of origin to perceive local events in Africa on a more continental scale.

Economic restructuring

Most African countries inherited large government bureaucracies from the colonial period. After independence, they expanded these institutions and added layers of activities in the primary and manufacturing sectors, such as state farms, mining companies and industrial holdings. A feature of the African economy since the mid-1980s has been the Structural Adjustment Policies (SAPs), aimed at implementing economic reforms including privatization of public enterprises, deregulation of prices, interest rates and overall financial liberalization. It was also aimed at attracting foreign investment and to improve efficiency of resource utilization. SAPs have direct impact on tourism by attracting investment in the tourism sector as well as increasing the inflow of the business market segment (Dieke, 1995). While the results of SAPs are debatable and even controversial, it appears that it will become a feature of the economic landscape of Africa in the next century, with its attendant impact on tourism.

Human resource constraints

Tourism requires a variety of inter-disciplinary competencies at various phases of its planning, development, marketing and management (ECA, 1992). Investment in the training activities that build local capacity in the tourism sector should ensure that Africans obtain maximum economic benefits through better-paying jobs, while reducing economic leakage that arises from hiring foreigners such as hotel managers. Ultimately, it also ensures development of indigenous tourism products as well as the delivery of quality services with staff who are knowledgeable about their own country and its attractions.

Regional cooperation

Regional political and economic unions that promote regional growth through easy movement of capital, goods, services and people have become a common feature of global interdependence. Africa has been rather unsuccessful at establishing lasting and viable economic sub-regional groups, even though such a large number of these organizations are scattered throughout the continent. Unfortunately, some, such as the East African Economic Community, which appeared to be the most viable regional organization in Africa, became a casualty of political differences between the member states (Kenya, Tanzania and Uganda) and broke up in 1977 (Delupes, 1969). Others, such as the Economic Community of West African States (ECOWAS), which was established in 1975, is ineffectual and has not delivered most of the programmes it set out to implement. The benefits that accrue to the tourism industry from regional cooperation cover almost every aspect of the sector's development. They include joint marketing programmes, human resource training, common transportation services, immigration, customs and health policies, standardization of research activities and classification of tourism plant (Teye, 1991; see also Dieke, 1998). Currently, the Southern Africa Economic Community (SADC) appears to be the regional organization with the greatest assets and potential in facilitating tourism development on the continent.

Other constraints

There are a number of other obstacles that would have to be overcome in order to develop a viable tourism industry in Africa. These include provision of adequate and basic infrastructure, including lodges, telecommunication and transportation services; overcoming health and medical challenges; strengthening weak institutional frameworks for tourism planning; encouraging effective community participation in tourism; promoting domestic tourism; effective utilization of the information technology, and minimizing the adverse economic, social and environmental impact of tourism. Ultimately, this means that what constitutes an appropriate form of tourism (Brown, 1998) at the country and local levels needs to be determined and then comprehensively planned in a sustainable manner.

Summary

This chapter examined the main issues that African countries will face in developing viable tourism industries in the new millennium. It began with a review of the international tourism industry in Africa within a global context. This was followed by a discussion of the reasons for and against tourism development in Africa during the post-independence period. It was concluded that these issues are even more relevant today and will present challenges in the future. Finally, a number of obstacles restricting tourism development were summarized as a basis for further discussion. An extensive list of sources follows this brief overview.

References

Adelson, C. (1976) Tanzania: Western tourism and African socialism. *Africa Report*, September–October.

Ankomah, P.K. and Crompton, J.L. ((1990) Unrealized tourism potential: the case of sub-Saharan Africa. *Tourism Management*, 11 (1): 11–28.

Ayi, N. (1974) Are we Ghanaians or semi-Europeans?, *Daily Graphic*, 3 January, p. 5.

Barnes, J. (1988) Africa makes a hard choice. *US News and World Report* June 27, 28-32.

Bell, R. (1987) Conservation with a human face: conflict and reconciliation in African land use planning. In *Conservation in Africa: People, Policies and Practice*. Cambridge: Cambridge University Press.

Britton, S. (1982) The political economy of tourism in the third world. *Annals of Tourism Research*, 9 (3): 331–58.

Brown, D.O. (1998) In search of an appropriate form of tourism for Africa: lessons from the past and suggestions for the future. *Tourism Management*, 19 (3): 237–45.

Bruner, E.D. (1996) Tourism in Ghana – the representation of slavery and the return of the black diaspora. *American Anthropologist*, 98 (2): 290–304.

Carter, S. (1998) Tourists' and travelers' social construction of Africa and Asia as risky locations. *Tourism Management*, 19 (4): 349–58.

de Kadt, E (1979) *Tourism; Passport to Development?* New York: Oxford University Press.

Delupes, I.D. (1969) *The East African Economic Community and Common Market.* London: Longman.

Dieke, P.U.C. (1993) Cross-national comparisons of tourism development: lessons from Kenya and the Gambia. *Journal of Tourism Studies*, 4 (1): 2–18.

Dieke, P.U.C. (1995) Tourism and structural adjustment programs in the African economy. *Tourism Economics* 1 (1): 71–93.

Dieke, P.U.C. (1998) Regional tourism in Africa – scope and critical issues. In Laws *et al.* (eds), *Embracing and Managing Change in Tourism- International Case Studies.* New York: Routledge, pp. 29–48.

ECA (1986) *Development of Tourism in Africa: the intra-African Tourism Promotion of Tourist Product.* Addis Ababa, Ethiopia: UN Economic Commission for Africa.

ECA (1992) *Directory of Vocational Training Facilities in Tourism in Africa.* Addis Ababa, Ethiopia: UN Economic Commission for Africa.

ECA/WTO (1984) Intra-Africa tourism cooperation, joint presentation to the regional conference on intra-African tourism cooperation by the ECA and WTO. Naimey, Niger, October 2–5.

Erbes, R. (1973) *International Tourism and the Economy of Developing Countries.* Paris: Organization for Economic Cooperation and Development.

Esh, T. and Rosenblum, I. (1975) *Tourism in Developing Countries – Trick or Treat?: A Report from the Gambia.* Uppsala, Sweden: The Scandinavian Institute of African Studies, Research Report 31.

Go, F.M. and Jenkins, L.K. (eds) (1997) *Tourism and Economic Development in Asia and Australasia.* London: Cassell.

Lea, J. (1988) *Tourism and Development in the Third World.* London: Routledge.

Lee, G. (1987) Future of national and regional tourism in developing countries. *Tourism Management*, 8: 2.

Novicki, M. (1983) Zimbabwe: tourism with a socialist slant. *Africa Report*, January–February, 49–53.

Nyerere, J. (1969) Essay, *The House Magazine.* Dar-es-Salaam, Tanzania: National Development Corporation.

Organization of African Unity (OAU) (1981) *Lagos Plan of Action for the Economic Development of Africa: 1980–2000.* Geneva, Switzerland: International Institute of Labor Studies.

Sako, F. (1990) Tourism in Africa: an expanding industry. *The Courier*, 122: 62–72.

Summary, R. (1987) Tourism's contribution to the economy of Kenya. *Annals of Tourism Research*, 14: 531–40.

Teye, V.B. (1986) Liberation wars and tourism development in Africa – the case of Zambia. *Annals of Tourism Research*, 13 (4): 589–608.

Teye, V.B. (1988) Coups d'état and African tourism: a study of Ghana. *Annals of Tourism Research*, 15 (3): 329–56.

Teye, V.B. (1987) Developing Africa's tourism potential: prospects and issues. *Tourism Recreation Research*, 12 (1): 9–14.

Teye, V.B. (1991) Prospects for regional tourism cooperation in Africa. In S. Medlik (ed.), *Managing Tourism*. Oxford: Butterworth–Heinemann, pp. 286–96.

United Nations (UN) (1986) *Africa's submission to the special session of the UN General Assembly on Africa's economic and social crisis*. New York: UN General Assembly.

Uweche, R. (ed.) (1975) Tourism, peace and sunshine. *Africa*, February, 73–4.

Williams, D. (ed.) (1974) Matchet diary . . .. from Ada. *West Africa*, 19 August, pp. 10–11.

World Bank (1996) *Annual Report 1996*. Washington, DC: The World Bank. http://www.worldbank.org/html/extpb/annrep96/

World Tourism Organization (WTO) (1991) *Impact of the Gulf Crisis on International Tourism*. Madrid: WTO Special Report.

World Tourism Organization (WTO) (1994) *Global Tourism Forecasts to the year 2000 and Beyond: Africa Volume 2*. Madrid: WTO.

World Tourism Organization (WTO) (1999) *Tourism Market Trends, Africa 1989–1998*. Madrid: WTO Commission for Africa.

World Tourism Organization (WTO) (2000) *Compendium of Tourism Statistics 1994–1998*. Madrid: WTO.

11

Asia Pacific

Kenneth Chamberlain

The financial crisis

In 1996 visitor arrivals in the area grew by 9.6%.
Confidence about the future of Asia Pacific
tourism was at its height. Yet, in less than a year,
the area dived from being the fastest growing
region to bottom place.

What happened? It all started on 2 July 1997
when the Bank of Thailand floated the baht. From
there the dominoes began to fall with great
rapidity. Currency values and stock markets
dropped dramatically. Korea is a case in point.
The won fell from around 900 to the US$ to
1960. The stock market index fell from almost
1000 to 300. Unemployment rose from 2.3% of
the labour force to 8.4% and the consumer price
index rose from 3.2% to 13.5 %.

Korea, Thailand, Indonesia and Malaysia were
hit the most. It was also felt strongly in Singapore,
Hong Kong and even the South Pacific. China
and South Asia felt it the least. Tourism was,
needless to say, badly impacted. In Japan,
outbound travel fell for 14 consecutive months.
Business travel between Asia's capital cities fell

by up to 30%. The focus of industry was on survival. Short-term needs created an environment of rate cutting. Yield was sacrificed for cash flow.

Overcapacity increased the impact on the hotel sector. Occupancy rates plunged by as much as 48% in some places. Hundreds of hotels have closed or become technically bankrupt. Among the airlines, all the performance indicators fell. Philippine Airlines closed altogether for a while. Hundreds of travel agents were reported to be in trouble. In Korea, the forecast was that only about half of the outbound travel agents would survive.

Why did all this happen? Contributing factors included the withdrawal of foreign short-term capital investments, bank loans and portfolio investments plus overvalued exchange rates and excessive credit expansion for speculation in land and real estate. In addition, there was declining relative competitiveness, a severe asset bubble and an insufficiently regulated and weak financial system. Export growth slowed. Current account deficits grew. The bubble was ready to burst. And, it did.

In many of the Asia Pacific countries a turn around began in the second half of 1998 and there was continued improvement in 1999. As the millennium closed Thailand and Korea were the real success stories. In Korea, the won rate rose 40% and its stock market by 123%. In Thailand, interest rates came down from the ugly 22% to 9%.

Visitor arrivals have risen in virtually all Asia Pacific countries and, by the end of 2000, totals were expected to have climbed back to where they were before the crisis, almost everywhere. This has been achieved at the expense of prices. In 12 out of the 16 Asian countries surveyed, hotel occupancy was up but room rates were way down. Low prices attracted more long haul visitors, especially Europeans and restimulated demand within the Asia Pacific region. Among airlines, flights are being added back and loads improved.

In summation, the Asia Pacific industry is now moving in the right direction all across the region. The weak have fallen by the wayside. The strong have a low cost environment in which to regroup and expand. Confidence is returning. One worry is that the recovery may be happening too fast and that renewed growth may lead to the underlying structural problems that contributed to the crisis being forgotten in the rush to chase new business and short-term gain.

Future trends

Globalization and liberalization

Most of us in the West see globalization and liberalization in a very positive light. If you speak to business people in Asia, you will find they see things from a quite different perspective. The 1999 UNCTAD report states:

> The humbling of the Asian tigers since 1997 has revealed the vulnerability of even the strongest developing economies to the powerful forces unleashed by globalization. While the developed world suffered little from the Asian crisis and even derived some benefit from it, the impact on the rest of the world has been dramatic. Growth in the developing world slowed from almost 6% in 1996 to under 2% in 1998.

Developing countries are being pushed towards greater liberalization and integration, to relax foreign investment rules, and to be more transparent. But, many Asians see that the countries in the region which were hurt the most by the crisis were the ones who pursued these policies and those hurt the least were the ones who did not. They see the process as being lopsided and feel that it is widening the gap between the developed and the developing worlds. A major problem is that it is moving too fast, faster than the structure and rules needed to manage it. In developing countries, the institutions, the systems and, for that matter, the mind set are often not ready for what is happening.

In tourism, power is increasingly being concentrated and there is concern that foreign multinational companies will take advantage of distressed situations and the low cost environment to gain a bigger share of the Asia Pacific tourism industry.

Greater understanding of the impacts on developing countries is needed. Without this, it is not hard to envisage conflicts and possibly renewed protection lying ahead, all of which could pose problems for tourism development in the region.

Consolidation

Perhaps the most significant development has been the creation of four major global airline alliances. Some Asia Pacific airlines, hit by the financial crisis, are signing up with one or other of them. More will no doubt do so. These alliances can use technology and their advantages of scale and reach to be a very powerful force in the Asia Pacific travel scene. Everyone in every sector of tourism is going to have to deal with that reality.

There is also consolidation going on in the Asia Pacific hotel and tour operator sectors. The financial crisis exposed the weak; the strong are buying the weak and others are looking for alliance partners so as to create a collective organization that is stronger, to build new regional distribution networks.

The message for the future, learned from the crisis, seems to have been 'do not get left out on your own'.

The Internet

Now the worst of the financial crisis is hopefully over, the Internet is the hottest topic in Asia Pacific tourism. Communication by e-mail is becoming standard practice. The proportion of travel companies with their own website or pages in a collective one is high. In part, this is a response to what is happening in the key generating markets. If one in every four German homes is online, they need to be online also. Internet sales are still small in percentage terms but are growing every month. In the future, the Asia Pacific travel industry will continue to develop its capacity to use the Internet and other information technology to advantage and will be a match for any region in these respects.

Distribution

It has been said that 'vertigo is caused by looking down from a great height or, in the case of travel agents, when faced by the prospect of zero commissions'. Impacted by the financial crisis, airlines operating in the region had to reduce costs and the floodgates are now open, releasing an onslaught on agents' commissions.

Agents are realizing that they have to make a fundamental change in the way they do business. Singapore's National Association of Travel Agents led the way in Asia when it resolved that it 'must prepare agents for a service fee environment'. It must convince them that their focus should be on serving their customers and charging for the services they provide. By eliminating so many of the weaker agents, the financial crisis helped to prepare the ground for this transition to be made.

Markets

Attracted by the low prices available as a result of the financial crisis, European tour operators are expanding their programmes and the North American market is once again on the wish list. Above all, however, there are three markets that will influence Asia Pacific tourism the most in the 21st century.

The first is Japan. It has been the dominant market for every Asia Pacific country. If you ask any of the region's tourism leaders about how the recovery will go, the answer is likely to be 'it all depends on Japan'. The view in Japan is that the economy has bottomed out, public confidence is recovering and travel remains on top of the wish list. The recovery remains slow but once confidence fully returns, the volume of Japanese travelling abroad will return to a pattern of sustained growth.

Then there is China and India. Each has a number of people in the middle class able to afford overseas travel that is already estimated to be bigger than the total population of all but a handful of countries and it is growing. No other region has potential markets on this scale. Both will inevitably impact the area's tourism in a big way in the coming century. A recent Kuoni study predicted that outbound travel from India will increase by 20% per year for the next five years. The World Tourism Organization (WTO) estimates there will be 100 million Chinese overseas trips in 2020. And most will be to other destinations in the Asia Pacific region.

Asia Pacific travellers

Australians and New Zealanders are experienced travellers, but the Asian outbound markets, on the other hand, are all new, most of them very new.

Japan started as a modern travel market in 1964 when exchange controls were lifted and it is now a relatively mature market. Travel is within reach of most people. The courier with the flag has largely gone; people are travelling with family members or a few friends. Growth is in independent travel with customized itineraries, and special interest travel is well established. Itineraries are not so crammed and even shopping is lower on the scale of preferences. These trends will continue.

The rest are really young markets. Restrictions on Taiwanese and Koreans travelling abroad, for instance, were lifted in 1988 and 1989 and it was only in 1992 that China relaxed its rules. In the early 1990s, the characteristics of their travellers were similar to those of the early Japanese tourists. Now these markets are maturing rapidly and catching up to where Japan is today. There is a growing amount of independent travel and an increasing number of people who expect to travel abroad at least once a year. One thing that is unlikely to change very much, however, is the length of their holidays, which will remain short.

National Tourism Organizations (NTOs)

Many governments are looking to reduce public expenditure on tourism and would like to see more private sector money in the tourism pot. For its part, the private sector is not particularly interested in putting in its money unless it has say in how that money is spent. In this situation, Nepal decided to close its Department of Tourism and establish an autonomous public/private sector tourism board. The Maldives set up a Tourism Promotion Board recently and Sri Lanka is on the same track.

One Asian Minister recently said: 'The government firmly believes that it should move out from conducting business and the private sector should do what it is good at, so that we can maximize the use of scarce resources (*The Island*, October 1999). With globalization, intensified competition and the impacts of information technology, it seems likely that this is the direction in which more Asia Pacific NTOs will be heading.

Cruising

Cruising has been around a long time in the South Pacific. The big new development is the recent growth of cruising in Asia. Cruising by Asians began to take off in earnest in 1990 and grew rapidly in 1993 when Star Cruises arrived on the scene. In 1998, the Port of Singapore handled over one million passengers. Most cruises are of three to four days' duration, which suits the urban Asian very well.

Star Cruises now operates cruise programmes based in Singapore, Hong Kong, Bangkok, Taipei and Osaka and has become the fourth largest cruise line in the world. Japan also has its cruise ships and in Korea, Hyundai Merchant Marine is filling two ships with a third on order. The potential of the Asian market is enormous and the future for cruising looks very bright.

Future growth

Forecasts

In the final part of this chapter, I would like to refer to the WTO *Tourism 2020 Vision* report. WTO says that, despite the financial crisis, the Asia Pacific region will grow faster than the others do and will pass the Americas to be second only to Europe in the number of visitor arrivals. I have my doubts, though, about the region receiving five times as many visitors in 2020 as it did in 1998. I question the forecast of 59.3 million visitors arriving in Hong Kong in 2020: that is 162 500 per day with perhaps 250 000 on a peak day, and if they all stayed an average of four days, that would mean there could be 800 000, perhaps even one million visitors in Hong Kong at one time. All I can say is that I would not want to be there or to have to go through Hong Kong airport!

Similarly, I worry about 141.5 million Japanese overseas trips at that time, not only from the demand viewpoint but also from the logistics of the situation. That figure breaks down to almost 400 000 leaving per day and over half a million on a peak day. Including arriving, departing and transit passengers, airports would be called upon to handle well over 1 000 000 passengers per day. And this in a country where, after many years of trying, Narita still does not have a second runway in operation.

With Asia's population and the growth of its middle class, there could well be the potential demand for international travel to create five times as many arrivals. But only if there were not five times as many people everywhere they went.

Restraints on growth

This is one restraint on growth that must be taken into consideration. Others are:

- Market pressure on governments to protect the environment and develop in a sustainable manner.
- Environmental and consumer protection legislation.
- The physical limits of the places every tourist wants to see and the impacts on them.
- Congestion at airports and in city centres. It might not be possible to move at all in some Asian cities.

- Destination opposition – the 'Not in my back yard' syndrome.
- Visitor expectations: surveys indicate that people are looking for customization, time efficiency, personal service and a unique experience plus the ability to relax and to get away from it all. These are not attributes that fit well with a five-times increase in visitor numbers.
- Quality: the more crowds, hassles and overdevelopment the more the quality of the visitor experience will be reduced.
- Prices: prices will rise if demand exceeds supply where space is restricted.
- Safety: aircraft disasters, air space congestion, civil disturbance, terrorism, health and natural disasters could all affect the desire to travel.

Domestic tourism

And then there is domestic tourism, a much-neglected aspect of the industry. It has been rising rapidly in the Asia Pacific region with the growth of the middle class and of car ownership. WTO has estimated that the ratio of domestic to international tourists may be as high as ten to one. In Thailand, for example, WTO forecasts there will be 37 million visitor arrivals in 2020 and, on a ten to one basis, that could mean 370 million domestic trips. Even if the ratio is only five to one, that is still 185 million. How much breathing room is that going to leave for the 37 million international visitors looking for a unique experience?

I feel that, at some point, a rising visitor quantity line on the graph will cross with a declining experience quality line and, together with the other factors mentioned, will restrain tourism from reaching the levels predicted by WTO.

The development matrix

Tourism has always been much better at building on strengths and taking opportunities than it has at correcting weaknesses. Its response to a problem has too often been to throw more promotion at it. In the 21st century, if quality is to be sustained and the optimum number of visitors sent home happy, tourism must be better at managing the framework within which the industry grows.

The restraints on growth that I have mentioned are all part of that framework. They are parts of a tourism development matrix which, in an ideal world, should all move together in the same direction and at the same pace. To begin to make that happen, we need to have decided where we want to go and how to get there or, in other words, to plan strategically. Whether or not such planning is both undertaken and implemented will have a significant bearing on the future growth of Asia Pacific tourism.

A responsible industry?

The WTO report comments on the degree to which markets are unsaturated and says 'International tourism can be seen to be an industry truly in its infancy'. As my earlier comments suggest, I disagree with that. I believe that the time has come for tourism, as one of the biggest industries in the world, to recognize that it has acquired responsibilities. This is going to be especially difficult in the Asia Pacific area since this is where there will be the greatest demand pressure. It is also where money talks and where return on investment talks the loudest. How the Asia Pacific region handles these responsibilities will say a lot about the future of its tourism industry.

But, whatever happens, the impact of Asia Pacific markets, destinations and its tourism industry on the world's tourism scene will be greater in the 21st century than it has been. As John Naisbitt has said, 'the West may come to need the East more than the East will need the West'.

Reference

Naisbitt, J. (1994) *Global Paradox: the Bigger the World Economy, the More Powerful its Smallest Players.* London: Nicholas Brealey Publishing.

12

The Caribbean

Auliana Poon

Introduction

The Caribbean is one of the most tourism-dependent economies in the world. It is estimated that tourism generates 560 000 jobs (directly and indirectly). Visitor expenditure contributed an estimated US$17.5 billion in revenues in 1998. The tourism sector represents about one-third of all regional exports. For islands such as Antigua and Barbuda and the Bahamas, tourism contributes most of the GDP.

It is imperative that Caribbean islands develop the strategies and take the necessary steps to ensure the sustainability and competitiveness of the tourism sector. The need to make the tourism sector work for the region is even more acute today in the light of key developments at the global level, namely the banana crisis and the deterioration of the manufacturing sector. In addition, many other developing countries (South Africa, Thailand) as well as developed market economies (UK and USA) and former Eastern-bloc countries (Hungary, China) are intensifying competition in the tourism market. Increased economic challenges in many tourist-destination countries is also pressuring outbound travel resulting in stark competition for the tourist dollar. Changes brought on by the rapid adoption of information technologies also pose a number of new challenges and opportunities.

There are many excellent initiatives taking place in the Caribbean that poise the region for further growth and competitiveness of the tourism sector:

- The Caribbean tourism industry is very competitive. The sector has not been weaned on protectionism as has sugar, bananas and import substituting manufacturing. Yet, the industry continues to hold its own in the international marketplace – countries such as the Dominican Republic, with superior price competitiveness, has been able to grow its industry by leaps and bounds.
- The highly innovative and dynamic all-inclusive hotel sector, led by Sandals and SuperClubs continues to post consistently superior performance. They are a driving force in the growth and expansion of the tourism industry.
- The cruise tourism sector is growing rapidly and the Caribbean continues to be the number one destination globally.
- There is growing concern and interest in sustainable development on the part of the public and private sectors. The Caribbean Action for Sustainable Tourism (CAST) led by the Caribbean Hotel Association (CHA) and initiatives such as the Caribbean Tourism Organization (CTO) regional annual conference on sustainable tourism are examples. In addition, many individual resorts and non-governmental organizations (NGOs) have won ecotourism awards.
- Progress has been made toward greater public and private sector cooperation, although much more work remains.
- The region is now marketed under one umbrella in Europe, with the assistance of the European Union.
- There have been several initiatives in the area of human resource development, although these initiatives are as yet inadequate to meet the needs of the region. One of these is CTO's initiative to establish a Caribbean Tourism Human Resource Council.

Importance of tourism and recent performance

Although the Caribbean region accounts for only 3% of international tourist arrivals, tourism plays a significant role in many Caribbean economies. The Caribbean (excluding Cancun and Cozumel) recorded 16.5 million tourist arrivals and 12.3 million cruise ship passenger visits in 1998. In 1997 gross visitor expenditure by all visitors to the Caribbean reached an estimated US$14.45 billion.

The total number of persons employed in accommodation establishments in the Caribbean in 1997 was estimated at 146 000. Available data suggest that total employment (direct and indirect) generated by tourism is about three times the employment in accommodation establishments (*Caribbean Tourism Organization*, 1997).

Despite temporary hiccups in 1973/74 (oil crisis), 1980/81 (second oil crisis), 1988 (Hurricane Hugo), 1991 (Gulf War) and 1995 (Hurricane Iris), stayover arrivals to the Caribbean continue to increase. However, while the trend in Caribbean tourism arrivals has generally been upward, this growth trend has not been the same for all islands. Different islands have experienced different levels of growth and have different levels of resilience to the global environment. An examination of the comparative rates of growth of Jamaica and Barbados, for example, shows that Jamaica has been far more resilient than Barbados and indeed the rest of the Caribbean during the 1980/1981 recession. A superior level of innovation in Jamaica (the development of all-inclusive hotels, for example), was certainly a contributing factor to Jamaica's superior performance.

As can be seen from Table 12.1 the cruise industry in the Caribbean has grown very rapidly and the rate of growth of cruise arrivals exceeded that of stayover arrivals in many years.

Table 12.1   Comparative growth of stayover and cruise arrivals, 1986–1996

Year	Stayover ('000)	Growth %	Cruise ('000)	Growth %
1986	8 460	6	5000	20
1987	9 590	13	5600	12
1988	10 400	8	6340	13
1989	11 170	7	6710	6
1990	11 850	6	7450	11
1991	11 650	−2	8700	17
1992	12 344	6	9400	8
1993	13 368	8	9615	2
1994	14 270	7	9790	2
1995	14 490	2	9710	−1
1996	14 838	2	10 696	10

The rapid growth and development of the cruise tourism industry opens key opportunities and poses a number of threats to the Caribbean destinations in which they operate. The environmental and economic impacts of cruise tourism are increasingly in question. Moreover, with its pace and magnitude of development, the cruise industry has almost appeared as a 'thief in the night', directly competing with land-based tourism.

The Caribbean is the most important geographic market for the cruise industry, accounting for over one-half of all cruises taken world-wide. According to informed observers the Caribbean is expected to retain its position as the dominant region for cruising for a number of reasons, including the region's proximity to the US market, its tremendous physical attraction and image of relative stability, and constraints to growth in some of the competing regions.

Strategic issues facing Caribbean tourism

Competitiveness

One of the key strategic issues facing the Caribbean tourism sector is that of ensuring the continued competitiveness of the sector in global markets. A number of factors will reinforce the competitiveness of the Caribbean tourism sector.

Human resource development   One of the keys to quality is the human resources that deliver quality services. The development of the human resource base of the Caribbean tourism sector is a key priority. There is an urgent need to invest in the training and development of human resources that would manage the tourism industry in an efficient, profitable and sustainable manner and also provide quality services to an increasingly demanding international clientele.

It is in the critically important field of human resource development that the accommodation sector faces its toughest challenge. In the increasingly competitive world of international tourism, the days of enthusiastic amateurs are over. Technical efficiency and professional service are the distinguishing marks of success.

Quality standard   It is also important that appropriate standards that meet global customer requirements are implemented. The problem of small hotels is the key concern. The Caribbean hotel sector, for a number of reasons, prefers to avoid any discussions or actions aimed at classifying its properties. More emphasis has been placed on developing and meeting certain minimum standards. However, much more work needs to be done in developing regional standards and re-developing and re-positioning the region as a destination of quality.

Ancillary services sector also needs attention. The ancillary tourism sector (which comprises a wide variety of services provided outside the hotel sector, including restaurants, ground tour operations, taxis, duty free shops, handicrafts, water sports operations, etc.) is generally not accepted as a mainstream component of the tourism product but operations within these services generally reflect the need for a closer examination of financial support systems, improved training and certification programs, and improved marketing skills.

Safety and security   Increasingly, lack of adequate security for visitors is becoming a major deterrent to the growth of healthy tourism in many destinations. The increasing trend towards harassment of visitors on the beaches and on the streets, the rise in crimes directed at tourists, and the open peddling of drugs is a growing concern for policy-makers.

Research and market intelligence   Another key pillar of competitiveness is research, information and market intelligence. The Caribbean needs to strengthen its information/intelligence base with which to monitor the tourism industry, anticipate change and identify policy instruments to address/control any adverse impacts anticipated. More research is needed to understand the dynamics of competition within the tourism industry – why some islands perform better than others; why do some sectors perform better than others (e.g. cruises and all-inclusive hotels compared with standard hotels); and what policy measures need to be put in place to ensure competitiveness of the industry. There is also need to focus research and efforts on the environment; monitor the impacts of tourism on the environment as well as the negative environmental impacts of other sectors (agriculture, manufacturing) which could have negative impacts on the tourism industry.

Use of technology   The Caribbean region will need to adopt strategies and the actions to put it in the forefront of technological change. It is in the marketing and distribution areas that the use of technology is most critical. Natural advantages (sun, sand and sea) are no longer sufficient to give the Caribbean the competitive edge in global markets. New technologies are driving the new tourism from the supply side. New technologies are making it possible to supply individual tailor-made holidays that are *cost-competitive* with mass standardized and rigidly packaged options. Technology is driving the new tourism. It is creating the basis for flexibility and individuality of the travel experience without necessarily increasing costs. The key differences in the old and new technologies are identified below:

- new technology is well developed;
- it is not simply the internet or a video brochure that is being used, but the whole *system* of information technologies;
- it is not only travel agents or tour operators or hotels that use the technology, but all suppliers and even consumers;
- the pace of adoption of the technology is rapid;
- technology creates new rules of the game for competitors and creates wealth.

Sustainability

It is a well-known fact that the tourism industry in the Caribbean is very dependent upon its environment. Tourism is a major user of the region's environmental resources (sun, sand, sea, nature, wild life, flora, fauna, reefs, nature reserves and national parks, etc.) Ensuring sustainability and protection of the environment is one of the key strategic issues facing the Caribbean region, and especially its tourism sector.

Environment aspects   With rapid growth of uncontrolled tourism development in the Caribbean, the fragile eco-systems of the region are exposed to an ever-increasing risk of environmental degradation which could destroy the very raison d'être of the Caribbean's appeal. A number of factors increasingly threaten the environmental quality of the Caribbean and hence the sustainability of the tourism industry. These include: poor sewage disposal; growing quantities of ship/boat-generated waste; beach erosion; destruction of reefs; water quality; overfishing; destruction of wildlife habitat; overcrowding; carrying capacity limits; treatment of solid waste.

Finding the balance with cruise tourism   The issue of sustainability is also at the heart of the debate on cruise tourism vs. stayover arrivals. Issues that need to be addressed in the cruise tourism industry are as follows:

- maximizing the economic contribution of cruise tourism through
    (a) increasing cruise ship purchase of Caribbean suppliers (an initiative already started by Caribbean Export Development Project of CARICOM);

(b) increasing absolute expenditure of cruise passengers (expansion of the range and quality of local crafts, activities, tours, duty free shopping and other items of interest for cruise passengers);

(c) converting cruise passengers into long-stay arrivals;

(d) increasing head taxes paid by cruise passengers;

■ determining the environmental impacts of cruise tourism and developing measures to minimize negative impacts. Areas to be addressed include: cruise ship dumping; identifying optimal carrying capacity for each destination, taking examples from the Bermuda model;

■ the need to understand the relative economic impacts of cruise and stay-over tourism.

Local involvement   A critical aspect of the sustainability of the Caribbean tourism sector is the meaningful involvement of the indigenous population in the production of and the benefits from the tourism sector.

Successful tourism destinations are those in which visitors feel a total sense of welcome – the locals that smile are not only those who are paid to smile (workers in the industry). Yet, so little effort and energy is spent on creating the reasons for locals to smile. Much of the effort of tourism authorities is spent on tourism awareness and 'smile training' – teaching locals about tourism and why they should smile at tourists. They fail to realize that unless locals feel tourism in their pockets and on their tables (food to eat), all the smile training will not help. According to an observer in the industry 'you do not teach people to eat, just give them the food'. Similarly, you do not teach locals to smile at tourists, just give them the reason.

It is believed that the responsibility for involving local communities in the tourism sector is the job of the government. Many private sector establishments operate in communities (many tourist attractions are located in communities where people live) and do not even think about the relationship that they build with their communities. Yet, they expect that their tourists will be safe and everyone will be smiling to them. The evidence suggests that it is those far-sighted entrepreneurs who build relationships with their local communities that are the most successful. Curtin Bluff Hotel in Antigua is a shining example of such involvement.

Unexploited and unexplored ways in which the established private sector can support community involvement in tourism include:

■ advertising local products and services;

■ sourcing goods and services from the community (e.g. eggs, bread);

- providing training and mentoring for small businesses that supply the hotel;
- out-sourcing certain services (laundry, gardening, water sports);
- employing persons (e.g. nannies) as free agents to build entrepreneurship;
- ensuring that community services are employed in building and construction;
- training and skills upgrading;
- employment from surrounding communities;
- identifying key opportunities for communities (e.g. production of fresh herbs; organically grown vegetables);
- introducing new services to guests (e.g. cooking classes in preparation of local food and local language training; story telling; traditional games, catch and release fishing and entertainment);
- featuring local cuisine on the hotel menu;
- identifying career opportunities for locals;
- encouraging staff and local schools to experience being tourists at the hotel.

The key approach to local community involvement in tourism is not aid, but private sector development in partnership with the local communities. As the saying goes, do not give people fish, teach them to fish.

Marketing and promotion

Effective marketing, promotion and product distribution is also key to the success of the Caribbean tourism sector. Here the issue is lack of adequate resources effectively to market and promote the region, effectively to distribute products in the marketplace and to adopt the necessary technologies for competitiveness.

Air access

Adequate, reliable and efficient air access is of paramount importance to the development and continued survival of Caribbean tourism. Caribbean destinations can fail or succeed depending on the actions of a single airline. Pan Am, for example, carried about 14% of passengers to Barbados; 17% of all seats to the Bahamas and 60% of all seats to the Turks and Caicos in 1991. When the airline shut down in 1991, Pan Am left many islands without access to a large part of their market.

The transportation challenge facing the region can be summarized as follows: how to guarantee air access with adequate capacity at competitive prices to all Caribbean destinations. Adequate air access is critical to the long-term survival of the Caribbean tourism industry.

Facilitation

There is need to facilitate the free movement of tourists and remove any barriers to the movement. Common issues need to be implemented as well as standardized immigration forms. The legal, policy and legislative framework for the development of the tourism sector needs to be put in place.

Economic impact

The tourism sector offers a number of opportunities for linkages, which have not been fully exploited. From organic food production and cut flowers, to health services, high fashion for the tropics and environmental services, the potentials are enormous. These potentials must be analysed on a sector by sector basis using new strategies of development based on the principles of product focus and production flexibility.

There is need to create more linkages between tourism and other sectors of the economy, particularly services of developing the axial potential of the tourism sector: using the presence of a tourism sector to develop other exports, e.g. sports, ecotourism, high fashion, environment services, health tourism.

Three key issues of economic impact have also been identified: the high leakage of the tourism sector and the low levels of linkages developed between tourism and the other sectors of the economy; the need for more research and analysis; and the need to develop strategies and actions to maximize the economic impacts of tourism.

Investment

Governments should seek to maintain an interest rate regime that is supportive to the tourism sector and, through fiscal incentives, encourage the banking sector to offer longer-term loans to the tourism sector. Consideration needs to be given to implementation of a taxation policy that seeks to minimize the tax burden placed on the tourism industry, given its competitive nature. Governments must ensure that careful consideration is always given to the potential impact of new tax measures on the tourism sector.

While there has been a large increase in investment in new hotel plant in the Caribbean in recent years, much of this has been restricted to relatively few countries. There is evidence from the previous studies that high tax regimes, bureaucratic delays and other factors inhibit the attraction of foreign investors to some countries in the region. Steps must be taken to eliminate as far as possible these barriers to investment and to attract new tourism investment to the region.

Lack of matching investment in essential infrastructure (such as roads, airports, seaports, electricity, water supply and telecommunications) has inhibited the development of tourism in some Caribbean countries. There is a continuing need for investment in the improvement of the region's tourism infrastructure, which also serves and benefits the local populations, if growth targets for tourism are to be realized. At the same time, greater attention needs to be paid to the preservation and development of the region's rich heritage of historic buildings as an important, but presently neglected, component of the region's tourism product. Expanded use also needs to be made of indigenous architecture, designs and handicrafts in the tourism sector.

Future prospects

In 1950, a mere 25 million persons crossed international borders world-wide; by 1990, 425 million persons travelled abroad; this figure is expected to reach 661 million in 2000 and 937 million (or double the number of tourists in 1990) by 2010. Consider that in Britain, Germany, Japan and the USA, more adults already travel during any particular year than visit a library, attend a sporting event or have gone to see a play or concert.

That the industry will continue to grow is not in question. However, it is increasingly evident that:

- the *rate* of growth will vary from country to country;
- the *distribution* of growth will shift;
- the *direction* of growth will change;
- the *capacity* to absorb growth will be limited for some countries.

The Caribbean Tourism Organization predicts a positive future for tourism arrivals where the Caribbean will receive 22.5 million tourists by the year 2000 and 37.9 million tourist arrivals by 2010. Tourist arrivals to the Caribbean in 2010 will be double those who came to the Caribbean in 1997.

The expected growth to the Caribbean by the year 2000 raises important questions. Will this growth impose limits to growth in some Caribbean islands? Do islands have the capacity to absorb more visitors? What are the environmental, social and other related limits to growth? Are there adequate skilled workers/managers and long term capital at reasonable rates of interest to fuel this expected growth? Are the infrastructure (ports, airports) adequate to facilitate this expansion? Are locals adequately involved in the industry?

13

Europe

Robert Cleverdon

Introduction

In product life cycle terms, Europe as a tourism destination has passed from the strong growth to the mature stage. Having led the expansion of tourism in the second half of the 20th century and been the principal tourist-receiving region, Europe has below-average growth prospects over the first two decades of the 21st century. However, while competition is eroding Europe's market share with virtually every country (and territory) in the world now embracing tourism as a key strategic economic sector, Europe will still record substantive growth. The reasons are as diverse as the forecast strong expansion over the first quarter of the century in outbound Asian tourism and growing tourism product diversification in European countries, catering for newly emergent market segments.

Forecasts of European tourism

The World Tourism Organization's *Tourism 2020 Vision* study has been finalized to be published in a series of volumes during 2000. Drawing on the volume dedicated to Europe *(Intraregional and Long Haul Flows: Europe)*, the following key factors and forecasts are identified:

- Forecasts of international tourist flows to Europe show that there will be 717 million arrivals in 2020. This represents an average annual growth rate of just under 3.1%, compared with the rate of expansion world-wide of approaching 4.2%, for a global total of 1.56 billion arrivals by 2020. Europe will retain its regional leadership of international arrivals but with a declining share from 59% in 1995 to 47% in 2020.
- Within Europe, the largest sub-region of Western Europe will show the lowest rate of growth between 1995 and 2020, at 1.9% a year. The Central/Eastern Europe sub-region will record the strongest rate of growth, at 4.4% a year. Southern Europe will see below regional average growth, at 2.6% a year, while the two remaining sub-regions will record better than average rates of expansion, i.e. Northern Europe 3.8% a year, East Mediterranean Europe 4.2% a year.
- Long-haul travel to Europe will grow, at just over 4% a year between 1995 and 2020 as against 2.9% for intraregional travel. None the less, there will still be a 6:1 ratio between intra-European and interregional tourists to Europe in 2020.
- Almost 200 million arrivals a year are recorded in the 22 countries bordering the Mediterranean Sea (including non-European countries with a Mediterranean coastline). Average annual growth of below 3% is forecast for the first two decades of the century, producing a volume of 346 million arrivals in 2020 for a global market share of 22%, as compared with almost 32% in 1995.
- The top three Mediterranean destinations in 2020 will remain the same, i.e. France, Spain, Italy. However, the strongest rates of growth among the Mediterranean countries will be achieved by two groups of countries: those in the rapid growth phase of development, e.g. Turkey and Egypt; and those rebuilding their tourism sectors from one form or another of disruption in recent years, e.g. the new countries of the former Yugoslavia, Lebanon, Libya.

Trends in the pattern of Europe's tourism

A number of researchers have presented information on likely future trends in Europe's tourism. A distillation of these is made from the following sources: the European Travel Commission's *Megatrends of Tourism in Europe (to the year 2005 and beyond)* (1999); the World Tourism Organization's *Tourism*

2020 Vision study volume *Intraregional and Long Haul Flows: Europe* (2000); that same body's *Strategic Issues for Europe,* arising from the June 1998 Leadership Forum of Advisers of the WTO Business Council; the European Travel and Tourism Action Group/European Travel Commission/British Tourist Authority August 1998 conference report *Marketing Intelligence for Planning the Future: Europe in the Global Context* (ETAG, 1998) ; and the issue of the *Tourism Trendspotter* bi-monthly service which identified eight trends for Europe's tourism (Tourism Trendspotter, 1999).

Increased competition

Stronger competition will come both from inside and outside the region. More Europeans will switch their holidays to destinations outside Europe. This trend is likely to outpace the rise in interregional tourists (where the biggest rate of increase will be provided by Asians) coming to Europe. Also, the increased range of goods and services competing for the prospective tourist's discretionary spend will be manifested in one respect through a growing number of leisure offers within a few hours' travel from many peoples' homes, such as theme parks, health and sporting clubs, cultural events, entertainment complexes etc. leading to more shorter-duration, closer-to-home trips. Demand will be diverted from longer trips further afield.

Changes in lifestyle

The fragmentation of household type and composition (i.e. less traditional family groups and more singles, single parents, couples without children), along with ageing of the population, is leading to a greater range of differentiated market segments and niches (and the need for tourist products to be developed for them).

The insecurity of tenure of employment is resulting in growing rather than lessening workplace pressure. The computer is proving not to be a liberating force reducing work but a facility which, because it can be accessed at all times, results in a blurring of work and leisure time. In consequence, there is occurring a rise of combined work and pleasure trips. The Scottish Tourist Board reports that more business travellers to Scotland are being accompanied by their families – not just partners but children too (Hay, 2000). This may reflect *inter alia* the increasing difficulty of scheduling a traditional summer holiday break given both partners in a household working, school term timetables, etc.

Another manifestation of the flexibility but 'tie' of the computer is likely to be the growth of holidays where the laptop and modem are taken along to enable daily contact to be maintained with the office, client, etc.

The growth of that group of consumers who are 'money-rich but time-poor' has spurred the expansion of the all-inclusive market segment – initially in the Caribbean, but now increasingly (though with a somewhat broader market segment focus) in Europe too. Of course, it is the 'money- and time-rich' consumers (the early retirees and others with protected pension incomes) who constitute the most potentially rewarding segments for the travel trade – particularly intra-European, and from North America and Japan into Europe. However, with the economies of the industrialized nations finding it difficult to finance the state pensions of the growing proportions of the older age groups, a consequence much discussed is the raising of the retirement age to 70 or over. This will dampen down demand from the most promising travel market segment.

Short breaks

From the first product and market developments in the 1980s, short break holidays have grown rapidly in popularity, and the signs are that this growth will continue. Short breaks now cover a wide range of types, i.e. from out-of-season promotions, to 'sampler' visits (a strategy used by many Eastern European countries), to luxury breaks, to thematic stays, to shopping trips, to concert/event visits. The pattern of a main holiday with a number of short break trips is a norm for increasing numbers of Europeans. In less strong economic times, the main holiday may be replaced by the short breaks.

It is this short breaks component which will be largely responsible for the growth rate in intraregional European tourist arrivals over the period to 2020 being as high as the 2.9% a year forecast by the WTO. This clearly demonstrates the difficulty of using 'arrivals' as the unit of measurement for forecasting tourism, but it is the only realistic option as the data availability for alternative (more useful) indicators such as nights or spending is much poorer across the countries of the world.

Growth segments

The European Travel Commission's *Megatrends* include the following market segments earmarked for especially strong growth: senior citizen travel, business travel especially in the MICE (Meetings, Incentive Travel, Conventions and Exhibitions) categories, visiting friends and relatives (VFR), city visits (especially for sporting and cultural events), winter sunshine and cruise holidays (which are expected to rise faster than either winter sports or summer holidays), day trips for varied purposes, adventure holidays and trips to 'off the beaten track' places (e.g. to the jungle in comfort and safety), society/association etc. group visits, and rural tourism.

Within the VFR segment the relative importance of visits to friends is reported by at least one destination to be rising faster than to family (Hay, 2000). This may be attributable at least in part to the expanding geographic boundaries of each individual's community of business and personal connections facilitated through the electronic communications age and the ease of travel. The spread of the impact of European air deregulation, noted below, could be a further positive influence. Given the key role of the 'friend' in the destination in influencing the potential traveller's decision to visit, destination marketing activities may in future include some undertaken in the destination itself targeted at residents with friends outside the area, e.g. money-off purchase or entry if accompanied by someone with a provable place of residence overseas or in some other part of the country.

Accommodation and catering

Again drawing on the European Travel Commission's *Megatrends*, it is anticipated that demand for three-star and budget accommodation will continue to rise, as it will for less formal types of accommodation (e.g. bed and breakfast, university facilities out-of-term). Hotel accommodation will be increasingly packaged, especially for short break pleasure trips. More hotel-created packages combining a variety of features will be offered through direct sell methods. More provision of in-house accommodation and catering at major leisure and sporting venues will be developed, e.g. theme parks, sporting, cultural, health centres and holiday villages. Second homes and timeshare will both continue to expand, resulting in increased homes for holiday rental.

Demand for catering is likely to polarize: with good quality, individualized small restaurants and inns maintaining strong demand despite the growth of chain and themed restaurants.

Technology

One-third of Europeans presently have access to the Internet, whether at home or at work. Between 1998 and 2000 e-commerce is estimated to have quadrupled, while marketing use of the World Wide Web increased from 44% of firms to 75%. Organizations like hotels (noted above), are increasingly developing their own marketing and sales packages communicated to individual market segments and niches. This is made possible by the large amounts of information which the current generation of electronic database systems can hold on individual customers. Electronic communications networks simultaneously support two important marketing strategies: segmentation and globalization. A supplier can contact the whole world, while creating specific products for very different market segments. Traditional marketing techniques are turned on their head: the supplier defines its own interface with the world (its web-site), stating what they have to offer, and the potential customer accesses it if it is of interest. The medium is also attracting new suppliers, e.g. the Microsoft Expedia site sells a wide range of travel and tourism services. While the threat to the traditional high street travel agent from this technology is real, there are also opportunities for agents to develop on-line product and service offerings since they can represent a variety of suppliers and give choice to the consumer.

The Euro

The January 2002 introduction of the Euro in 11 European Union member states seems less likely to have the wholesale impact on the region's travel and tourism than was widely assumed to be the case when the dates were finalized and the 11 committed to it in 1999. Generally speaking, the main benefit to tourism will come from increased intra-European travel, with the following main impacts arising from the Europe's introduction: holidaymakers saving on converting cash and credit card bills; greater predictability of costs for travel companies booking overseas; more transnational tour operating businesses resulting in better deals for consumers; the loss of fee and commission income from foreign exchange business; greater price transparency leading to more harmonizing of air fares. The single currency could provide a strong marketing tool for incoming tour operators offering multi-country Euro zone holidays to travellers from interregional markets.

Airline deregulation

European air deregulation has produced a number of new, no frills airlines, some independent, others as subsidiaries of the major carriers in response to the upsurge in consumer interest (including from business travellers) to cheaper air travel. Though the low cost airlines operate between secondary airports they have been successful in fuelling the growth of the short breaks market segment in particular. Despite the demise in late 1999 of one of the original entrants, Debonair, the prevailing high level of standard European air fares (which are set to ensure that the business traveller pays a high premium through the condition that a Saturday night should be spent away from point of origin for any concessional fare to apply) offers scope for the continued incursion in the European air travel market by the low cost carriers. Whether this will be a strand of the big carriers' business or whether genuine competition will continue through the success of the independents remains to be seen. The dice are loaded against the independents if the US deregulation experience is replicated.

The dilemma for destinations is that while they wish to encourage the new market segments able to visit their attractions through the low fares, they do not want to risk alienating their existing (by and large higher spending) clientele. Selective market segmentation is needed to realize the optimal potential across the whole range of opportunity segments.

The consequence of the increased power of the major airline groupings (e.g. Star Alliance, Oneworld partnership, North Atlantic Excellence alliance, North-West-Continental alliance, all of which have European airline involvement) is that Europe's regional airlines are joining up with the alliances because they are finding themselves squeezed between the premium and low cost carriers.

Sustainable tourism

As tourism in Europe continues to expand and tourists become more aware of socio-environmental aspects of their activity, there will be rejection of certain operator practices as well as of destinations that do not pursue sustainable strategies. The issue was a focus of the WTO Business Council's Leadership Forum of Advisers which in its *Conclusions: Strategic Issues for Europe* warned that those European cities and regions which are totally built and developed will need to look at measures like the decommissioning of existing bed stocks, replacing sub-standard hotels or, at the very least, regenerating bed stocks or resorts, if they are to satisfy the more demanding tourist of the future. New partnerships and models will be needed in order to create sustainable tourism.

The evidence to date as to the degree of commitment of either the industry or the consumer to sustainable practices in travel and tourism is not conclusive. Despite initiatives like Green Globe, there is one line of argument that states that consumers are able to afford to be concerned about the environment presently because economic performance in the industrialized countries is solid (Willmott, 2000). From the industry standpoint, it is perhaps telling that only 200 out of 16 000 tourism businesses in Scotland have signed up for a Green Business scheme operated by the authorities (Hay, 2000).

Taxation

The European Travel Commission's *Megatrends* document, while optimistic about Europe's prospects, warns that external conditions and government attitudes are uncertain and growth can no longer be taken for granted, especially since increasing tax and regulation are eroding Europe's competitive edge.

The ETC particularly bemoans the fact that the European Union has no coordinated tourism policy or strategy , and that the weak voice which tourism has in putting forward its case holds back the creation of favourable conditions for profitable and sustainable development. It argues that this vacuum in the policy area at a time of great change needs to be filled with a strong and collective presentation on agreed key issues by all the main sector organizations consulting and cooperating together.

Congestion and capacity

The capacity of airports and air traffic control systems, along with road congestion at peak times and in popular tourist destinations, will lead to both delays in travel and abandoned plans to travel with a nearer-to-home activity or a non-travel alternative being chosen in preference (Todd, 2000). Combined with approaching ceilings in travel time availability in several Western European countries like Switzerland, the challenge to the industry will be to find ways to achieve growth despite the squeeze on capacity growth and congestion. It is in respect of an area such as this that a European-wide strategic approach may prove most valuable.

References

European Travel Commission (1999) Megatrends of Tourism in Europe (to the year 2005 and beyond). Unpublished draft. ETC.
European Travel and Tourism Action Group (1998) *Marketing Intelligence for Planning the Future: Europe in the Global Context.* ETAG/ETC/BTA.
Hay, B./Scottish Tourist Board (2000) Conference Interventions. Tourism and Hospitality in the 21st Century, University of Surrey.

Todd, G. (2000) World Travel and Tourism Today. Conference Paper. Tourism and Hospitality in the 21ˢᵗ Century, University of Surrey.

Tourism Trendspotter (1999) Eight trends for Europe. *Tourism Trendspotter* (Crusader Publications), 1 (4): 2–4.

Willmott, M. (2000) The World of Today and Tomorrow. Conference Paper. Tourism and Hospitality in the 21ˢᵗ Century, University of Surrey.

WTO Leadership Forum of Advisers of the WTO Business Council (1998) *Conclusions: Strategic Issues for Europe.* Madrid: World Tourism Organization.

WTO (2000) *Tourism 2020 Vision: Intraregional and Long Haul Flows,* Volume 4, *Europe.* Madrid: World Tourism Organization.

Appendix: WTO Europe sub-regions

Central/Eastern Europe

Armenia, Azerbaijan, Belarus, Bulgaria, Czech Republic, Estonia, Georgia, Hungary, Kazakhstan, Kyrgyzstan, Latvia, Lithuania, Moldova, Poland, Romania, Russian Fedn, Slovakia, Tajikistan, Ukraine, Uzbekistan.

Northern Europe

Channel Is, Denmark, Faeroe Is, Finland, Iceland, Ireland, Isle of Man, Norway, Svalbard Is, Sweden, United Kingdom.

Southern Europe

Albania, Andorra, Gibraltar, Greece, Holy See, Italy, Malta, Portugal, San Marino, Spain, Yugoslavia SFR (Bosnia Herzogovina, Croatia, Slovenia, Macedonia, Yugoslavia).

Western Europe

Austria, Belgium, France, Germany, Liechtenstein, Luxembourg, Monaco, Netherlands, Switzerland.

East Mediterranean Europe

Cyprus, Israel, Turkey.

14

Middle East

Salah Wahab

The Middle Eastern travel market

Key trends in international tourism show that tourist arrivals across state boundaries reached about 625 million in 1998 worldwide. International tourism receipts (excluding international transport) increased by just 2% in 1998 over 1997 to US$ 445 billion, which was mainly due, perhaps, to Asia's financial crisis. The Middle East was the second fastest growing region in 1997 after Africa, registering an increase of 6.1% in arrivals and 10.5% in tourism receipts over 1996. In 1998, tourism in the Middle East grew much faster than the world average – by 5.3% in terms of arrivals and 6.4% in terms of receipts.

The Middle East region enjoys a competitive advantage in its attractions, consisting of unparalleled cultural and religious wealth, its still unpolluted and unspoiled beaches and the well-known warmth and generosity of its people. The WTO 'Vision 2020' forecast 19 million tourist arrivals in the Middle East in the year 2000, 37 million tourist arrivals for 2010 and 69 million for the year 2020. This represents an average rate of growth of 6.7%, compared with a world average rate of increase of 4.3% (WTO, 2000).

The Arab Middle Eastern travel market was a predominantly business market. Gulf travellers, for instance, were mostly business-oriented and did not give much attention to leisure travel, at least in the Arab world. However, other Arabs such as Egyptians, Tunisians, Syrians and Lebanese, have been travelling for leisure for a relatively long time. As an illustration, well-off Egyptians were accustomed to spend their summer holidays in Lebanon and Syria in addition to Europe since the dawn of the 20th century. The Gulf people started their leisure travel to Lebanon, Syria and Egypt in addition to European countries perhaps in the 1960s. They used to buy villas and flats as second homes to visit in urban centres and in resorts. More recently the Arab leisure market has become large enough to justify dealing with it as an important market, particularly after some Arab investors became interested in new resorts in certain Arab countries such as Egypt, Lebanon, Syria and Tunisia.

The Arab travel market has its own peculiarities, depending upon the character and temperament of the Arab traveller/tourist in various Arab countries. Irrespective of the many links and common features that tie Arabs together, their motivations and behavioural patterns differ. The combination of business and leisure is perhaps the most striking purpose of travel besides visiting relatives and friends. The Arab market segments, whether economic, social, cultural/educational or geographic, dictate variations in attitudes and travel patterns. Urban settlers would have different motivations and attitudes than rural people, which is a distinction that is common to most nations of the world: the distinction may be more prominent with Arabs.

Factors influencing the tourist traffic in the Arab Middle East

Positive factors

■ Worldwide economic recovery with the countries of the region contributing to resumed economic growth.
■ Growing interest of the populations in developed countries in the culture and ways of life of people of developing countries.
■ Scale and variety of natural and cultural tourist attractions and development in the Arab world.
■ Growth in tourist-generating markets which results in the increase in the number of consumers with sufficient discretionary income to travel outside their own country.

- Expansion of international airline connections between tourist-generating countries and main Arab destinations.
- As a result of the up-swing in Middle East traffic, charter flight traffic is expanding.
- Easement of currency and travel regulations affecting foreign tourists.
- Growing impact of computer technology on distribution systems.

Negative factors

- The negative image that used to exist about some countries in the Middle East region characterized by low hygiene standards, tourist harassment, moderate safety records in air, sea and land transport, standing tensions and political upheavals.
- Lack of sufficient infrastructure and major tourist development projects in some destinations.
- Insufficient numbers of skilled personnel and ineffectiveness of education and training programmes.
- Risk of conflict between tourist developers and local communities concerning sustainable tourist development projects.
- Low level of environmental conditions in some towns and localities.
- Ineffective marketing and promotional efforts exerted by some countries of the region.

Trends in the Expanded Middle East in 1997

The Expanded Middle East (EME) covers the following three sub-regions: Middle East, Northern Africa and Europe–Mediterranean region. Many of the countries of the EME have experienced unrest and tensions. In some countries, the security of foreign tourists was seriously threatened while in others tourists were the target of terrorist movements and attacks. Many destinations in the region would therefore benefit significantly from Middle East peace agreements.

Some traditional destinations of the region have already invested heavily in tourism and they are reaping benefits of such investment. Other countries, particularly those of the Gulf, are realizing the importance of investing in tourism as a tool for development and are adopting progressively measures to create a better climate for potential investors, both within and outside the region.

All three regions taken together registered almost 36 million tourist arrivals in 1997, generating an estimated US$ 22.8 billion in tourism receipts, or an average of US$ 633 per tourist arrival. This average conceals significant differences between one sub-region and another. The average receipts per tourist arrival in Northern Africa were US$ 343 against US$ 871 for the East-Mediterranean Europe and US$ 582 for the Middle East region (WTO, 1998). The share of the EME in world tourist arrivals was 5.9% and in world tourism receipts 5.1%. This share has fluctuated only marginally on a year-to-year basis. Compared to 1996, this share has increased in terms of tourist arrivals (5.6% in 1996), and tourism receipts (4.9%).

In 1997, countries most visited by European tourists were Tunisia (2.1 million), Egypt (nearly 1.9 million), Syria (286 000), Dubai in the United Arab Emirates (183 000 in 1995) and Jordan (171 000). Growth in European tourism to the region since the late 1980s is attributable in large measure to the tourism development promotion of Egypt. Lower real air fares make the countries of the region more 'price accessible' to European holidaymakers. The continued significance of the region in international trade has generated substantial extra business tourist volumes from Europe. The principal tourist-generating market to the Middle East is Saudi Arabia (intraregional traffic). As to inter-regional travel, Germany, the UK, United States, France, Italy and the Netherlands constitute about one-third of the tourist traffic to the region.

Insofar as outbound travel from the region is concerned, Middle Eastern residents have increased the volume of their overseas travel noticeably. The most favoured destinations for Middle Eastern tourists are tourist destinations in the region (intraregional), such as the Gulf states, Egypt, Lebanon, Syria, Jordan and Tunisia. The next favoured destination regions are Europe, North America and East Asia. Data on outbound tourism by the residents of Middle Eastern countries are inadequate to conduct any detailed analysis. Such data are not recorded by separate country of origin for Arab travellers between many states. Moreover, some governments regard these data as politically sensitive. Likewise data on expenditures overseas by country are not reliable and are not even available in most countries of the region.

A new regional tourism association, called the Middle East Mediterranean Travel and Tourism Association (MEMTTA), was created in October 1995 at an international economic conference in Amman, Jordan. Its goal is to pave the way for increased tourism development in the region and at the same time, forge bonds between private sector tourism interests that will help ease some of the political tensions in the region. Cyprus, Egypt, Israel, Jordan, Morocco, Palestine, Tunisia and Turkey signed its charter.

In March 1996, a 'conference of peacemakers' was convened in Sharm-el-sheikh, Egypt, and was attended by leaders of 27 nations, including a broad swath of the Arab World. They joined in a sweeping condemnation of bombings and vowed to cooperate in cracking down on terrorist attacks and in promoting peace throughout the Middle East.

The private sector should become more active, experienced and more participative in achieving economic growth. Middle Eastern tourism will continue to benefit from moves towards more free-market economies and the search for alternative growth sectors in the economies. Many Middle Eastern countries see tourism as an excellent developmental tool, which can fulfil balanced and sustainable growth.

Changing market segments, product development and marketing strategies

Growth of tourist outbound travel and purpose of visit

The tourist demand for outbound travel is growing due to the enhanced discretionary incomes and increase in the reasons for travel. Visiting friends and relatives (VFR) still occupies a large portion of the tourist market in the Middle East. Continuing advances in computer technology and the even more rapid growth in the use of these developments for business applications is likely to restrict the expansion of business travel. Companies are now applying technology more and more as a substitute for a business trip where possible.

Patterns of holiday travel

The Middle East region has developed its tourism not on the basis of beach resort holidays as so many long-haul destinations from Europe and North America have done, but on the basis of the rich cultural and religious heritage of the countries of the region. It is the birthplace of three major world religions: Christianity, Islam and Judaism. The archaeological sites in Egypt, Jordan, Lebanon and Syria have constituted the attractions for foreign tourism for decades. However, these sites clearly have finite carrying capacities. The tourist authorities in Jordan strictly limit new hotel development expansion in the ancient hidden city of Petra because of concerns that consequent large increases in tourist numbers will cause irreparable damage to the antiquities. The same concern prevails now in Egypt, particularly in the Valley of the Kings in Luxor's West Bank, where studies to limit the numbers of visitors are in process.

Many of the countries of the region now embrace tourism as part of their economic development strategies. There is consequently a need to develop more natural and archaeological sites for tourist use and/or to diversify the types of tourism catered for, including beach tourism. The region possesses a wide array of natural as well as cultural and historical resources, including the Mediterranean, Red Sea, Arabian Gulf and Indian Ocean coastlines. These offer considerable potential for beach resort development. The Middle East is the first logical interregional tourist destination for the European tourist market because of its geographical proximity, but the unsettled political climate of the region over recent decades has prevented both interest and the flow of investment in coastal tourism. The expansion of European beach resort tourism has been to the west (e.g. to the Caribbean and North America) and to south and south-east Asia (e.g. Goa in India, Sri Lanka and Thailand). The governments of the region, including Egypt, recognize that the Middle East tourism product should not be developed solely as an extension to the Mediterranean resorts of Spain, France and Italy. It should be manifested through facilities and attractions, which are an expression of the cultural heritage and intrinsic features of the Arab people of the Middle East. The recent growth in European interregional tourism has been based on long-haul beach resorts reflecting the 'trend-setters' move away from the closer to home destination areas towards far flung destinations which are perceived as 'exciting and unspoilt'. Marketing activities by many of these destinations and improved air transport access, including through charter operations, have ensured that the momentum of trend has been maintained. The North American and Asian origin markets (principally the United States, Canada and Japan) are geographically more distant form the Middle East region than is Europe. The lure of the region for the tourists from these markets will remain predominantly its culture and heritage, with beach resorts constituting relatively limited appeal until late in the forecast period.

In volume terms, Europe will remain the largest potential interregional market for the Middle East. Yet Europe is a mature tourist-generating region and overall could be approaching its ceiling (both in terms of free time and personal income) for tourism growth potential. The Middle East region will continue to attract for some years before ceiling limitations come into effect. None the less, ceiling constraint on the European market in the mid- to long-term will be of increasing concern to tourism planners in the region.

Quality and quantity

An important question for the Middle East is how tourist traffic in general and intraregional tourist movement in particular could be economically, socially and environmentally viable.

As Middle Eastern tourist products are mostly quality products, they should be addressed to quality markets. While quantity (number of tourist arrivals and tourist nights) count in placing the tourist destination among the leading places to visit, quality is becoming more and more a decisive criterion in the economic viability of tourism as a productive industry. How quality tourist flows could be marketed is a technical and professional question that requires expertise and know-how that cannot be explained in the present chapter. On the other hand, service quality in tourism is a cornerstone in the competition between destinations.

The full range of elements, features and characteristics that go to make up any tourist experience is quite wide and varies from one customer to another, but good field research in tourist motivations would help in diagnosing those desired components of the tourist experience. Among these would be quality of attractions, facilities, safety, superservices, good general atmosphere, comfort, warmth friendliness, care, immediate corrective action for any default, etc.

Tourism and sustainability

International tourist markets are becoming increasingly conscious of the need for sustainable tourism development, which meets the needs of present tourist and host regions while protecting and enhancing opportunity for the future. Tourists are more knowledgeable about their possible contribution to the degradation of nature and culture and are increasingly scrutinizing tourism development occurring in a country or region before making their choices. Knowledge leads directly to interest in the intrinsic features of countries and regions.

In practice, few tourists undertake a holiday solely related to nature or a country's culture. Despite the upsurge in awareness and interest noted, the avid ecotourist will remain a small market segment. However, an increasing proportion of tourists will include a nature or culture component in their holiday (as a day trip for example). Even more will select a destination, which has an environment-friendly approach to its tourism development. Marketing strategies (supported, of course, by appropriate product development) should stress this sustainable approach to tourism development. This can influence the destination decisions not only of special interest culture or nature-oriented tourists, but also of tourists wishing to pursue conventional general interest pursuits such as beach or touring holidays.

Tourist product development in the region could fall under four categories namely:

- Full development of tourist resorts, e.g. in Egypt, the Gulf of Aquaba, the Red Sea coast, the North West coast and North Sinai, Mutrah/Muscat, and Salala in Oman, Aquaba in Jordan, Jumeira Beach in Dubai, Lattakia in Syria.
- Creating new and re-establishing tourist destinations of Oman, Yemen and eventually Iraq. Libya, once freed from the economic blockade, could be developed as a potential tourist destination provided that tourist awareness of the population and efficient tourist training could be conducted.
- Reconstruction of secondary existing tourist-oriented cities in Jordan (Jarash) and Syria (Aleppo and Homs).
- Restoration and improvement of prime historical attractions and archaeological sites, such as the Giza pyramids area, Valley of the Kings and Fayoum in Egypt, Petra in Jordan.

Future prospects

Although 'growth sustains growth', which means that tourism in the Middle East would continue to grow, this does not necessarily apply at continuous high rates of expansion. Some air transport studies show that the Middle East will match the world's average for all scheduled air traffic growth but will lag behind slightly in the expansion of international route traffic. The *Economist* study 'International Tourism Forecasts to 2005' shows that tourism expansion prospect in the Middle East would average 4.3% a year.

WTO forecasts to the year 2000 and beyond suggest more than 4.5% annual growth. This average rate of increase is low when compared with the rates of growth achieved and/or anticipated by a number of countries in the Middle East region for their inbound tourism traffic. Some of these forecasts are close to or in excess of 10% a year. Egypt is one of these countries while some important European tourist-generating markets such as Germany, the UK, France and Italy, responding to the good resort developments in Egypt, are expected to achieve faster rates of growth. This would be contingent upon continued stability in Egypt and in the whole Middle East region.

The development potential of tourism in the Middle East looks good but the question is how much would its average growth rate be? Accurate scientific forecasting is difficult as almost all base years are exceptional years because of the repetitive negative events that occur in the Middle East, i.e. conflicts, wars and terrorist acts. If real sustainable peace and stability prevail, the Middle East would become a tourist heaven. Beside peace, perhaps the three most pressing needs for action both by individual countries and on a collective basis, are:

- Encouragement and generation of investments in and resource commitments to the region's main tourism sectors including air transport, accommodation and recreation.
- Image improvement: substantially increased and well-planned focused aggressive marketing and promotional activities are necessary to win the conviction and confidence of potential tourists of the major tourist generating markets that the Middle East region has a competitive advantage in offering a wide range of bona fide holiday destinations that cater for almost all forms of tourism.
- Developing more effective safety and security measures to guarantee a more stable tourist climate that contributes to longer-term tourism development programmes in the face of international competition.

Moreover, a revival of the consciousness of Arab solidarity and realization of exogenous risks and dangers that threaten Arab identity in the age of globalization should result in more solid and substantial efforts to constitute Arab economic and tourism integration. These would lead to a brighter future through complementary productive endeavours, among which Arab intraregional tourist traffic would be one effective operational tool.

References

Economist Intelligence Unit (1995) *International Tourism Forecasts to 2005.* London: EIU.

Wahal, S. and Pigram, J. eds (1997) *Tourism Development and Growth.* London: Routledge.

WTO (1998) *Tourism Market Trends 1998.* Madrid: World Tourism Organization.

WTO (2000) *Tourism 2020 Vision: Intraregional and Long Haul Flows*, Volume 4, *Europe.* Madrid: World Tourism Organization.

15

North America

Suzanne Cook

This chapter examines North America – specifically the United States, Canada and Mexico – as origin and destination markets for international tourism. It provides statistics on the size and scope of international tourism, how North America fits into the whole, and analyses international tourism performance in the United States, Canada and Mexico in the 1990s. The chapter also reviews some major factors likely to affect international tourism to and from North America in the future, and includes official forecasts where available.

The Americas

The Americas (including North, South, Central America and the Caribbean), home to nearly 800 million people, 14% of the world's population, is second as a regional destination for international travel, after Europe. The Americas received nearly 123 million international visitors in 1998, up 41% since 1989 and comprising 19% of all international tourist arrivals. International tourist receipts (excluding international fares) have increased more than twice as fast as arrivals. The Americas received 27% of international tourism receipts or US$120 billion. Receipts in the Americas rose 99% over 1989. South Asia (117%), Africa (114%) and the East Asia/Pacific region (101%), however, enjoyed larger gains.

These differential growth rates have resulted in a loss of share of arrivals for the Americas, falling from nearly 26% of the total in 1970 to 19% in 1998. The region, however, has seen a small increase in its share of international tourism receipts, rising from 26.8% in 1970 to 27.3% in 1998, due primarily to the changing composition of visitors to the region.

North America

The remainder of this chapter deals with North America alone, including the countries of the United States, Canada and Mexico. In 1998, the US was placed third as an international visitor destination, losing its second place ranking of the year before to Spain. The US hosted over 46 million international arrivals, 7.3% of the world total, in 1998.

Mexico and Canada are considerably smaller inbound markets, receiving 19.8 million (3.1%) and 18.8 million (3.0%) international arrivals, respectively. In total, then, North America hosted over 85 million international visitors in 1998, 69% of the Americas' regional total and 13% of all international arrivals.

North America, however, accounted for a significantly greater share of international receipts, 20%, due largely to the influence of the United States. In 1998, international tourism receipts in North America totalled US$88 billion. The US garnered 81% of this, or over US$71 billion, making it the largest international destination in the world in terms of receipts. The US, while hosting only 7.3% of arrivals, received 16.2% of receipts, due to the longer stays and higher spending patterns evident among many of its visitors.

Canada came in ninth in tourism receipts in 1998, capturing US$9.1 billion (2.1% of the total), while Mexico received US$7.9 billion (1.8%). In both cases, their shares of receipts were smaller than their shares of arrivals, the reverse of the pattern evident for the United States.

United States

According to Tourism Industries/International Trade Administration in the US Department of Commerce, the US has benefited greatly from this international tourism boom. International arrivals in the US increased 28% since

1989 to total 46.4 million in 1998. In 1998, however, international travel to the US declined nearly 3% from its record high level of 47.8 million international visitors in 1997.

This decline in arrivals also generated a similar decline in international travel receipts in the US in 1998. Receiving a total of US$71.1 billion in international tourism receipts, however, the US remained the top international tourism receipts earner in the world, well ahead of second place Italy, with US$30 billion in receipts.

As an origin, the US is the second largest outbound market in the world, following Germany. Since 1989, the United States' outbound international tourism market has increased more than its inbound market, rising 37% over the 1990s to total 56.3 million in 1998. Over the period, international departures from the US have shown a rather steady increase year after year, with the exception of 1991. In response to the Persian Gulf War and an economic recession at home, US residents reduced their outbound travel by nearly 7% that year.

International payments by outbound US travellers increased nearly twice as much as did departures – 61% during the past decade to reach US$53.7 billion in 1998.

To summarize, the United States experienced slower growth as an international tourism destination than as an international tourism origin of international travellers. But, because of the changing country composition and nature of its visitors, the US actually enjoyed a much greater increase in receipts than in payments during the same period. As a result, it increased significantly its international travel trade balance from a surplus of US$5.2 billion (including international passenger fares) in 1989 to US$18.7 billion in 1998.

US markets

The US is quite dependent on its two neighbours, Canada and Mexico, for many of its international visitors. In 1998, these two countries accounted for nearly half of the total, while overseas origins generated the remaining 51%.

This represents a major shift, however, from 1989, when Canada produced 42% of all international visitors to the US, as compared to only 29% in 1998. Ten years earlier, Mexico generated 19%, about the same share as today, while overseas countries generated only 38% of all international arrivals in the US, compared to 51% in 1998.

The real growth in international travel to the US, therefore, has been from overseas markets. While all international travel to the US increased 28% between 1989 and 1998, arrivals from overseas origins grew more than twice as fast, 69%, to total 23.7 million in 1998.

The year 1998, however, was not a particularly good one for international travel to the US, reflecting a continuing slide in arrivals from Canada, which first started in 1992 in the wake of a weakening Canadian dollar. Travel from Canada declined a significant 11% in 1998 to total 13.4 million arrivals as the Canadian dollar sunk to historic lows. This decrease was almost completely offset by the gain in the United States' second largest country market, Mexico, with a 10% increase to top the 9 million mark in 1998.

Both these markets are extremely sensitive to exchange rates between themselves and the United States. Economic problems in Asia, volatility in South America and a sluggish economy in Europe all contributed to the 2% drop in overseas visitors to the US in 1998. Overall, inbound international travel to the US declined 3% in 1998.

Europe is the United States' top regional origin, from which 45% of its overseas visitors embark. Asia/Oceania accounted for 31% of all overseas visitors to the US in 1998, followed by South America (12%), the Caribbean/Central America (8%) and Africa/Middle East (4%).

Three of the United States' top overseas country markets are in Europe – the UK, Germany and France. The UK is the United States' leading European market, with nearly 4 million arrivals in 1998. Germany produced 1.9 million visitors to the US in 1998. Japan, however, is the largest overseas country market for travel to the US, generating 4.9 million arrivals in 1998. Since 1989, travel from Japan has increased rather significantly (+59%), although it was down 9% in 1998, less than might have been expected given the Asian financial crisis. Other Asian countries, however, posted even more significant declines, such as South Korea (−51%) and Taiwan (−13%), as origins of international travel to the US in 1998.

Brazil stands out as the real star in terms of growth over the past decade, increasing its production of visitors to the US by 172%. Today, Brazil is the United States' fifth largest overseas market.

International travel from the US

Outbound international travel from the United States has shown strong growth throughout the 1990s, increasing 37% overall. In 1998, the US experienced a record year for outbound tourism with departures totalling 56.3 million, up 6% over 1997. Growth was particularly strong in travel to Canada (+11%), as the same exchange rates that kept many Canadians away from the US stimulated US travel to Canada. Travel to overseas destinations was also strong, up 7% over 1997 and a well-above-average 56% over 1989.

Among US travellers visiting overseas destinations, Europe is the most popular, garnering 45% of the total in 1998. Asia/Oceania received 21% of US overseas departures, while Central America and the Caribbean receive a combined total of 19%.

With approximately 11 million US visitors, Europe is more than twice as large as a regional destination for overseas travel from the US than the second most popular, Asia/Oceania. In 1998, US travel to Europe grew 14% but even more so to South America (17%), the fourth largest overseas destination for US departures.

By country, the UK benefits most from outbound US travel, receiving 3.6 million US visitors in 1998, a gain of 2% over the prior year. France was the second most popular destination of overseas US travellers, followed by Italy and Germany. Over the past decade, Italy has seen the greatest growth in US visitors (+60%), receiving almost 1.9 million in 1998.

Travellers to and from the US

So, who are these people behind these impressive numbers? We know that the worldwide international travel community consists of a relatively very small number of people. The WTO estimates that today only about 3.5% of the world's population are international travellers. That translates to about 200 million people out of a global population of 6 billion.

- This small group of people take lots of trips; they tend to be repeat visitors to their destinations and, therefore, over time they have become very experienced, sophisticated and demanding travellers.
- Most international travellers, like a growing percentage of the population in many of the developed nations of the world, are middle-aged.
- Not surprisingly, international travellers tend to be quite affluent, especially US outbound travellers to overseas destinations.
- Leisure purposes dominate international travel to and from the US.
- International travellers tend to take substantially longer trips than do domestic travellers: overseas travellers to and from the US average more than 15 nights.

Canada

Let us look now at another North American travel market – Canada. Canada's inbound international visitor market is less than half the size of the United States' and has been on a slightly slower growth curve. Since 1989, international arrivals in Canada increased 25% to reach 18.8 million in 1998. Growth came primarily from overseas and less so from the US. Because of this, Canada has enjoyed a dramatic increase in tourism receipts, which more than doubled from US$6.7 billion in 1989 to US$13.9 billion in 1998. This surpasses the United States' growth in receipts of 99%.

The big difference between Canada and the US is Canada's declining outbound market. This is due exclusively, however, to the big drop-off in overnight visits to the US as mentioned before. Canadian departures to the US were 12% fewer in 1998 than in 1989. On the other hand, departures to overseas destinations grew 41% among Canadians, as compared to the 56% growth in US travel to overseas countries during that period.

Again, reflecting the fact that overseas destinations now capture a much larger share of Canadian outbound travel – where travellers spend more time and money than they do in the US – payments of outbound Canadian travellers soared 62%, despite the decline in departures.

To summarize, unlike the US, in the 1990s Canada showed greater growth as a tourism destination than as an origin. But like the US, because of the changing country composition and nature of its visitors, Canada enjoyed a much greater increase in receipts than in payments during the same period. As a result, Canada's travel deficit fell to US$2 billion in 1998, down 45% over 1987 and its lowest level in 12 years.

Despite the significant increase in overseas arrivals in Canada, the US remains its number one source market, with nearly 80% of its total inbound market coming from its southern neighbour in 1998. The share coming from overseas origins, however, rose from not quite 18% in 1989 to 21% in 1998.

Europeans made up 56% of Canada's overseas market in 1998, increasing their visits to Canada by 37%. Three of Canada's top four country markets are in Europe. Growth has been particularly strong from France and Germany over this period. Travel from Asia grew 25% between 1989 and 1998, but was down a dramatic 19% in 1998.

Mexico

In Mexico, the Americas dominate international travel. In 1997, nearly all international tourist arrivals in Mexico (18.9 million) came from this region. Travel from Europe to Mexico totalled 347 000 arrivals that year.

In 1998, there were nearly 10 million Mexican international tourist departures. The vast majority of these (9.3 million) were destined to the United States. After the US, the next most popular destination for Mexican international travellers are Italy, Spain and Canada, with around 100 000 visitors each.

Forecasts

Forecasting international travel in total and between countries can be a difficult task in that there are so many factors that can affect it. There are currently several trends favourable to the growth in international tourism.

Population growth, immigration and an ageing population in many developed nations of the world will continue to have profound impacts on the travel industry in North America. For example, the ageing of Baby Boomers (those born between 1946 and 1964) in the US, and similar trends in other leading developed nations in Europe and Asia, have produced and will continue to produce significant gains in the numbers of people in the middle-aged and older categories, those groups most likely to travel internationally.

Where the economy goes, so goes the travel industry. The travel industry in North America is also likely to prosper over the next several years thanks to steady growth in the economies of the US and Canada, and renewed growth in Europe and Asia. DRI/McGraw-Hill, the econometric forecasting firm used by the Travel Industry Association of America, projects that real GDP will increase in the 2.5–3.5% annual range for each of the major world regions between the late 1990s and the early 2000s.

These positive factors are reflected in the bullish outlook for international tourism presented by the World Tourism Organization (WTO). According to WTO, total international arrivals are predicted to rise to 668 million in 2000, top 1 billion in 2010 and reach nearly 1.6 billion in 2020. This represents a growth rate of about 4.1% a year. Spending by these travellers is expected to increase even more, so that spending in the year 2010 is expected to be US$1.6 billion – nearly four times more than in 1998.

Prospects are also improving in the United States. According to Tourism Industries, short-term growth in arrivals may be slow but expected recoveries will spur the US into a record breaking international visitation level in 2003 when international arrivals will top out at nearly 55 million.

Growth between 1998 and 2003 is expected to be 18%. Arrivals in the US from Canada should total over 15 million by 2003, as the recent strength of the Canadian economy is expected to reverse the decline in travel to the US in the 1990s.

In Mexico, stability of the economy is also expected due to the US$24 billion financial agreement reached with the International Monetary Fund, World Bank and Inter-American Development Bank. Assuming sustained growth in its NAFTA partners which would also help support Mexico's upward GDP trend, arrivals from Mexico to the US should grow steadily by over 3% a year to reach 10.6 million by 2003.

And, overseas arrivals in the US are expected to continue to grow the fastest, 22% over the next five years to total 28.9 million arrivals in 2003. Growth should be strongest from Venezuela (+38%), the UK (+27%), Argentina (+25%) and Germany (+23%).

Growth is expected to be even stronger in international travel to Canada, up 20% between 1998 and 2003. Travel inbound to Canada from the US is projected to reach 18.3 million arrivals in 2003. This long-term forecast assumes continued growth in the US economy and benefits of the Open Skies agreement.

The outlook for France is decidedly upbeat, due to pent-up demand for travel to Canada among the French and a resilient economy. The outlook for Germany is less favourable and it will take some time for the German economy to rebound. The forecast for Japanese travel to Canada is negative as well. Canada expects to start to see small increases from the Japanese market.

Looking even further ahead, the WTO predicts that the East Asia/Pacific region will continue to be the world's fastest growing tourism regional destination in the upcoming decades, overtaking the Americas as the world's number two receiving region, holding a 26% share in 2020 as against 15% by the Americas.

The top ten receiving countries will change significantly with China (currently not even in the top ten) becoming the leading destination in 2020, with a predicted 130 million arrivals. France, the US and Spain will be in second, third and fourth place. Hong Kong, if treated as a separate entity, will also become one of the main destinations. Also entering the top ten will be the Russian Federation.

179

In terms of generating countries, Germany will remain number one as it is today. The next largest will be Japan and the United States, followed by China in fourth place. The Russian Federation will also become a major outbound tourism country by the year 2020.

16

South America

Regina Schlüter

Introduction

South American countries have realized that tourism is an excellent way to diversify their economies. Every day more and more capital is being invested in infrastructure and at the same time there are a number of initiatives to attract foreign capital, especially geared to financing hotels and other kinds of accommodation for tourists. In addition to the traditional options of 'sun and sand' holidays, as well as ecotourism and cultural tourism, it is now possible to witness the rise of cruise tourism, with cruises towards the Antarctic becoming increasingly popular.

South America benefits from 14.9% of the total of arrivals of international tourism to the Americas and its proportion of income stands at 12.6% (WTO, 1999). According to data from the World Tourism Organization (WTO, 1999) arrivals of foreign tourists reached 18 247 000 in 1998, amounting to a growth of 15% compared to the year before. This growth is reflected in receipts, which during this period amounted to US$15 075 million, that is an increase of 11%

over 1997. During the period between 1989 and 1998 arrivals grew at an average rate of 9.1% and income at 13.2%. The principal market for South America is regional; Europe and the United States are the principal long-distance markets.

The most important countries in terms of attracting international tourism to South America are Argentina, Brazil and Uruguay (Figure 16.1), although Uruguay finds itself only in eighth position as regards tourist income, preceded by Argentina, Brazil, Venezuela, Chile, Colombia, Peru and Paraguay in that order (Figure 16.2).

Brazil (14.7%), Peru (10.4%), Chile (9.2%) and Colombia (9.1%) are the countries with the greatest growth in arrivals during the period 1989–98. Surinam (21.2%) and Paraguay (21.1%) demonstrate the greatest percentage of income in US$ during the same period (WTO, 1999: 211).

The Tourism Survey Panorama 2020 (WTO, 1998) predicts that in this new millennium the annual growth in tourism in South America will be 4.9% compared to North America where there will be a decrease of 3.6% a year.

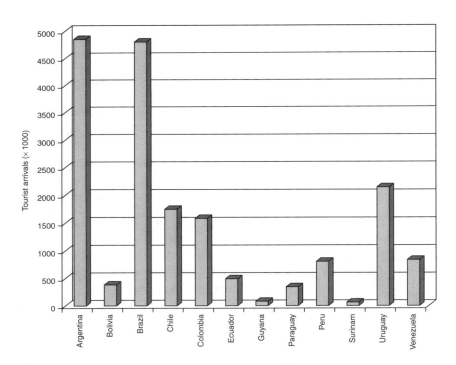

Figure 16.1 South America's tourist destinations, 1998

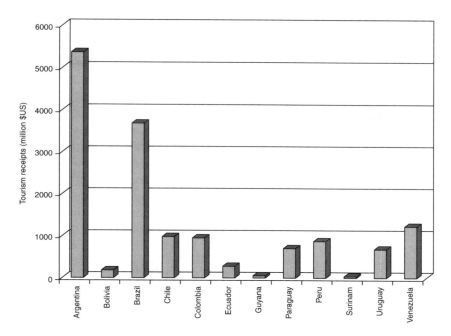

Figure 16.2 South America's tourist receipts, 1998

It is generally considered that ecotourism allows for a greater participation by the local population in its development. This is due to the fact that it is practised on a small scale, thus achieving a less conflicting relationship between visitors and those visited. Income gained by those offering services complements traditional sources of income. The growth in participation on the part of the local population has added to a commitment towards the environment and led to ecotourism being regarded as one of the most popular expressions of the sustainable development of tourism. There is every reason to hope that this will continue. In many South American countries rural tourism is another form of tourism that is considered sustainable.

Ecotourism and rural tourism as forms of sustainable tourism

The 1970s witnessed a growing concern for the deterioration of the environment and this led to the creation of what became popularly known as ecotourism. In South America the Galapagos National Park (Ecuador) was an important ecotouristic destination well before the term 'ecotourism' was coined. On the threshold of the new millennium two parks of the subcontinent are growing in popularity: the Amazon and Patagonia. Bolivia is looking for a strategy of sustainable development within the parameters of 'eco-ethno' tourism while Peru can count on an alternative in adventure tourism.

Ecotourism in the Amazon region

The Amazon region includes the river of the same name and its 1100 tributaries. It covers an area of 7–8 million km² and has a population estimated at 20 million inhabitants, one million of whom are aborigines belonging to 420 ethnic groups. The Amazonian rain forest has a great variety of medicinal plants and also a great richness in fungi, bacteria and insects that constitute an important basis for the development of biotechnology (SUDAM/OEA 1997).

The efforts made by Brazil to position itself in the extraregional ecotouristic market are best known. The extraction of minerals and the exploitation of the forest are still the dominant economic activities, but the government as well as the private sector are trying to develop ecotourism, which is growing rapidly and has a conservationist nature as well as permitting a sustainable way of life for the local population and the generation of income for companies in the area (Chun, 1995). The region has a great capacity to develop ecotourism and thus attract considerable international tourism. Other attractions are of a historic and cultural character, as well as scientific interest, technical activity and programmed events (SUDAM/OEA, 1997).

While there is evidence that in the 1960s there were already travel agencies specializing in ecotourism, the boom took place between the end of the 1980s and the beginning of the 1990s. An ethical code of the practice of ecotourism was established in 1996 (Pires, 1999).

The Pantanal is another region of Brazil being developed for ecotourism. Its system extends to the neighbouring countries of Bolivia and Paraguay and it is considered one of the greatest concentrations of fauna on the planet as well as being one of the most important natural nurseries in the world (SUDAM/OEA, 1994b). While the region started to receive sporadic visitors from the 1960s it was not until the 1990s that the area witnessed an accelerated influx. The arrival of visitors brought economic benefits to the region and cattle-estate farmers saw in tourism an excellent opportunity to increase their earning power. However, given the considerable fragility of the ecosystem, conservationist groups are afraid of the negative impact that might be generated. With the objective of minimizing this negative impact, a number of programmes which aim to preserve the environment and educate the local population have been implemented. The objective is to transform the Pantanal into an important destination within the context of international ecotourism, which allows for a sustainable development for the whole area in the new millennium. With this in mind, a convention will be signed between the Inter-American Development Bank (IDB) and the Brazilian government to develop a programme that will improve the existing infrastructure.

Penguins, whales and elephant seals on the Atlantic coast of Southern Argentina

Tourism in Argentina has always been closely linked to the National Parks and the network of provincial reserves. As a result of the success of the tourism-protected area formula a system of fauna reserves was established in Patagonia along the southern Atlantic coast with the objective of favouring economic growth by attracting the market segment interested in contact with nature. At the present time, the system of fauna reserves protects whales, penguins, sea elephants and seals and a great variety of birds. It extends from the Southern 41° parallel to the extreme south of the continental coast of Argentina.

The creation of this system of protected areas positively influenced the reproduction of coastal fauna and allowed for the consolidation of growth of tourism in the area. The area which most benefited from this was the city of Puerto Madryn given its proximity to the Valdés Península Reserve, which was added to UNESCO's World Heritage List in 1999.

From the Andes to the Pacific: the search for sustainable development in Argentinian and Chilean Patagonia

In the Andean-Patagonian mountain range of Argentina, National Parks are the principal attraction for tourism. They consist of a number of settlements and their surrounding areas and allow for the growth of non-conventional economic activities such as the cultivation of berries and aromatic plants (Schlüter, 1999). Away from the protected areas farmhouses constitute an accommodation option for visitors which leads to additional income for those families that make their living from sheepfarming. At the same time, in areas of considerable interest to tourists, small enterprises have sprung up as 'ecolodges' administered by people who live in the area and who apply a conservational approach both to the management and practice of recreational activities.

In Chilean Patagonia rural tourism is benefiting from important development. It started almost two decades ago in the surrounding area of Puerto Montt, in the south of the country. Szmulewicz (1995: 204) points out that the area was colonized by Germans who transplanted their distinctive architectural style to Chile, which, added to the extensive availability of wood, led to large houses being built. The houses were of a very high standard in terms of construction. In the 1980s, when young people moved to the cities in order to find work, most of these houses became unoccupied. At the same time the south of Chile was becoming a popular tourist destination, not only for Chileans but also for foreign tourism (mainly Argentineans). The houses were refurbished and converted into tourist accommodation with or without breakfast.

Ethnoecotourism in Bolivia

Bolivia is known as 'The country of the High Plateau', given that Lake Titicaca, its most representative site, is to be found there. It can count, at the same time, on traces of a rich pre-colonial past and a very considerable jungle. As Bolivia is unable to offer the 'sun and sand' option, the government looked for a way, from 1994, to base a strategy for sustainable development on a product called 'Ethnoecotourism from the Amazon to the Andes' (Vera-Mendia, 1999). This concept aimed to integrate the physical, biological and cultural diversity of Bolivia, emphasizing not only the variety but also the quality of the environment. From a practical point of view, ethnoecotourism consists of different kinds of nature tourism in close association with the culture of the place. Vera-Mendia (1999: 364), optimistic about the possibilities for ethnoecotourism in Bolivia in the 21st century, states that:

It is the instrument for a model of socio-economic development based on sustainable use, this being harmonious, not wasteful of natural resources or the national heritage. It is based on the capacity of the pre-hispanic population in Bolivia to present itself to the world, expressing its cultural characteristics. At the same time, in order to enhance diversification of tourism in Bolivia, a number of specialized options has been developed, taking into account the nature of national geography. Among these specializations are to be found pot-holing, mountain climbing, fishing, walking, bird-watching, scientific tourism and archaeological tourism.

Ecotourism and adventure tourism in Peru

While it is the case that ecotourism is different from adventure tourism in that the latter implies activities with a certain degree of risk, in the Andean environment simple contact with nature implies a certain degree of risk in itself. This is the case in Peru, where the most important natural and cultural sites are found at high altitudes, which implies physical discomfort for people of advanced age or with precarious health.

Among the most promoted areas of the Peruvian Andes are the Huascarán National Park and the Inca site of Macchu Picchu. The first offers mountain climbing and trekking (Morales-Arnao, 1994), which can also be practised on the four trails that lead from Cuzco towards the Inca fortress of Macchu Picchu. The trails allow for the appreciation of this UNESCO World Heritage site as well as a number of other interesting sites in the Sacred Valley of the Incas.

Tourism in the South American Caribbean

The first tourist product for the international market to be developed in South America was sun and sand holidays. Colombia and Venezuela have the great advantage of having coasts on the Caribbean Sea and thus benefit from the flow of tourism to that region. While Colombia is currently associated with social problems deriving from the struggle against drug trafficking, it can still offer tourists, mostly from Europe and the USA, two popular and traditional resorts: Santa Marta and Cartagena de Indias. The San Andrés Islands are also an important destination.

Venezuela also benefits from a considerable flow of tourists heading towards the Island of Margarita in the Caribbean. However, the search for more sustainable forms of tourism has led to the practice of ecotourism in National Parks (M. Ascanio, 1999) and has fostered travel to various areas of the country characterized by considerable natural beauty but at the present time without the necessary infrastructure or equipment for tourism.

With the objective of offering the visitor a way of life similar to that of the native population, and using the natural geography to promote tourism, the idea of tourist camps has been initiated. A. Ascanio (1997: 159) states that:

> The tourist camps in Venezuela are very different to those known as camping in other countries. In Venezuela the tourist camps in the jungle, the plains or even in the mountains offer a habitat designed using the

indigenous type of housing. For example, in the plains and the jungle can be found a kind of accommodation known as *churuta* and this adapts well to the environment and the climate. In the mountain area, old country houses are being remodelled and cabins are being built while, in the open countryside, a shelter is being built from which to hang a number of hammocks.

A programme of inns for tourists has recently been implemented in Venezuela. This has enabled all those who own an attractive dwelling in a rural setting to offer accommodation to tourists. The inns, combined with the organization of walks and excursions, have led to the development of new routes which are attracting more and more tourists to the area. (A. Ascanio, 1997)

Beach tourism in Brazil

Brazil was among the first South American countries to compete in the interregional market with its 'sun and sea' product. In the early 1970s a chain of seaside resorts along the Atlantic coast, from Rio de Janeiro to Santos, was developed for both domestic and international tourism. These resorts attracted mainly tourists from Argentina, who also visited the beaches that stretched from Santos to Porto Alegre (Schlüter, 1998). Later, Brazil started exploiting a number of tourist developments in the northwest of the country, with the objective of capturing an important international market. Another important element is the creation of a number of nature reserves.

Culture as a tourist resource

South America counts on important traces of its pre-colonial culture, among which are the outstanding archaeological heritage of Inca civilization, the most important example being Macchu Picchu in Peru. There are also a number of colonial cities, most of which are included in the World Heritage List of UNESCO. Among them are Lima (Peru), Quito (Ecuador), Colonia del Sacramento (Uruguay), Olinda (Brazil) and Cartagena de Indias (Colombia).

South America also offers a wealth of socio-cultural expression in which pre-Columbian rituals are mixed with elements introduced by the former colonial powers and influenced by the African slavery system. However, the Rio Carnival is the only socio-cultural product that is highly competitive in the international market (Schlüter, 1998).

Facing the challenges of the 21st century, communities located at a short distance from popular coastal tourist destinations have also sought to benefit from this flow of visitors, developing products based on popular festivals or gastronomy. This is the case of Blumenau (Brazil) and Gaiman (Argentina). Blumenau, in the state of Santa Catarina, is a community whose inhabitants descend mostly from Germans. It is located next to Camboriú, Florianópolis and Laguna, important sun and sand destinations in the South of Brazil. From the early 1980s a 'Beer Festival' or 'Oktoberfest' was organized which has its roots in an important event held annually (actually in the month of September) in Munich, Germany (Machado, 1996). In the coastal region of Argentinian Patagonia, the small town of Gaiman has sought to develop its economy by offering the classic 'five o'clock tea', which has become known as 'Welsh tea' (Schlüter, 1998: 186).

Concluding comments

South American countries can count on excellent natural resources to attract international tourism, both from neighbouring and distant countries. Efforts are centred on achieving the sustainable development of tourism in the subcontinent. However, it is still the case that there are not sufficient studies to determine whether development within the concept of sustainability can realize, in the long term, the necessary benefits to achieve the desired profitability of companies, the improvement of the quality of life of the resident population, tourist satisfaction and care of the physical environment.

There are already signs that sustainability is not an easy road to follow and is likely to be beset by many problems in this new millennium. Small undertakings can count on the benefits offered by the Internet but they will have problems in making themselves known to potential tourists. Longed-for community participation in the future could easily degenerate into apathy (Romero-Mayo, 1997; Masri de Achar and Robles-Ponce, 1997) if the inhabitants do not feel sufficiently involved in decision-making and in the sharing of benefits. There is the danger that as the new millennium advances, the environment will be increasingly exposed to pollution with the result that the tourist market could be damaged.

References

Ascanio, A. (1997) El programa de posadas y campamentos turísticos venezolanos. *Estudios y Perspectivas en Turismo*, 6: 157–16.

Ascanio, M. (1999) Una aproximación al ecoturismo en Venezuela. El Parque Nacional Henri Pittier. *Estudios y Perspectivas en Turismo*, 8: 274–90

Butcher, J. (1997) Sustainable development or development?, In M.J. Stabler (ed.), *Tourism and Sustainability. Principles to Practice*. New York: CAB International, pp. 27–38.

Chun, M. (1995) The future model rainforest lodge. IICT training academic native craft center. In D.E. Hawkins, M. Epler Wood and M. Bittman (eds), *The Ecolodge Source Book for Planners and Developers*. North Bennington: TES, pp. 107–9.

Coriolano, L. (1996) Turismo e degradacaö ambiental no litoral do Ceará. In A. Lemos (ed.), *Turismo: Impactos Socioambientais*. Sao Paulo: Editora Hucitec, pp. 93–103.

Machado, E.V. (1996) Festas de outubro em Santa Catarina. Notas para compreensäo de suas influencias na (re)organizacäo do espaco. In A. Lemos (ed.), *Turismo: Impactos Socioambientais*. Sao Paulo: Editora Hucitec, pp. 241–60.

Masri de Achar, S. and Robles-Ponce, L. (1997) *La industria turística hacia la sustentabilidad*. Mexico: Editorial Diana.

Morales-Arnao, C. (1994) El turismo de aventura en el Perú. *Estudios y Perspectivas en Turismo*, 3: 162–71.

Pina Mendonca, E. (1995) Bahia – leading tourism development in Brazil: investment opportunities. In Ministry of Tourism of Israel (ed.), *Investments and Financing in the Tourism Industry*. Madrid: WTO, pp. 174–8.

Pires, C.C. (1999) Management in ecotourism agencies and their insertion in the context of sustainability. *Turismo: Visäo e Acáo*, 1 (2): 45–6.

Rivera, J. (1993) Project for regulating and developing ecotourism in Amazonia. Proceedings of the World Congress on Adventure Travel and Ecotourism, Manaus.

Romero-Mayo, R. (1997) Dilemas del turismo ecológico en el Caribe Mexicano. *Revista Mexicana del Caribe*, 2 (4): 80–129.

Ruschmann, D. (1997) O ecoturismo no Brasil. Proceedings of the World Ecotour '96, Rio de Janeiro.

Schlüter, R. (1998) Tourism development: a Latin American perspective. In W. Theobald (ed.), *Global Tourism*. Oxford: Butterworth–Heinemann, pp. 216–30.

Schlüter, R. (1999) Sustainable tourism development in South America. The case of Patagonia, Argentina. In D. Pearce and R. Butler (eds), *Contemporary Issues in Tourism Development*. London: Routledge. pp. 176–91.

SUDAM/OEA (1994a) *Oferta turística da regiäo Amazonia brasileira*. Belem: Pará.

SUDAM/OEA (1994b) *Diagnóstico do desenvolvimento de ecoturismo no Pantanal brasilerio*. Belem: Pará.

SUDAM/OEA (1997) *Recursos Naturais na Amazonia*. Belem: Pará.

Szmulewicz, P. (1995) Agroturismo en el sur de Chile. *Estudios y Perspectivas en Turismo*, 4: 201–15.

Vera-Mendia, J. (1999) Turismo en Bolivia. Propuesta para categorizar la profesión del guía de turismo. *Estudios y Perspectivas en Turismo*, 8: 351–65.

World Tourism Organization (1998) *Turismo: Panorama 2020. Nuevas Tendencias*. Madrid: WTO.

World Tourism Organization (1999) *Tendencias del mercado turístico: Las Américas*. Madrid: WTO.

Part
III

Sectoral Futures

17

Which way for tourist attractions?

Victor Middleton

What are we talking about?

As we contemplate the trends in the new millennium, it is curious that tourist attractions in the UK and elsewhere are still broadly defined and assessed from a traditional 1960s resource-based definition of sites or places 'where it is feasible to charge admission for the sole purpose of sightseeing [and where] the primary purpose is to allow public access for entertainment, interest or education, rather than being primarily a retail outlet or a venue for sporting, theatrical or film performances'. The UK definition further notes that attractions 'must be open to the public without prior booking . . .' (*Sightseeing in the UK*, 1998).

Primarily heritage-orientated, this definition includes:

- Historic properties
- Museums, galleries and science centres
- Wildlife/aquarium attractions

- Botanical and other gardens
- Country parks
- Heritage and other visitor centres
- Leisure/theme parks
- Cathedrals and some churches
- Other attractions, such as industrial archaeology sites, steam railways and farm-based attractions

Within this definition, the UK had an estimated 6164 attractions in 1998, drawing around 400 million recorded visits per annum. Only 7% of all attractions (428), however, including those that are free, achieved over 200 000 visits per annum. Between them they achieved just over 225 million visits or 57% of all recorded visits in 1998. The 428 comprised 111 country parks, 73 museums or galleries, 60 historic properties, 40 leisure parks, 31 wildlife attractions, 16 gardens, 10 visitor centres and 87 'other'. These attractions draw on an audience of UK and overseas staying tourists but the bulk of all visits are day visits from home in leisure time.

These estimates are based on recorded visits and estimates of visitor volume at known attractions. In other words, they are supply-side estimates of demand and many of them at free attractions are 'guesstimates'. This author believes that, while the available data are indicative of the utilization of traditional attractions, they tell us nothing about the total demand potential for visitor attractions, especially if the attractions are outwith the traditional tourist board definition.

Market demand for traditional attractions falters as supply increases

The UK evidence, based on surveys of known attractions, reveals some clear trends. Table 17.1 shows 20-year trends on an index basis for the volume of visits recorded at four main types of attractions in England. Table 17.2 notes growth in the number of attractions entering the market. Bearing in mind that newer attractions tend to be larger on average than existing attractions, there is no doubt that capacity in the UK increased faster than demand in the last two decades of the 20th century. The UK enters the 21st century with an excess of capacity that has major economic implications for future viability. Reflecting the size characteristics noted in Table 17.3, the majority of visitor attractions are not profitable in a normal industrial sense and their return on capital is inadequate. Five key points help to explain the implications for the future of the three tables.

Table 17.1   Trend in number of visits to attractions in England, 1978–98

Year	Historic properties	Gardens	Wildlife sites	Museums and galleries
1978	100	100	100	100
1982	85	98	85	91
1990	112	139	127	112
1994	109	162	111	119
1996	116	174	117	121
1998	117	170	129	121

1978 = 100. 1978 was chosen as the base year because it was the high level of the 1970s.

Table 17.2   Years in which UK attractions first opened to the public

First opening	Historic properties (%)	Gardens (%)	Museums and galleries (%)	Wildlife (%)	All (%)
1990–98	9	19	16	26	20
1980–89	17	26	28	29	27
Sub-total	**26**	**45**	**44**	**55**	**47**
1970–79	15	18	20	19	19
1960–69	8	13	10	11	8
Pre-1969	51	26	26	15	26
Total	100	100	100	100	100
Number known in 1998	1418	347	1724	300	5890

Table 17.3   The small size of tourist attractions in the UK

Visits per annum	%
Less than 1000	10
1001 to 10 000	32
10 001 to 50 000	34
Sub total	**76**
50 001 to 200 000	17
More than 200 000	7
Total	100

- The volume of visits to main attractions has grown over 20 years but at a very low rate. The average growth disguises losses in volume of 20% or more over the period for many established attractions that make a charge for admission.
- Around one-half of all known attractions in the UK opened in the years between 1980 and 1998. The impact of many large new attractions to celebrate the millennium is yet to be felt.
- The average size of tourist attractions in the UK is small – with an average of 46 000 visits per annum to attractions that charge; 76% of all attractions record no more than 50 000 visits a year.

The economics of the sector are confused by the fact that ownership is split between government and its agencies, local government and the private sector (including not-for-profit trusts). Reflecting public sector ownership, 42% of recorded attractions within the official definition do not charge for admission and they receive over 50% of all visits to attractions. An even larger percentage are dependent on one or other form of public sector subsidy for survival. Not shown in Table 17.1, available evidence indicates that demand has been rising faster at free attractions than at those that charge. From 1989 to 1995 the private sector attractions achieved total growth of just 3.3% in total visits.

To cope with weak demand, a typical resource-based response is to put up prices ahead of inflation. Between 1989 to 1995, for example, notwithstanding the UK's worst economic recession in half a century, prices at charging historic properties rose by 75% against a 29% increase in the UK retail price index. Annual revenue increased but rates of increase of this order for a largely unchanged product are not sustainable in the face of other competition.

In common with other industrialized countries, the 1980s and early 1990s were years of extensive urban decline and dereliction in many parts of the UK. Global economic competition forced the closure of large sectors of traditional manufacturing and extractive industries in areas once dedicated to coal mining, iron and steel making, shipbuilding, textile industries, fishing and the associated trades that supplied them. The European Commission, national governments and local government endeavoured to alleviate the social hardship caused by this decline and to promote other forms of post-industrial economic activity that could generate employment and wealth creation. Leisure and all forms of cultural and heritage activity together with tourism and hospitality have been high on the development list for all such areas.

In the UK much of this thinking came together in the government funded Garden Festival movement of the 1970s that changed national attitudes to visitor attractions as an engine of redevelopment and created major one-year visitor attractions on reclaimed derelict land in cities such as Liverpool, Glasgow, Gateshead and in the former mining valleys of South Wales. Visitor attractions were identified as one of the government's chosen vehicles for focusing regeneration possibilities and changing attitudes to modern forms of employment. Following much the same philosophy, the UK's Millennium Dome, itself built on previously poisoned land used for gas making, is being used to trigger economic regeneration in the Greenwich/Woolwich area south of the Thames and carry eastward the momentum of the Docklands Development north of the river.

The size of UK tourist attractions shown in Table 17.3 explains why Middleton (1990, 1998) and other authors have noted the extent to which many traditional tourist attractions, especially in the heritage sector, are still operated in effect as cottage industries. Middleton uses the term *management deficit* to summarize what is arguably the principal structural weakness in the traditional attractions sector that frequently inhibits the development of effective responses to its difficulties. For example, in 1998 only 17 charging attractions in the UK achieved at least 1 million visitors and 12 of these were in or near London (including Windsor Castle and Legoland). Within the sector, entering the new millennium, effective, continuous market research is still unusual; traditional publicity is used but branding and marketing is weak and much of it is provided on an amateur basis or through public sector agencies and committees often lacking commercial visitor management skills.

The underlying consumer demand for leisure-based attractions is growing strongly

By evaluating the available research evidence from the consumer side rather than the supply side one gains insights and a new perspective into the demand for and supply of attractions for leisure day visits. It is possible to provide at least a broad estimate of the overall size of the UK market by combining information from surveys of UK domestic tourism (United Kingdom Tourism Survey, UKTS) and overseas tourism to the UK (International Passenger Survey, IPS) with data from the *UK Day Visits Survey* (UKDVS). The latter is a survey commissioned jointly by the Department for Culture, Media and Sport (DCMS, the sponsoring government department for tourism in the UK) and a consortium of the national agencies responsible for recreation and tourism. It measures all leisure trips from home regardless of duration and by agreement between DCMS and tourist boards, a *leisure day visit* is defined as being of more than three but less than 24 hours away from home for any 'non-regular' purpose not connected with the daily routines of work and sustenance.

Leisure visits cover recreation, sport and informal leisure including walking, driving for pleasure as well as visiting traditional attractions. Very importantly in reviewing the market for attractions, it also covers non-regular shopping excursions, non-routine eating and drinking out and all forms of cultural and entertainment choices that are associated with mobile populations in post-industrial societies.

Drawing on a recent report (Middleton, 1999), it is possible at least broadly to quantify the total potential market for leisure attractions in the UK over a year. The UK generates, in rounded terms, some 1500 million potential leisure day visits. This is the total market in which traditional attractions are competing on the threshold of the 21st century. It is nearly four times larger than the estimated number of 400 million visits to traditional attractions noted earlier. It is not possible to plot this growth statistically over the years because comparable back data on leisure day visits from home are not available. But a combination of rising income per head and greater personal mobility as well as the massive commitment of commercial money to the developments noted in the next section provides all the proof that is needed of recent and anticipated strong consumer interest and market growth. While the traditional attractions market shows only slow growth overall and decline for many, the new leisure market is booming and prosperous.

A new formula for leisure time destination attractions – funded by massive private sector investment

Since the economic prosperity years of the 1980s and the economic boom years that followed the 1990/92 recession, large commercial operators in the hospitality industry as well as in retailing have analysed consumer leisure trends generally and noted the rapidly growing demand of a mobile society for eating and drinking out, health and fitness clubs, a range of family focused recreation activities, entertainment, cultural activities and live shows and, especially in the UK, multiplex cinemas. These trends have combined with remarkable commercial synergy with another major growth sector of more affluent societies – shopping as a leisure activity.

The development of shopping malls in the United States dates back to the 1960s, of course, but in its more modern form it effectively crossed the Atlantic in the mid-1980s and was remarkably successful in the form of pioneer developments in the UK of large, one-stop, under-cover, multi-component centres, as at Gateshead Metro Centre, Merry Hill (Dudley) and Meadowhall (Sheffield).

In the 1990s, stimulated by the evidence of success of the 1980s centres and the emergence of a buoyant economy combined with the knowledge that the government would impose a halt to all new out-of-town developments after 1997, there was an astonishing scramble to develop sites with the essential motorway access and economic potential in all parts of the UK. There are now around ten major complexes each attracting more than 25 million visits a year and many more at around the five million visits level. All are providing for a remarkably similar combination of retail, leisure, entertainment and catering offered in an integrated 'one-stop' under-cover complex with easy access by car and operated for at least 12–18 hours a day. The key concepts or principles in this development are *leisure destination, entertainment, family day out, multiple facilities, dramatic architectural forms and internal ambience, and something for everyone.* With the somewhat smaller-scale development of designer outlet villages since around 1993/4, the leisure destination formula is an internationally powerful formula for profitable development. The new wave of destination attractions has moved through mainland Europe for most of the same consumer-related reasons as in the UK.

The one-stop leisure/retail/entertainment complex development is highly profitable because it fits perfectly with a multiple car owning society that is 'money-rich and time-poor'. It has developed in the 1990s from a retail concept, although retail remains a key element, into quite a new animal – destination leisure centres, often identified as 'parks' or 'villages' to sustain the day out concept. Opened in March 1999 and located in a former chalk quarry between the M25 and M2 in Kent, the largest development in the UK and Europe to date is Bluewater Park. Owned by Lend Lease, an Australian-based developer which has some 40 other centres around the world, it comprises 1.7 million square feet, over 300 shops and car parking for some 13 000 cars. Larger than most town centres and aiming for around 35 million visits a year, Bluewater is truly a 'new resort for the 21st century'. Under its roof it provides an indoor 'tropical rainforest', a 'town square' and a street café leisure environment within a spectacular setting more reminiscent of Disney than traditional shopping malls (Middleton, 1999). 'In order to satisfy consumer expectations of a complete day out experience ... leisure facilities ... will be centred around three themed "village areas"' (South East England Tourist Board, 1998). The size of the new centres is contrasted with the largest traditional attractions in Table 17.4.

Table 17.4   A comparison of traditional and new UK attractions (visitor numbers)

Blackpool Pleasure Beach	7.1m	Bluewater Park	30–35m
Madame Tussauds, London	2.8m	Trafford Park	30–35m
Alton Towers	2.8m	Lakeside – Thurrock	20–25m
The Tower of London	2.5m	Meadowhall	20–25m
The British Museum (free entry)	5.6m	McArthur Glenn	5–6m

The new 'resorts': business strenghts

The new leisure destination centres or 'resorts' have the following characteristics and business strengths:

- They are large-scale complexes capable of sustaining between 5 and 35 million visits a year.
- They are open for 15 (and up to 24) hours a day, 363 days a year – under cover – providing for maximum dwell time on site.
- Free at point of entry, often with sheltered walkways from the car parks.
- A safe, graffiti-free, patrolled, clean, air-conditioned and relaxed environment designed and managed around consumer interests – uniformed staff are available as 'hosts' to guide and help visitors.
- Multiple product base – retailing, themed catering and bars, entertainment, recreation, family and health facilities – select your own experience.
- Spectacular surroundings with space for live shows, events and exhibitions and architecture designed to appeal to the imagination.
- Multiple repeat visits and excellent prospects for developing a loyal clientele using databases and relationship marketing.
- Professional management, strong branding and typically linked into international alliances, often making designer label products available at advantageous prices.
- Appreciating capital assets, with profitability ploughed back into refurbishment.
- Attractive to private sector investors such as pension funds and investment trusts seeking profitable growth and attractive to public sector planners for the economic benefit they bring, often to formerly derelict industrial sites.

Traditional attractions: business weaknesses

The contrast with the business weaknesses inherent in many traditional attractions is stark. Most are:

- Stand alone, the majority on a very small-scale basis with less than 50 visits on average per day.
- Short opening hours – short dwell time on site of 2–3 hours, many not open every day.
- Seasonal demand – often weather-dependent.
- Up front, very visible charge for admission – either at a car park or a reception building or kiosk.
- Many with a long-standing public sector management ethos and a single/limited product focus designed and managed around the resource needs rather than consumer interests.
- Mostly once only visitors with few reasons for repeat visit (cost of attracting first time visitors rising).
- Revenue inadequate for the essential refurbishment cycle so that major changes are unusual and visible dilapidations are all too often evident.
- Weak management/management deficit. Often with only weak links to other businesses.
- Unattractive to private investors since very few offer growth prospects in capital asset and revenue growth terms.
- Often unattractive to the public sector as it seeks to limit and withdraw from its revenue funding commitments.

Concluding thoughts

The way ahead for visitor attractions is clearly dividing between the traditional and the new. The 1960s supply side definition of traditional tourist attractions has been overtaken by subsequent developments and it now serves to obscure rather than clarify real trends. In answer to the classic business strategy question, 'what business are you really in?' the answer for a growing number of attractions is leisure and entertainment, not tourism.

The new leisure destination attractions are the new resorts for the 21st century. Just as seaside resorts met the needs in Northern Europe of railway excursionists at the end of the 19th century, so modern out of town leisure/entertainment destinations meet the needs of modern mobile post-industrial consumers.

Looking ahead, the number and size of the new resorts and the sheer sameness of much of the product offer may carry with it the seeds of decline from

Table 17.5 Approximate number of UK attractions opening and closing since 1978/80

Type of attraction	Opened 1980–98	Closed 1978–98	Total[a] in 1998
Historic properties	370	113	1418
Gardens	156	51	347
Museums and galleries	760	246	1724
Farm attractions	210	49	249
Wildlife attractions	165	36	300
All attractions	2770	776	5890

[a] Total reporting on this issue (5890) compares with 6164 known attractions in total for UK in 1998.

fashion. There is a danger that much of the provision will be seen as bland, standardized, synthetic and boring after the first flush of novelty and convenience has worn off. Creativity, originality and individuality do not sit easily with lowest common product denominators often associated with large-scale provision.

In the traditional tourist attraction sector there are uneasy, often unspoken compromises as to what extent they should be judged to be businesses and to what extent they are a core part of public sector provision, publicly funded for the conservation of heritage, the good of the visiting public and quality of life in the areas where they are located.

As for the way ahead for traditional attractions, a war of attrition seems inevitable in which many existing attractions will continue to fail and be closed. This is not a new process as Table 17.5 shows. Survivors will make best use of their unique blend of originality and personality but systematic collaboration will be the hallmark of survivors. The core solutions as identified by Middleton (1998) will include:

- Quality assurance to attract customers and encourage repeat visits.
- Integration wherever possible with other services associated with post-industrial society, such as education for life, speciality retailing, the arts and other cultural provision.
- Networking using modern information and communications technology (ICT) for communication, management training, research, branding, marketing and customer access.
- Association, strategic alliances and sometimes collocation for attractions to achieve the economies of scale essential to efficient and cost-effective management and marketing.

Source note

Most UK statistics on attractions are drawn from *Sightseeing in the UK*, an annual statistical report published by the English Tourist Board (now the English Tourism Council).

References

Middleton, V.T.C. (1990) *New Visions for Independent Museums in the UK.* Chichester: Association of Independent Museums.

Middleton, V.T.C. (1998) *New Visions for Museums in the 21st Century.* London: Association of Independent Museums.

Middleton, V.T.C. (1999) The new resorts for the 21st century? In *Insights.* London: English Tourist Board.

Museums & Galleries Commission (1998) *The Domus Database.*

South East England Tourist Board (1998) *Bluewater: Retail Tourism in the South East.* Tunbridge Wells: SEETB.

18

Hospitality and the tourist of the future

Michael Olsen

Opening thoughts

In anticipating the future, the key challenge is to identify emerging patterns from the complex array of information that lies before us. This assumes that leaders of organizations will be in a constant search for ideas that will offer opportunity to lead their competition at every chance. This requires not only the ability to synthesize the patterns emerging from all sources of information, experiences and exchanges; it also requires creativity in order to develop a vision out of what all this means and how it can then be used to develop competitive advantage. In doing so, that leader must avoid what Linden (1998) refers to as 'the tyranny of the near past'.

The meaning of this is for many that they are unable to see the emerging patterns because they are anchored in the comfort level of the present and recent past. And as complex and uncertain as the environment is these days, it is often safer to cling to the tyranny of the near past rather than risk bold new initiatives to capture the customer of tomorrow.

The purpose of this chapter is to attempt to break with the past and offer another view of the future and how the customers of tomorrow will differ from those of our near past. These views have been developed over five years through a series of 'Visioning the Future' workshops and think-tanks, which have been conducted by the International Hotel & Restaurant Association. These sessions have produced ideas, feedback and discourse from more than 5000 industry professionals who have either participated in, or received the messages from, the results of these efforts. The task put forth to participants in each case was to try to answer the questions in Box 18.1. In other words, attempts were made to solicit their foresight regarding the future. As such, their views represent a collective view of emerging patterns from professionals in more than 20 countries across the globe. This chapter is a synthesis of those ideas.

Box 18.1   How will you interact with the guest of the future?

- How will the guest be travelling in the future?
- How will the guest be communicating in the future?
- How will you distribute your product to the guest in the future?
- What new customer benefits will the guest demand in the future?
- What competencies will be necessary to serve the guest in the future?
- What standards will be accepted in the future?

Underpinnings influencing the customer of tomorrow

Throughout the last 20 years of the 20th century the distinction between the business traveller and leisure traveller became blurred as people tried to pack into each trip an opportunity to conduct business as well as attempt to take some time for themselves. It can be anticipated that this desire will not change in the future. In fact, it may even be heightened as individuals find themselves in a more complex and uncertain world that no doubt will add stress to their lives. Globalization and the dawning of an information age have helped to bring on much of this complexity and uncertainty.

Globalization itself is complex. It is a phenomenon that often defies simple understanding using basic concepts familiar to most. The terms like economics and free trade are now blended with ideas like geo-political and ecological sustainability. The complexity of the world today will serve as an underpinning shaping business forces and customer behaviours well into the 21ˢᵗ century. It implies that the simple rules used to try to analyse and describe hospitality customer behaviour will be insufficient in this growing web of local, national and international relationships between businesses and their customers. The task of trying to understand these relationships in order to anticipate customer needs will be daunting indeed, maybe even impossible. It is clear that customers will be perceived as more fickle if attempts to describe their future behaviour use dated concepts in simple isolation.

The information age will also create more challenge in terms of trying to understand the customer. This is partly a function of what Tapscott (1995: 58–9) refers to as the convergence of computing, telecommunications and content. This union of three industries will bring the customer into closer contact with their world and at a speed and clarity that has yet to be experienced by them. As Davis and Meyer (1998: 6) state:

> Almost instantaneous communication and computation, for example, are shrinking time and focusing us on Speed. Connectivity is putting everybody and everything online in one way or another and has led to the 'the death of distance', a shrinking of space. Intangible value of all kinds, like service and information, is growing explosively, reducing the importance of tangible mass.

Their thesis is that the world is becoming a 'blur' as a result of their conceptualization of this concept as a formula that states, *Blur = Speed × Connectivity × Intangibles*. It seems clear that speed and connectivity will continue to influence how we live our lives. We will become used to receiving information instantly when we want it as we continue to become more connected to each other. It is also clear that this concurrence will result in a better-informed consumer. For, in addition to speed and connectivity will come increased transparency with regard to each and every purchase decision that this customer will make.

This transparency will be a function of almost perfect information available on all the offerings of products and services that are made by sellers. This near perfect information will exist regarding the physical products that are offered because they are easily described, observed and measured. And because of this, information will be similar to what is often referred to as *word of mouth* commentary but the difference will be that it will now be available for the world to see and even hear.

More challenging will be the management and marketing of the third element of the formula, *intangibles*. Most firms that provide services including hospitality services offer intangibles. However, they are difficult to describe or even measure. They often are characterized by such terms as: *feel, comfort, experience, look, satisfaction*. In each case, these terms are very personal and defined by the customer based upon their perceptions, attitudes and beliefs. It is the intangibles that will drive customer behaviour and motivation in the future as they seek to obtain satisfaction and value from all the experiences related to their purchase. The level of satisfaction anticipated will drive their view of the economic value of the offering of the enterprise. Here again, information will drive how many view the quality of the intangibles and their subsequent value.

When you combine the cumulative effects of globalization and information most individuals are overwhelmed. Yet, judging by all the emerging patterns identified by participants in the think-tanks and visioning workshops, this will continue to be the case. Thus, consumers will be in search of ways and means to reduce this confounding environment. While it is difficult to predict how they will accomplish this, it is clear that they will expect those who plan to offer them products and services to help simplify their world. This will no doubt translate into a new set of new standards for making the offering, delivering the products and services, and following-up on it all. The firms that can do this with the greatest amount of integrity, reliability, consistency and honesty will be the long-term winners of tomorrow's hospitality customer.

The customer of tomorrow[1]

The consumer of tomorrow can be viewed using the metaphor of the historic tribal community. Members of the tribal community lived, defended and often gave their lives protecting the tribe; such was their loyalty. In contrast, tomorrow's consumer, whose attributes are listed in Box 18.2, will have little tribal loyalty at all – or at least not enough for which to sacrifice one's needs. This future consumer feels compelled to remain in search of new tribes, always looking for the best deal or new community. In other words, this new consumer is *fleeting and irreverent* when it comes to remaining loyal to the tribe. The consumer of today, and more so of tomorrow, will be much like a mercenary. She or he will sell out to the highest bidder and the company that offers the best value proposition. In today's terms, this usually translates into competition among travel and hospitality providers to create and manage the best guest loyalty programmes. The future, however, will take this concept much further. Beyond this threshold, the price of loyalty will be superior products and services that add real and significant value to the guest. Determining what that means for each and everyone is no small challenge, especially in the context of the 'blur' environment referred to earlier by Davis and Meyer.

Box 18.2   The Tribal Traveller

- Fleeting and irreverent — brand loyalty will probably go to the highest bidder unless the brand is unquestionably value positive
- Seek entry into tribal groups that satisfy specialized needs in discontinuous patterns — the mall of life via your favourite chat room
- Acquiring product knowledge through several filters — most likely non-human — the personal agent — Wildfire, the ultimate
- Will sell information about themselves for overall value; money, integrity, authenticity, honesty and reality

---

Whereas the historic tribal member was born into and died as a member of the same tribe, tomorrow's member will hold many tribal affiliations. The historic member had little choice in this case, for seldom would she or he be accepted into other tribes, nor experience what membership was like in others. Today, the information highway permits access for the modern day tribal traveller to a number of tribes or communities depending upon his or her needs at the moment — almost like shopping in the *mall of life*. Thus, whether it comes to sports, clothes, music, books, art, travel or hospitality, tomorrow's consumer will enter as many or as few tribes as necessary to satisfy their needs.

This can be experienced today by simply entering into any on-line chat room — a modern-day version of the tribe. It is not uncommon to find that participants enter just to see what the discussion is like, often doing so in both audio and video mediums. If they find it boring or not of interest they move on. If they like it, they enter into the exchange until they grow tired and move on. While many are just shopping for interesting dialogue, others are more specific about what they are seeking. It is difficult to know what they are looking for or how to keep them interested. If one is a hospitality enterprise seeking to attract this type of traveller, it is important to be able to reach them at the time they are looking, capture their interest and make joining your tribe worthwhile. This cannot be done by yield management systems, as we know them today. It will require something different.

That something different may take the form of a *personal agent*. The personal agent is the non-human tribal warrior driven by artificial intelligence software programs and neural networks. It is programmed initially by the human tribal traveller but then continues to learn by itself what drives this human in terms of desires. It does this by remembering each decision made by that traveller throughout the decision-making process. Once enough of a history has been experienced, this software agent is often free to act on behalf of that person when choosing what products and services *or tribes* to enter. This tireless agent is constantly looking out for the interests of its master. It can shop many tribes, far more than the human wants or has the time to explore. An early example of this form of technology at work can be seen by TheTrip.com's IntelliTrip product. With just a few quick keystrokes, a consumer can quickly and easily shop multiple on-line travel services for the best airfares or hotel rates. In this new model, the consumer never even visits the web-site of the service provider or supplier. Such a model poses a great challenge to the firm trying to reach the customer and appeal to his or her desires through the filter of the personal agent.

This new consumer will be more confident in all types of transactions involving the information highway. The personal agent will do most of the information gathering and analysis. This analysis will be objective, based upon previously established criteria set out by the consumer and built upon by the learning capabilities of the software. Armed with better information, the decisions will be more rational, turning basic ones like airline and hotel reservations into more of a commodity exchange process. Price and location will often be the determining factors.

In this context, consumers will actually control more of this exchange process. Therefore, they will determine who will have information about them and how much they will acquire. They will demand to receive value for providing this information. One does not have to look too far to see the frequent flyer points awarded these days for those customers who are willing to fill out the market research forms. In other words, the consumer will be happy to sell information about themselves to the tribal masters who are willing to pay the price so long as the end result is better value in the consumers' eyes. Without question, consumers will continue to become more powerful in this new environment.

What will be essential in this new era of information exchange will be the *integrity of the overall process*. Consumers will not accept the transfer of information about themselves from one tribe to another. They will seek and obtain control of this. The selling of name lists from one company to

211

another will extract a high cost if the consumer does not want this to happen: the cost will be abandonment of the tribe. With so many alternatives available, either through human searches or those done by non-human personal agents, and the lack of loyalty by the consumer, the firm will never be able to maximize the economic lifetime value of that consumer who has felt violated. As consumers become more comfortable in this new role, those firms that have been passively trying to hang on to that value will find themselves deserted, often forever. For the hospitality enterprise, there is little that can be done to prevent this.

Of course, many are trying to prevent this growth in consumer buying power. The industry consolidation that is occurring either through strategic alliances or mergers and acquisitions is one example. Although this consolidation is driven by many other factors besides this one, it is one way of balancing the growing power of the tribal traveller. And while this will work temporarily, the inevitable consequence is that these mega corporations will still have to compete for the consumer's loyalty through price and reward systems, bringing about further commoditization of the industry's products and services.

One alternative to this unpleasant thought is for the hospitality enterprise to expand its domain, to think beyond the present boundaries of food, accommodation and transportation. In the future, these will only be seen as elements of some greater whole. There are many who feel that this greater whole will be the entire travel experience, which will be part of the emerging *experience economy* (Pine and Gilmore, 1998) in the developed world. This suggests that if the hospitality enterprise seeks to compete in the future, it will be required to enter into the desired portfolio of providers that will meet the *experience* requirements of the guest. Figuring out how to do this will be no easy chore.

Other drivers of change

It is no secret that in the Western world the average age of the population is increasing. The so-called Baby Boomers are turning 50 on a daily basis in large numbers. This demographic shift in the part of the developed world that possesses the greatest spending power will pose one of the more interesting drivers of change in the hospitality industry.

The first major concern of this group of customers will evolve around safety and health. Consider first just the physical aspects of ageing, like the ability physically to get around. If this group is experiencing the normal consequences of ageing, it is not likely that they will want to be climbing mountains, forging streams or crawling through antiquities. Thus, physical limitations will drive destination choice. That future consumer will want ease of access and assurances that they will be able to get around comfortably.

The second consideration regarding the ageing process is the ability to fight disease. Evidence suggests that there is a growing spread of disease occurring as a result of both new and old bacteria and viruses. Further, the globalization of the food chain has resulted in widespread food-borne illnesses across the globe. This is expected to continue as globalization envelops the world. This puts at risk those who, either through the natural ageing process or as a result of other disease, have experienced a suppressed immune system function. They will be more concerned about their ability to meet the challenges of these threats when they travel, especially if there is reason to suspect poor medical care at the destination.

This future customer will also avoid those destinations that create risk to safety and well-being brought about by increased crime, nationalism or growing threats from fanatical groups seeking to right wrongs they perceive have been done. As the gap between the *haves* and *have-nots* continues to grow, this can be expected to be more of an influence upon travel than most currently realize.

The uncertainties and complexities of the world appear to be creating a need for the consumer of tomorrow to seek answers as to why this is so. They find it hard to understand the brutalities occurring in the former Soviet Union and the continuation of ethnic groups maintaining old hatreds. Extremist groups and their behaviours are equally as puzzling. There is also a growing guilt regarding the gap between the *haves* and *have-nots*. In response, there is a movement to righting the wrongs that have been done. This again appears to be the collective guilt of those living in developed countries who are now looking back over a lifetime and becoming concerned that they, in their rush to accumulate wealth, may have forgotten a few things along the way.

Many refer to this shift as a new spirituality. This does not necessarily mean a movement closer to some God as much as it means a re-evaluation of the values that have guided development over the past century and a half. The consumer is in some ways going to continue to try to right the wrongs of the past. This is very evident in the new social responsiveness observed by many companies. For example, both consumers and investors are rewarding those firms that have aggressively addressed environmental concerns or social injustices. They are doing so with capital, a powerful motivator in today's global economy. The pattern seems clear here: tomorrow's consumer will demand greater social responsibility by all firms and will reward this with their pocket books. This may indeed be the new spirituality.

Lastly, the consumer will demand greater levels of integrity and honesty in their dealings with them, workers and society in general. A higher standard of quality, responsibility and message will be expected. And if they don't find it, they will be able to let the world know immediately. No executive today or tomorrow will want, nor can afford, to let this happen. Everyone will be held more accountable in this new transparent environment.

Concluding thoughts

The information age and globalization will continue to drive changes in the way the consumer of tomorrow will do business with companies in the hospitality industry. This consumer will demand greater assurances of quality, safety and well-being. They will look more for intangible experiences that match their wallets and physical capabilities. Their loyalty will be easily transferable, making it more difficult to keep them. Their demands will be relentless as they seek to maximize their wishes and economic realities.

The question becomes, is the hospitality industry ready for this new consumer? Many would argue no. They believe that the industry is more concerned about financial engineering as a way of producing wealth as opposed to meeting the challenges of the consumer of tomorrow. If this is true, then it is very unfortunate. It leaves little optimism regarding the ability of firms to compete in the future. As theory has it, firms that are in co-alignment with the forces driving change in their environment and invest in competitive methods to meet the opportunities they present will be successful going forward (Olsen *et al.*, 1999). As this chapter has tried to point out, the forces and patterns are clear as to where the consumer is headed. So, for those firms that follow this principle, the new millennium will be a fun place to be; for those that are guided by *the tyranny of the near past*, they will continue to long for the good old days when the consumer remained with one tribe for life.

Note

1   This section was taken in part from Olsen and Connolly (1999).

References

Davis, S. and Meyer, C. (1998) *Blur, the Speed of Change in the Connected Economy*. Reading, MA: Addison Wesley Longman.

Friedman, T.L. (1999) *The Lexus and the Olive Tree*. New York: Farrar, Straus and Giroux.

Linden, E. (1998) *The Future in Plain Sight*. New York: Simon and Schuster.

Olsen, M.D. and Connolly, D.J. (1999) Antecedents of technological change in the hospitality industry. *Tourism Analysis*, 4 (1): 19–28.

Olsen, M.D., West, J. and Tse, E. (1999) *Strategic Management in the Hospitality Industry*. New York: John Wiley and Sons.

Pine, B.J. II and Gilmore, J.H. (1998) Welcome to the experience economy. *Harvard Business Review*, 76 (4): 97–105.

Tapscott, D. (1995) *The Digital Economy*. New York: McGraw–Hill, pp. 58–9.

19

The future of cruising

Bryony Coulson

An introduction to cruising

The UK cruise industry is young and growing rapidly – 140% in the past five years alone. This is due primarily to the introduction of tour operators entering the UK market and the increase in new ship builds. Cruise lines are investing heavily in the future of the cruise market, with the planned launch of more than 50 new ships over the first five years of the new century. The average age of a British cruise passenger is now 55, but in recent years cruising has attracted younger passengers, with 12% being under 35.

The industry is supply-led, and owing to slower growth in the maturer North American domestic market the American-based cruise companies are putting more effort into marketing and sales from the UK and Europe, with a resulting increase in traffic.

Cruising meets with all of the requirements that customers expect from a holiday with exotic destinations, luxury staterooms, exceptionally high standards of service, the opportunity to meet new people, a wide range of gourmet cuisine on offer, and the activities and entertainment onboard all included in the price. Generally, the only items not included are shore excursions, port taxes, gratuities and drinks. However, some of the luxury cruise lines do include these in the holiday price, so apart from the odd massage and bottle of bubbly, there are no hidden extras whatsoever.

Cruising can appeal to everyone, no matter what their budget or interests. Activities onboard range from aerobics to aromatherapy, art auctions to rock climbing! Cruising is attracting more families, with a wide range of children's facilities and childcare on board. There is also a length and type of cruise to suit everyone, whether it is a mini-cruise for three or four nights, a seven or fourteen night fly cruise, a scenic river cruise or a relaxing three week voyage on a working ship.

The roles of the PSA and PSARA

The Passenger Shipping Association (PSA) is the trade association for cruise and ferry companies operating in the UK. The PSA offers its members advice and information on subjects ranging from safety to statistics, acts as a bonding authority for non-licensable activities and runs a conciliation and arbitration service.

One of the main functions of the PSA is to act as a forum for discussion on areas of mutual interest. This is achieved by lobbying the government and the EU and working with other bodies, including the Association of British Travel Agents (ABTA), the Chamber of Shipping and the Council of Travel and Tourism. The PSA also runs a generic PR campaign promoting cruising to the public.

PSARA (Passenger Shipping Association Retail Agent scheme) was formed in 1987 to train and educate travel agents to help increase their cruise sales. The scheme, which is self-funded based on contributions from both the cruise industry and retail agents, provides an extensive programme of nation-wide training seminars, a cruise manual, ship visits, educational materials, newsletters and a freephone helpline to achieve this aim. It is an important factor in the growth of cruising traffic in the UK and is steadily increasing its membership in the travel agency world.

Current cruise statistics

For the fifth year in a row, the number of British cruisers in 1998 grew by 20%. More than 700 000 British people took a cruise in 1998, 635 000 of those an ocean cruise and 65 000 a river cruise. The most popular destinations continue to be the Mediterranean followed by the Caribbean, Scandinavia and the Baltics, with a third of British cruisers coming from the North of England and a quarter coming from London and the South East.

Cruising has a higher commission than other products and is becoming much more popular with British holidaymakers because cruises give clients greater satisfaction than any other type of holiday and therefore produce a high percentage of repeat business. Cruising only makes up 3.7% of the UK holiday sector and as less than 2% of the people who can afford a cruise actually do so, there is a vast untapped market.

The development of cruise ship design

Since its inception in 1844, when P&O claimed to have invented the first deep-sea cruise, the industry has come a long way. However, it is only in the past 20 or so years of its 155-year history that the industry has seen most of its most dramatic increase in ship size. In terms of gross registered tonnes (grt), the early 1970s saw Royal Caribbean order the 22 945 grt *Song of Norway*. However, by the mid-1980s ships of about 45 000 grt began to emerge on the market. By the early 1990s Carnival's Fantasy class, the largest cruise ship series ever built, had taken the tonnage levels up to the 70 000 grt mark. In 1996 the 100 000 grt mark was passed with the launch of *Carnival Destiny,* with dimensions that preclude her from transiting the Panama Canal.

According to a recent study by Ocean Shipping Consultants, the present cruise ship order book is about 60 vessels with a combined capacity of over 93 000 berths. The new generation of 'post Panamax' ships will account for 19 ships with 50 000 berths or 25% of the current fleet of 217 000 berths.

The 'post Panamax' ships have ushered in a new era of 'floating resorts' offering a wide variety of entertainment and activities including rock climbing, state of the art health clubs, a variety of dining options, spacious cabins with interactive TV and a high proportion of balconies. With 'floating resorts' the itinerary of the ship becomes less important and to increase onboard spend it is in the interest of the cruise line to encourage passengers to stay onboard.

The quay length will curtail the length of future ship designs . Plans for 'Super Wide' cruise ships are beginning to develop on the drawing boards of major shipbuilders. The ship is constructed with a large central atrium accommodating the public areas overlooked by cabins. Therefore cabins can be sold with balconies which can be seafacing or facing inwards.

Globalization and cruise ship deployment

The cruise map of the world has seen dramatic change since 1960, when most of the world's cruise liners were positioned in the Caribbean and seasonally in the Mediterranean and Alaska. Nowadays the Caribbean is a seasonal destination accommodating 100 000 berths in the winter but only 41 000 in July, whereas the Baltic will attract 37 000 berths in July 2000.

The US cruise industry is showing some signs of reaching maturity in that growth rates have slowed down and recently faltered, although penetration of the domestic market is four to five times that of the UK market. The leading cruise lines are adopting a more global strategy by positioning their ships in the Mediterranean throughout the summer and even in the Indian Ocean in the winter months.

The main thrust to globalization of the cruise industry is investment and the growth of the world's cruise fleet. New, bigger ships are cheaper to operate and therefore force smaller ships to operate new itineraries. Additionally, of the 6 million people cruising in 1999 more than 50% are repeat passengers and therefore demand a range of new itineraries to choose from.

Socio-economic trends are influencing the demand for cruising. Emerging middle classes in countries such as Korea and Brazil produce new markets of educated and wealthy potential customers. Similarly political and international events open up new cruise opportunities. The fall of the Berlin Wall saw an increase in both river and ocean cruising in Eastern Europe and the former Soviet Union. Similarly, the Barcelona Olympics produced a sophisticated hotel infrastructure which attracted cruise activity. It is anticipated that the forthcoming 2000 Olympics in Australia will stimulate demand for cruising in Australasia. Indonesia is seen as the sleeping giant of the Far East, with more water than land combined with a rich cultural and historical background it is a potential target for European and Australian markets.

Distribution technology – its impact on the cruise industry

Current agent distribution systems

Around 85% of cruise bookings are presently being sold through travel agents. In the UK the travel agency market is dominated by multiple travel agency groups, which are vertically integrated with ownership of airlines, tour operators and retail outlets. The major multiple groups are Thomas Cook, Carlson World Choice, Lunn Poly and Going Places.

Technology

There has been a generally slow uptake of newer technology due in part to incompatibility with back office functions. 'Viewdata' continues to be widely used, although Royal Caribbean is the only cruise line offering the facility to book via Viewdata and GDS. It is estimated that one in ten bookings are presently made via Teletext and a recent report estimates that the present £12m spent per annum on holidays bought via the TV will grow to £2 billion by £2003.

The Internet

The Internet is cheap, quick, convenient, 24 hour and global and the phenomenal growth in the use of the Internet is forcing suppliers to provide improved information and services. An estimated 18 million European households were on-line in 1998 with a forecasted 80 million by 2002. Virtually all PSA members have a web-site, although Royal Caribbean is the only PSA member to have a real time booking facility on their site. Of UK agents presently 28% have web access (16% in 1996). Considering that 62% of people using the net do so to access travel information, there is a threat that the role and service of the high street travel agent will be threatened, although most on-line travel sales presently include air tickets and hotel room bookings. Although some direct purchasing is inevitable, generally the more complicated and expensive products such as cruises continue to be sold on a face-to-face basis. Additionally, cruising is still an unfamiliar type of holiday to the majority of people and therefore prospective buyers will have a wide range of questions and misconceptions, which are not easily answered through the on-line sales process.

Digital television

This is the interactive technology of the future. It is estimated that within 10 years all UK TVs will be digital, with free set-top boxes accelerating the transition. Unlike a PC, watching television has the advantage of being a shared family activity and therefore offers a more conducive and compatible way to shop for a holiday.

The impact of technology on suppliers

Cruise web-sites are already proving very popular. Technology is bringing cruising to life in ways previous media failed to do; for example, Princess

Cruises' web-site has a live link with the bridge of the *Grand Princess* filming the progress of the ship. Electronic 'word of mouth' recommendations via chat forums will become a powerful consumer tool. The Internet and specifically e-mail will offer frequent and cheap relationship management, instant personalized communication and feedback. Large cruise lines are increasingly distributing pre-booking information direct to customers via the web and the fastest growing sector of Internet users are females aged 55–60, which is the exact profile of the typical cruise purchaser.

The impact of technology on distributors (travel agents)

Although electronic media cannot replicate the experience of shopping, retail agents do have to have access to the information that their customers can get on line and be fully aware of the available sources of information. Proactive cruise specialist agents will not have to fear the Internet if they become electronic information brokers, offering well-researched advice and third party endorsement. Also, as more commoditized travel products adapt more easily to direct sell, agent reliance on cruising will grow.

The future

The cruise industry is confident that the total number of cruise passengers worldwide will increase to the 12–13 million required to fill the extra berths that will be on sale by 2005. Reflecting the substantial investment required to build these giant ships, typically in the region of $450–500 million, ownership is limited to the industry's largest players, namely Carnival, Royal Caribbean and P&O, although other smaller operators have also ordered new builds to serve their markets.

20

Transport: the tail that wags the dog

John Seekings

As we step into this new millennium, we must ask whether life is going to change. The basic theme of this chapter is that the relationship between the tourism dog and its transport tail is going to change. Unless the tourism industry fully understands, anticipates and influences these changes, the outcome may well be unfavourable in that the tourism dog will in the future be hindered rather than helped by the action of its transport tail.

Without transport there is, by definition, no tourism. This means that, although transport accounts for only a part of the tourism business, without it there is no tourism business. The future of transport is thus pivotal to the future of tourism. However, transport is pivotal not only to tourism. It is pivotal also to the economy and indeed to society. As a result it has always attracted the interest of politicians and rulers. The earliest road systems of the Roman Empire – and indeed of most, if not all, later empires – were built for strategic reasons, without thought for tourism. The Duke of Wellington opposed the construction of railways on the grounds that it would result in the working class becoming ungovernable. Construction of a Channel Tunnel was obstructed for a century on the grounds that it would facilitate any invasion of Britain. The roads of Scotland were built by the English army to uphold Union. The first canal network of Europe was built to allow rapid Spanish troop movement throughout the mutinous Netherlands. The first aeroplanes were conceived a hundred years ago as weapons of war and it was not until the middle of the 20th century that governments finally recognized that they should be mainly considered as instruments of peace. More recently, the 747 jumbo jet only came about in the 1970s because the US government had already funded its massive engines to power a giant military freighter.

It is precisely because transport developments invariably come about for reasons that have nothing to do with tourism that it is notoriously difficult to predict far ahead how the transport tail is going to wag the tourism dog. This is abundantly evident in the inaccuracy of any transport-related predictions. As a result, serious transport forecasters seldom look more than ten years ahead. And the most far-sighted serious prediction of which I am aware is that for airport capacity in the south east of England – 30 years ahead, with any data beyond 20 years being viewed with extreme caution.

In the past the political interference with the transport market has been mainly directed at promoting or protecting particular aspects of the transport system which are considered to be either in the public interest or in vote-catching interest. Two very recent examples can be offered from the UK. To encourage private funding of the bridge connecting the island of Skye to the Scottish mainland, the government obliged the state-owned ferry operator to withdraw its Skye service, despite the fact that the profits from this service supported the loss-making services on the rest of its network. A condition attached to the latest extension of Eurotunnel's concession was that no other tunnel operator would be permitted by the governments of the UK and France for a period of 50 years. However, transport predictors are now faced with a new generation of 'Iron Dukes' who would like to suppress transport in some way or other. Despite the awful experience of Montreal's Mirabelle, more governments are insisting on developing airports which are too remote to be of interest to air travellers or to airport workers: Oslo is one recent example. Addis Ababa is probably another. Milan might well prove yet another. A recent example from Britain was the last Conservative government's capitulation, apparently on vote-catching grounds, to the environmental lobby and scrapping its long-overdue road improvement programme.

This chronic, built-in habit by governments of interfering in transport matters, and thus distorting the working of the market, is the basic reason why predictions on future developments have to be taken with great suspicion. But even if this habit were to be curbed, prediction would still be dubious, except in the short term, because of the peculiarly complex nature of both demand and supply which together form the transport market.

Demand

It is often wrongly supposed that transport demand is all about people being moved from one place to another, from A to B, and then, in the case of tourism, back from B to A. This error is often evident in academic discussions on air transport where airlines are viewed as offering a single homogeneous product and are then accused of superficially 'differentiating' their products in order to establish a distinct identity in the marketplace. In real life the demand for any transport service is extremely complex. To start off, it is essentially a derived demand in the sense that it is only demanded as a response to demand for something else. In the case of tourism this is the demand to do something in a place other than the normal place of work or residence. This immediately introduces an unpredictable variable for the transport forecaster: how will people split their time in the future between in-home or in-office activities and out-home or out-office activities? The poor forecaster can only be sure of one thing: that the split will change one way or another. But which way it will change, when and how much; these defy prediction simply because there are too many unknowns. So the forecaster assumes that the split will remain as it is even though it does not, thus creating another reason why so many forecasts are wrong. This tells us that we should all be placing much higher priority on distinguishing between demand for tourism products and demand for alternative non-tourism products. A start has been taken by the World Tourism Organization (WTO), whose preliminary view is that increasing pressure on people's personal time is going to tilt the balance in favour of non-tourism products. For what it is worth, my view is that this particular prediction is wrong.

Supply

To some extent this fundamental split between tourism demand and non-tourism demand will be determined by the view taken in the marketplace on the other features of transport service which together will not only determine whether we travel but also which travel mode we choose, should we decide to travel, and indeed which particular service and carrier we choose. Principal among these features, other than physical transplant, are the following: speed, frequency, comfort, safety, availability, information, access and – last but not least – price. Before briefly examining each of these in turn it is worth noting that on balance – with the possible exception of price – the overall quality of transport is likely to continue to improve significantly. This suggests that the tourism versus non-tourism demand split is more likely to be determined by the relative prices of tourism and non-tourism products rather than by the pressure felt by people on their time.

Speed

In assessing the value placed on speed it is important to take account not only of time saved but also of reduced journey time. For most people the ideal is instantaneous travel, not only because it would release more time for doing other things – including doing nothing – but also because it would remove the many unpleasant aspects of travel that have to be endured in order to be transplanted. This means that we all display a stronger preference for speed, and for paying a premium price for speed, than can be explained by the value placed on time saved. My favourite example of this is Sydney harbour, where it is evident that many people choose to pay extra for a faster ferry, only to spend the time saved enjoying doing little or nothing. Most of the unpleasant features, like the expense of travel as compared with non-travel, are self-evident. However, one feature deserves to be better understood: it is the dislike of not being in control. Transport planners everywhere fail to give enough weight to this factor. It is the main reason why the motor car has become the dominant mode of transport for tourism. And it explains why forecasts for rail travel are persistently over-optimistic. Again, my prediction is that this preference for personal control – as opposed to being under the control of others – is certain to become an increasingly important factor in transport and this is bound to favour the car over the train or the aeroplane.

Frequency

Frequency is another feature of transport that is often misunderstood by planners. Frequency seen as being low is not only seen as being inconvenient, it is also a potential waste of time and therefore equivalent to slow service. Most public service vehicles, notably trains, are so large in relation to expected traffic that economic operation can usually be achieved – except on a few high-volume routes – only by reducing frequencies to levels that are often unacceptable in the marketplace. This is going to become a major problem for airlines at the ever rising number of points where inadequate airport capacity obliges the use of aircraft so large that frequency suffers.

Comfort and safety

In an effort to compensate for the innate unpleasantness of travel, vehicle manufacturers and operators over the past decade have gone to great lengths to improve travel comfort and safety. In terms of comfort, the results have been spectacularly successful, particularly in the case of the motor car where the occupant today is often more comfortable than he or she would have been at home! Perhaps the main failure in terms of comfort has been failure by public service operators to match seat-pitch to customer expectations. Whereas the typical car seat has become an armchair, the seat in a modern aeroplane or coach is increasingly akin to a barstool. For those unwilling to pay the normally excessive price of business class travel, this factor is already driving traffic away from air travel to surface travel. As far as safety is concerned, the actual improvements which are going on in surface travel, and which are likely to continue in the future, are not being matched on the aviation front where safety rates appear at best to have stabilized. Airline leaders are now becoming alarmed by the threatened public perception that air travel is unacceptably dangerous. As railway operators have recently discovered in Britain, public perceptions of safety have more to do with media coverage than with actual safety levels.

Availability

The actual presence of a convenient seat to the desired destination – a situation covered by the jargon term 'availability' – is obviously a basic element in any transport service. Here the future prospect is dominated by funding, in particular of infrastructure. Until now governments in one way or another have funded virtually all transport infrastructure. This investment has seldom yielded an economic return to the governments concerned, and in many cases it has even been proved intrinsically uneconomic. The TanZam railway is perhaps the most spectacular recent example of such a white elephant. But any transport economist is ready to provide any number of disturbing examples. However, there is no doubt that governments almost everywhere are increasingly reluctant to pour money into transport infrastructure. A topical example is the great difficulty being experienced by its sponsors in raising funds for the ultra high-speed magnetic railway between Berlin and Hamburg.

Despite the great attraction of this project, if only as a working model for later applications, the current prospect facing the sponsors is not optimistic. On a smaller scale, there are now similar doubts about the viability of earlier plans to modernise the trunk railway linking London and Glasgow via Britain's west coast. This reluctance to invest in transport infrastructure reflects several converging forces: pressure on governments to achieve balanced budgets and low levels of indebtedness; growing realization that the private sector – and this means, ultimately, the travelling public – can and should bear the costs of infrastructure; and finally, that a growing body of voters are ready to vote against any transport project which they consider to be against the public interest, regardless of whether or not it is actually against the public interest! The net effect is that in the coming decades it is certain that transport infrastructure will either be lacking or will result in transport services becoming more expensive. This effect will not be evenly felt. My guess is that this problem of infrastructural constraint is going to be most severely felt in the most developed so-called Western world; this could lead within 20 years to major change in the global distribution of tourism.

The same forces, which are encouraging governments to behave less generously over provision of transport infrastructure, are persuading governments to be less generous in their subsidy of uneconomic state-run or state-backed transport services. Western governments have now, with few exceptions, withdrawn from the subsidy of operations by their national airlines. It is most unlikely that Western governments will continue pouring subsidy into rail operations other than for metropolitan commuters (where the sheer number of affected voters would result in a politically unacceptable outcry). An early casualty of this could well be Amtrak. Heavily subsidised rail operations of most European states – notably, France, Germany, Spain and Italy – are surely bound to be curtailed. It is no coincidence that it is these same countries which are busy persuading the European Commission to shoulder the burden of rail funding. It needs a bold forecaster to predict the future tourism implications of this particular situation.

Marketing

In contrast to the political uncertainties over infrastructure, there is little doubt that the prospects in regard to two other essential elements of transport service – provision of advance information to potential customers and facilitation of purchase (known as access in the jargon) – are both certain and positive. Thanks to electronic technology we are standing at the dawn of a new and improved era, a true paradigm. More than any other aspect of transport operation, these two elements – which can perhaps be better described jointly as marketing – are already resulting in a transformation of the quality of the entire transport product. A good example can be seen in Berlin, where it will soon be possible for intending passengers to discover immediately by mobile phone in how many minutes the next bus of their choice will reach the nearest stopping point. Because tourism more than any other economic activity involves communication over relatively long distance, it is a reasonable guess that tourism in general – and transport in particular – will become a primary beneficiary of the electronic revolution. The impact of this is already being felt but it is as yet too diffused to show up in statistics. It is not too fanciful to hazard a guess that this factor alone could account in the long term – i.e. more than ten years ahead – for an extra one per cent growth per annum. If other factors were broadly balanced this would mean a jump upward in the long-term annual growth of world tourism from say four to five per cent.

Price

The final essential element in transport to consider is price. Here the critical factor would appear to be the cost of fuel. Despite two major so-called fuel crises, first in the early 1970s and again in the early 1980s, we went through the 1990s living through a period of relatively cheap fuel prices. Paradoxically, this was the result of the two 'crises' which brought about a desperate but astonishingly successful search for new fuel reserves. This in turn created a relatively short-term excess of supply over demand from which the world economy is now starting to retreat. As the most price-sensitive user of fuel, airlines are again proving to be the first to suffer. In the case of surface transport, the effects are masked by discriminatory taxation which so distorts the market that accurate forecasting requires advance knowledge of how politicians are going to tax (as well as subsidise) the various competing forms of transport. However, it is reasonable to guess that conventional fuels are slowly going to become less readily available and will tend to become more expensive. This means that transport products will generally become more expensive, and therefore less economically attractive, than non-transport products, until alternative fuels become available in abundance, as is certain to happen within our 30-year time frame. Unfortunately for the forecaster, nobody yet knows exactly when this will happen!

Vehicles

Last to consider among the mysterious variables that confront the forecaster are the changing characteristics of vehicles and indeed the emergence of new forms of vehicle. It is interesting to reflect that few of the significant vehicular changes that have actually taken place were accurately predicted in advance. When these fundamental changes take place, it is invariably the result of an invention aimed at solving a non-transport problem. The application of coal and later of oil and most recently of gas to generate power; the invention and development of electricity; the development of the train and the aeroplane: none of these started life as projects to promote passenger travel. One of the very few exceptions is the reciprocating engine, which immediately spawned the motor car, and which is still today in its many derivative forms the foundation stone of the transport industry. In contrast there is no shortage of forecasts for exciting new devices that have in fact failed to work as passenger vehicles. Vertical take-off. Hovercraft. Rockets. My guess is that in the coming 10–20-year time frame, beyond which it is imprudent to look, there will be no revolutionary changes on the vehicle front. I am quite sure that space travel, even in the limited form of recreational space stations, will not become of any significant commercial importance. What in fact will happen is a slow, gradual, steady adaptation of existing technology to take advantage of new materials and processes – which will usually have evolved in areas other than transport – and to respond to the changes which I have attempted to describe. The many different forms of vehicle which will surely emerge in the next 10 or 20 years are indeed the subject for another occasion. For this chapter, the main message is that the realistic future will be determined not by the vehicle but by the political and economic environment it which it is allowed to operate.

As indicated in my introductory remarks, my assessment of the overall situation is that we now stand at a turning point. Throughout the past century we enjoyed dramatic improvements both in vehicles and in the way they can be used by tourists. In contrast, looking a quarter of a century ahead, we see few dramatic improvements in vehicles and many possible limitations on the use of vehicles. We may well therefore find ourselves in a new situation where improvements in our vehicles are outweighed by restrictions inflicted by governments on the use of our vehicles. This possibility – of transport becoming a hindrance rather than a help – will ultimately turn on our success at persuading the makers of laws, regulations and infrastructure that tourism is so politically important that it must not be restrained by inadequate transport. From now on the dog must take control of its tail.

21

The future of timesharing

Nelson Hitchcock

Introduction

Over the 1990s alone, timeshare has come a long way. New markets and consumers are coming on stream, sales are buoyant, legislation is in place in most markets, satisfaction levels amongst purchasers are high, and the public image of the product has improved considerably. Moreover, timeshare has now reached the point where it is becoming ever more an integrated part of the 'mainstream' holiday market. Integration is a theme that runs through this chapter; for whilst timeshare is a distinct product with unique properties, requiring specialist skills and knowledge to bring to the market, its long-term future is inextricably linked to that of the broader hospitality and travel sectors wherein vertical and horizontal integration are reshaping supply and distribution channels. Implicit in the above is the spectre of consolidation, branding, segmentation and other drivers of change.

A global industry

Timeshare is a global industry, with more than 5000 resorts and 4 million owners spanning all continents. Although timeshare emerged first in Europe during the 1960s, it was in the United States where it burgeoned, especially after the introduction of the exchange function in the mid-1970s. The United States currently accounts for 35% of all timeshare resorts and 48% of all timeshare owners, though its percentage share of the world totals will inevitably decline as the industry continues its geographical expansion. Indeed, growth in the European market has been particularly strong throughout the late 1980s and 1990s, making it the second largest market with 31.5% and 26% of timeshare resorts and owners respectively (RCI Consulting, 1999). These two key regions are annexed by a number of smaller established markets and, moreover, the emergence of new markets: India and Asia, Central and Eastern Europe, and the Middle East, for example.

At a global level, growth throughout the 1980s and 1990s was considerable, albeit from a low base in the early stages. In the late 1990s, growth in resorts and owners has levelled off to more sustainable figures of around 7–8%. Although not strictly comparable, as a point of reference it represents twice the growth rate of supply in the hotel sector in 1998. In terms of sales, the worldwide industry totalled over US$6 billion in 1998, double the volume processed in 1990 at the start of the decade.

Whilst the aggregate figures give a broad overview of the industry as a whole, it is important to recognize that they mask differences between markets. It is difficult to categorize Europe, for example, as one market, when in reality growth rates vary between constituent countries, reflecting their different and particular characteristics and nuances. In some cases the performance of the timeshare industry in a given country is linked to general macro economic conditions, and Russia is perhaps an obvious, albeit extreme example. More often than not, however, there is no direct correlation between economic growth and that of sales in an industry that is overwhelmingly supply-driven.

A changing industry structure

The composition of the industry is changing, and the pace of change looks set to increase in the coming years. Key drivers of change include the entry of branded hospitality corporations and vertically integrated travel companies, linked to a general trend towards consolidation.

Consolidation, hospitality groups and clubs

The recent takeover of US timeshare group Vistana by Starwood Hotels & Resorts is symptomatic of timeshare's transition from an industry comprising large numbers of localized independent companies to one comprising a smaller number of branded global players. To date, this has been a gradual and largely US-centred process: timeshare has been home to a number of large branded companies, including the oft-quoted hospitality groups such as Hilton, Hyatt, Disney and Marriott, for some time. Over the next five years or so, however, the pace of change is likely to increase and, moreover, embrace more fully regions outside of North America. It is no coincidence that virtually all of the leading hospitality companies have looked at, or are looking at, formally entering the timeshare industry. The obvious question to ask is: 'What is motivating these companies to enter the timeshare business?' And the answer is simple: new revenue streams and new profits. Of course, the viability of each project has to be viewed on its merits, and the operational nuances of a mixed-use or separately run site are manifold. Yet, on a general level the hotel and timeshare products are a good fit, and the natural overlap between many operational and promotional functions means that the two businesses complement rather than compete with each other. (For a detailed review of the issues pertaining to hotels and timeshare see, for example, Dean, 1993; Sweeney, 1993; RCI Consulting, 1999.) This trend is set to intensify in the foreseeable future, proving mutually beneficial to hospitality and timeshare industries alike. For the timeshare industry, the association of well-known brands not only brings credibility, it also provides a sustainable platform for future growth.

But the consolidation process currently under way in the timeshare industry is not exclusively hospitality-driven. Growth via acquisition and merger is a strategy being pursued by a number of specialist timeshare developing companies, the most obvious example being the Sunterra Corporation. Sunterra is a relatively new company, which has grown ten-fold between 1995 and 1998, largely through acquisition. Last year it sold US$352 million worth of inventory, making it second only to Marriott in terms of global timeshare sales (Vacation Ownership World, 1997, 1999). These are US-based companies with global reach and inventory – so they operate in Europe and other regions as well as North America. Further, they are also companies that operate club products utilizing 'points'.

The move towards holiday clubs and points

Of course, points-based products and holiday clubs are nothing new. Hapimag, a pioneer of European timeshare, has operated a points-based product since the mid-1960s and points have dominated the South African market for several years, for example. But the move towards this form of product has gathered momentum in recent years, especially in the major markets. There are currently many successful clubs operating in Europe in addition to the afore-mentioned US-based concerns. Generally, the clubs grow not in an organic fashion, but by acquisition and merger – that is to say, they acquire specific inventory or whole resorts, which then become part of a club's network of inventory, which, in turn, is made available to its members. The larger the number of resorts and resort destinations the club has, the greater the choice offered to the member and potential member. Coupled with the flexibility of points, which enables members to vary their vacation patterns according to needs and lifestyle, the club concept has much appeal.

Whilst this shift presents potential difficulties for small developers – in terms of maintaining an independently successful operation – it does not mean that large and small operators cannot co-exist. But co-existence for independent operators will probably entail a re-focusing of business strategy and a review of options such as segmentation and niche marketing, perhaps.

One thing is clear, however: holiday clubs and the points-based timeshare product is here to stay. And these are not hollow words; for we at RCI Europe have already shown our commitment to the points club product through the acquisition of Club Resorts International (CRI) earlier this year. CRI is now up and running, and forms the European arm of RCI's Global Points Network (GPN) which is to be rolled out in full in the near future. GPN will not only ensure that RCI continues to operate at the heart of the industry, but it also provides an opportunity for smaller developers to embrace the club concept and continue to compete in an increasingly competitive marketplace.

Travel trade distribution

Timeshare is also attracting interest from major vertically integrated travel groups, which are set to initiate a new wave of change in product delivery. Groups such as Thomas Cook and Airtours bring to the product additional brand visibility and increased public awareness and acceptance. To date, the exposure to timeshare of tour operators and the high street travel agents has been limited, but what activity there has been has proved successful. Indeed, RCI Europe recently established a programme to promote timeshare-based holidays with Seligo, the UK's leading worldwide accommodation reservation specialist. The promotion is then distributed through independent travel agents. The initial stages of the project suggest that it will be a promising venture.

And this is the central message with regard to travel trade groups – that the potential here is vast, and could transform the way in which timeshare is sold. The retail branch networks of the major travel chains are a powerful distribution channel that could bring the timeshare product to a much larger and more diverse consumer base. This, in turn, integrates timeshare still further into the mainstream holiday market and increases the potential for cross-marketing activity for all concerned. Most important of all, however, the consumer is afforded easy access to the timeshare product via a familiar and trusted mechanism – the agent in the High Street.

Moving more towards a customer-driven market?

Over time, the increased sophistication and diversity of distribution channels will bring the timeshare product more in line with traditional holiday products by eroding the dominance of supply over demand. At present, applying the traditional concept of a market to timeshare is problematic because the notion of 'natural' demand does not apply. That is to say that the product is 'sold' rather than 'sought', meaning that the size of given countries' customer bases are largely a function of sales and marketing activity by developers and marketing companies as opposed to indicators of consumer demand. And, price competition is something that the industry has hitherto lacked courtesy of limited supply outlets and a lack of pricing transparency. Of course, this system has worked spectacularly well for many companies, in many regions, and for many years – and, generally, the very high quality of the product has ultimately converted prospects into sales. But as the industry matures, so it embraces the trappings that accrue to mature markets everywhere, including greater competition, price transparency and concomitant developments such as a vibrant resale market. The latter is already growing, proliferation being speeded via the Internet, technology that will, in turn, increase the ability of consumers to 'comparison-shop' with regards to new as well as second-hand goods.

Product trends

It is not just the way the product is sold and distributed that is changing, the timeshare product itself is becoming more diverse and segmented. The traditional beach, mountain or country club product will always be mainstays of timeshare, just as they are mainstays of holiday products in general, but time-share is evolving ever more into a lifestyle product, catering to activity-based and niche markets. Indeed, the products now embraced by timeshare include cruise ships, golf, skiing, narrow boats, hotels, villas and even caravans courtesy of Resort Parks International (RPI), a subsidiary of RCI Europe.

Another avenue proving increasingly attractive to developers is the urban market. High profile examples here include the Manhattan Club in New York and the Edinburgh residence in Scotland, allied to a number of properties in London, Paris, and other cities across the globe. The urban sector thus far has grown quite modestly, perhaps because the increased profile and attractive-ness of timeshare has coincided with a property boom in the major cities, and the return on investment has to be measured against that generated from other options such as serviced apartments (Anthony, 1998). Clearly, both of these factors act as broad constraints on the cumulative expansion of the urban market, but they need to be set alongside the potential benefits such as all year round seasons and the possibility of attracting corporate customers. One thing is clear – the city locations currently operating timeshare are both popular and successful, and I believe that the urban market is set to be a major growth sector over the next five years, fuelled in part by the involve-ment of the hospitality companies noted earlier.

Then there are the points-based products mentioned earlier. Points are essentially currency: owners can choose the number of points they want to purchase and, because they know in advance the number of points needed to secure their desired holiday experience, they can use them in a flexible way. Whereas traditional timeshare has operated around predominantly fixed weekly intervals, points open up new permutations, enabling owners to choose the number of trips – and combinations (e.g. short breaks mixed with longer holidays) – taken per year, which can be varied to the full value of points held. Ultimately, points are a vehicle for the delivery of a true integrated lifestyle product, where timeshare becomes one piece of a larger jigsaw embracing hotels, cruises, car rentals, package deals and a whole raft of other products and services that can be accessed by a universal points currency. Some leading hospitality companies have operated points systems for some time. The associated loyalty schemes, and those of airlines, operate around transferable currency. In the future, it is likely that timeshare will become an integrated part of an expanded currency-based system, offering consumers ever more choice and control over their holiday experiences.

And then there is the service that is most associated with my own company, RCI – exchange. This will continue to be the oil that lubricates the industry, operating at the very heart of the timeshare business as it has since the early days back in the mid-1970s. The ability to exchange was the catalyst for the growth of timeshare in the late 1970s and 1980s. This continued through the 1990s, and the exchange function will continue to add value to the time-share product in the future. Of course, no business can afford to stand still, and that is why RCI has embraced the points business. This will comple-ment our core exchange business and provide a solid platform for future growth. Both of the two major exchange companies have vast timeshare expe-rience and knowledge, growing resort networks and member bases, and exchange will continue to be a major factor in the success of the industry as it heads towards maturity.

Public image, satisfaction and the consumer

It is no secret that, throughout its short life, timeshare has attracted negative coverage from the media, resulting in public wariness concerning the product. This has largely been due to a focus on isolated sales abuses by a minority of companies in the early years, obscuring the positives such as product quality and high satisfaction amongst owners. However, the image is improving. In the United States, the combination of effective consumer legis-lation, the entrance of well-known brands, the efforts of a well-funded and organized trade body – American Resort Development Agency (ARDA) – and a high quality product backed by efficient exchange networks, has effec-tively refreshed the image of timeshare. The most recent survey by RCI Consulting (1998a) into the public image of timeshare in the United States, found that 31.6% of consumers were interested in purchasing a timeshare interval, up from 27% in 1992. Although direct survey data for other regions are limited, this gradual improvement in public perception is also evident.

In Europe, we have worked closely with the new trade body – Organisation for Timeshare in Europe (OTE) – in promoting the industry and educating the consumer about the product. Virtually all of the EU countries have now passed the Timeshare Directive, affording consumer protection to potential purchasers, and the press coverage of timeshare is much more balanced and positive than was once the case. A good example of this is Germany, a market in which the image problem had been particularly pronounced. In 1996, over 80% of press coverage of timeshare in Germany was negative; by 1998 it was just under 60%; we project that the positive will outweigh the negative over the next few years (figures based on circulation: according to unpublished internal RCI research). Of course, the German market still represents an ongoing challenge, as do many other markets, but the point to emphasize is that the image of timeshare is moving in the right direction. As to the future, strong and well-funded trade bodies are essential to ensuring that this continues – and I believe that, over time, OTE will do for the industry in Europe what ARDA has done for it in North America.

Consumer profiles, product penetration and satisfaction

Typically, timeshare consumers have tended to be well-educated married couples between the ages of 40 to 60 with above-average incomes. The key purchase motivations are the opportunity to exchange, quality of accommodation, value for money (e.g. RCI Consulting, 1998b). Penetration levels tend to be higher in the upper income brackets. In the United States, for instance, penetration rates vary from 1.8% amongst purchasers with incomes of US$35–50 000 up to almost 6% amongst buyers with incomes of over US$100 000 (RCI Consulting, 1998c). In general, this reflects the fact that it is not until later in life that most people have the disposable income to purchase the product. But the demographics of new buyers may change over time, with a larger percentage of younger buyers possibly coming on stream as (a) the availability of consumer finance increases, rendering the product more affordable, and (b) more diverse 'lifestyle' products attract hitherto untargeted sections of the population (e.g. singles, sports/activity-oriented buyers, double-income families with no children, etc.). In addition, the consumer is becoming better educated and more sophisticated. In part, this is linked to the educational and awareness programmes of the trade bodies and exchange companies allied to an improving press mentioned earlier. More than this, however, the customer of the future will benefit from, amongst other things, the Internet and other technology that will facilitate easier comparison shopping and aid informed choice.

One thing above all is clear, and that is the vast size of the potential market for the product in all corners of the globe. Even in countries with the highest penetration levels, such as the United States and the UK, less than 5% of all households with a minimum income of £22 000 currently own timeshare (RCI Consulting, 1998c; UK figures based on unpublished RCI research). And this is potential growth in a product that achieves very high satisfaction rates amongst owners. Numerous studies over the past five years have pointed to satisfaction rates of between 80 and 90% ('satisfaction' here referring to the combination of 'very' and 'somewhat' satisfied results from questionnaire-based surveys) across all regions (e.g. Ragatz Associates, 1995; RCI Consulting, 1997, 1998b).

Conclusion

Summing up, it is clear that timeshare is an industry witnessing considerable change. It is becoming more global, attracting larger, sophisticated and well-capitalized players. In conjunction with technological advances that enable consumers to compare prices, this will lead to a more competitive business climate, forcing smaller players to review strategies or succumb to consolidation. This process is inextricably linked to the growth of points and holiday clubs, and the ability of companies to capture niche and sheltered markets. Moreover, the future is a regulated place – if Europe and the other regions that have enacted consumer legislation mimic the experience of the United States then regulation may have a short-term impact on sales, but will serve as a solid platform for long-term growth.

Last, but by no means least, penetration rates are still relatively low even in the major markets, and new markets are coming on stream across the globe each year. This is good news for an industry that is becoming more integrated into the mainstream travel and tourism market, leading to improvements in product delivery. This, in tandem with the already high quality of the timeshare product, bodes well for the industry. Ultimately, I believe that the changes currently under way will benefit the customer – and providing the industry does not lose sight of that, it faces a bright and profitable future.

References

Anthony, D.S. (1998) Urban timeshare . . . a new wave in the industry?, *Hospitality and Leisure Executive Report*, 5 (3).

Dean, P. (1993) Timesharing opportunities for the hotel sector. *Travel & Tourism Analyst*, 4.

Ragatz Associates (1995) *The World Wide Resort Timeshare Industry*. American Resort Development Agency.

RCI Consulting (1997) *Timeshare Purchasers in France, Germany, Italy and Spain: Who They Are, Why They Buy*. Eugene, Kettering: RCI Consulting Inc. Europe.

RCI Consulting (1998a) *The Public Image of Resort Timesharing*. Eugene, Oregon: RCI Consulting Inc.

RCI Consulting. (1998b) *The Benefits of Owning Resort Timesharing: A National Survey of Resort Timeshare Owners*, 1998 edition. Eugene, Oregon: RCI Consulting Inc.

RCI Consulting (1998c) *Timeshare Purchasers: Who They Are, Why They Buy*, 1998 edition. Eugene, Oregon: RCI Consulting Inc.

RCI Consulting (1999) *Timeshare Industry Overview '99.* Eugene, Oregon: RCI Consulting Inc.

Sweeney, J.F. (1993) Hotel and timesharing mixed use. *Developments,* November (American Resort Development Agency).

Vacation Ownership World, January 1997.

Vacation Ownership World, January 1999.

22

The tourism marketplace: new challenges

Daniel Affolter

A growth market with intensive competition

Leisure travel today has become a basic need and turned into a commodity. The desire and urge to travel and 'go some place' is nowadays viewed as a matter of course. By and large, it can be said, no matter what the circumstances, people will make time and means available to travel. They may undertake a short trip, an extended vacation some other time, vary the standards and so on, but travel they will.

The growing demand has led to a rapid expansion of the travel industry. Today we are facing substantial excess capacities. Air and other transportation capacities are available in abundance. Tour operators produce travel packages in ever larger quantities and at the destinations guests, decision-makers and product managers are lured not only with attractive rates, but with promotional support and a range of incentives as stimulants to fill the wide offers of accommodations. Holiday prices show a clear downward trend; it is noteworthy in this context to recall the availability of travel and its cost some 30 years ago compared to today's virtually limitless possibilities and low costs.

In line with the development of increasing volumes of vacationers and tourism in general, the industry has undergone and still is undergoing a process of change and concentration. Different skills and competences are required to succeed in the highly competitive volume market in the lower and mid range than in the segment of niche markets for the more discerning traveller.

While operators of niche products continue successfully to occupy their positions and hold their own markets, a process of concentration in the volume market has been initiated among a handful of large internationally operating travel groups. Given the fierce price war taking place in the high volume market and the big investments and competences required in IT for processing and distribution, significant volumes and turnovers are needed for a profitable operation. These are not feasible without concentration and though this process has been going on for some time, it will continue even further.

IT – motor in competition

The dramatic development in the IT field has also had its impact on the travel industry and is a major motor to stimulate competition. In the volume business it is today without a doubt the single biggest factor that contributes to an operator's competitiveness, in fact a high degree of IT know-how can assure the competitive edge over the competition.

IT is not only the key to lower operational costs and higher productivity, it opens new avenues in marketing and sales, be it direct sales, interactive TV travel shops or transactions and ultimately one-to-one marketing via the Internet. To implement these new technologies, which are here to stay, and make them work by giving the consumer extra value and convenience, requires substantial know-how and competence in IT technology and the skill to combine these new technologies with the requirements and mechanics of the travel business as well as with the changing consumer behaviour.

Pressure to change by changing consumer behaviour

Consumers for any type of product or service are today vastly different from what they were not long ago. The relentless flow of information to which we are all exposed on a daily basis, the readily available information, facts and details, literally available at our fingertips, on almost any topic, provides today's consumers with a competence not existing in earlier times and confidence in defining their requirements and making their choices and decisions. And they make use of this increased self-reliance by letting the markets know. They buy what they want, or do not buy if it is not there, rather than simply buying what the market suggests one should buy.

This combined with the strong trend to individualism, or individual lifestyles, by the modern consumer, has not left the travel industry without impact. The increasing amount of spare time and growing importance of leisure activities, the desire for more frequent but shorter trips and holidays, have caused the travel industry to adapt. New travel products are on the market; flexible individual travel programmes have out-ranked the regimented group travel packages, which at one time formed the bulk of leisure travel. In addition the increased transparency of market and product information has enhanced price awareness among consumers and as a result further raised price competition in the industry.

Tourism market workflow

Through changing consumer behaviour and the entry of new technologies, the traditional workflow link in the travel market is also undergoing decisive changes and the once clearly separated roles and functions of its principal participants are being redefined. The borderlines of their respective activities and market audiences are getting more and more blurred with increasing overlapping.

Electronic platforms, like global distribution systems (GDS) and other booking systems, are not only the line of contact to tour operators and travel agents; new technologies offer new opportunities for new channels of information, marketing and sales straight to the end consumers. This will shift the established balances of the workflow in the industry. On the downside, by pursuing this option, suppliers will have to add significantly to their marketing and advertising budgets as well as work on their IT competence and exposure. Widening the marketplace, dealing through more channels and selling to a larger number of buyers in different segments will increase the importance of yield management for best use of capacities and maximizing revenues.

What goes for one participant in the change process of the workflow will of course apply to others, too: tour operators will equally take full advantage of the newly available technologies in their efforts for most effective distribution, including direct marketing to end consumers. With growing complexity of the markets and the consumers being overwhelmed by a multitude of information sources and a continuous barrage of direct marketing via conventional and electronic channels, consumers will have fewer ties and emotions toward a specific product, service or brand. Apart from the many ways and means to foster customer relationships, a precisely defined and strictly followed brand policy will become a key criterion. A strong brand underlies perceptions and signals reliability and stability – elements by which the vast majority of consumers are, to a greater or lesser extent, mostly unwittingly, influenced, and will be more so in the future. Strong brands will also in our business increasingly make the difference between making or losing a sale.

Despite commission capping and the threat of direct sales by tour operators and suppliers, the retail industry will not be forced out. In fact, through the new technologies new opportunities arise beyond merely reducing operational costs. The range and depth of available information on products and services in combination with the retailer's skill to draw on this immense pool of data and render it quickly at the customer's disposal highlights the strength and added value of the retailer's advisory competence and care. The new media are perfectly suited to provide individual, custom-made and yet efficient advice and recommendations to the retail clientele, and complete transactions on their behalf, any place, any time and over distance. The speed of communication can be accelerated to the customer's own pace. The challenge for the retail industry is to profile itself as a 'counsellor' and service provider, away from the image of a mere outlet.

Tomorrow's consumer

Tomorrow's consumer will not only add further to his or her personal know-how and competence, but become also more and more demanding and expectant. Market transparencies will increase and knowing that information is available, consumers will expect to be given the relevant details and information without having to gather it on their own. The times when selections and decisions are made on price alone are – apart from specific bargain offers – largely gone.

'Best value for time and money' is not just a buzzword, though it can have different meanings for different people. With the increasing individual lifestyle mentioned earlier, the trend for individualism in travel is also growing. As travellers gain more routine, they become receptive to and eager for new innovative products and look more often now for new experiences and adventures rather than just 'another vacation'.

In general, public trends, moods and value thinking will have to be taken more and more into account. On the issues of ecology, for example, there is a slowly awakening trend detectable, putting eventually if not a halt, a brake on certain developments in world-wide tourism. Apart from a minority, people are hardly yet at the point where they would refrain from buying a specific travel programme for ecological considerations unless it would severely affect their own personal comfort and experience during their travel. But what is likely to happen when an operator's reputation suffers on environmental grounds is that consumers might stay away from an entire brand. Such developments are impossible to predict, but nowadays they must not be ignored.

Challenges of the new tourism marketplace

Let me summarize the key issues ahead of us. The direct access to everyone, the wealth of information and density of communication made possible by new technologies and the changing consumer behaviour will place the customer at the centre of the new marketplace. All active participants in the market, suppliers, tour operators, retailers and new industry entrants, will be increasingly vying directly for consumers' attention. For consumers this development is two-sided, yet the additional benefits of more choices and options and of low prices outweigh the extra task of sifting through the information, separating the unwanted from the useful and desirable and making appropriate comparisons. The decision-making process may not always become simpler.

The highly competitive business environment with its low elasticity of prices in the market together with the new consumer expectations, force tour operators to generate high volumes and come up with products at attractive prices. These products have to be flexible so that they can be tailored individually to a complete holiday programme according to the clients' liking.

The complexity of the handling of such products requires sophisticated IT systems. Quick and easy access to a tour operator's products and uncomplicated, 'user-friendly' booking and order-processing through innovative IT systems are becoming as decisive for success as a good travel product at a fair price. IT issues become of utmost strategic importance.

In the growing myriad of propositions and choices in the market, consumers will look for orientation and guidance, a spot with which they can identify and find some common values. A strong brand will stand out as a marker and have a drawing effect. Weak brands will go by largely unnoticed and its products and services will consequently be in low demand.

Finally, there is an increasing awareness of health and security. While it seems accepted that certain risks and hazards in travel like anywhere else, be it through 'force majeure' or otherwise, can never be ruled out entirely, the tolerance and willingness to accept mishaps and incidents and bear the brunt of the consequences are diminishing. Risks to the travellers' well-being and safety may arise anywhere through political developments, dangers to public health or natural forces. Consumers want to know in unambiguous terms that someone is responsible for their respective activities and that they are accountable. Obligations and responsibilities of suppliers, providers and intermediaries will increase, as well as expectations by the public that all realistically feasible considerations and precautions are taken and appropriate information is provided. It is evident and must be understood that product liability on the part of all of us in the travel industry and its inherent risks and implications will continue to rise.

23

Travel distribution systems: one-to-one marketing

Maggie Bergsma

What is one-to-one marketing?

One-to-one marketing encompasses a set of marketing techniques aimed at selling to the individual. Instead of selling one product at a time to as many consumers as possible, it is about selling as many products and services as possible to one customer using databases and interactive communication. What is important in the one-to-one marketing is not how much you know about all of your customers that counts but how much you know about *each* of your customers. This means you no longer have to be a giant to win against one. Relationship or one-to-one marketing applies to everyone in the 'people' industry, especially that of tourism. It involves getting to know your customer by asking questions of your existing and potential clients. The answers are the key to learning about the individual and must be remembered, recorded and used to give customers new ideas and create new sales. Often the client does not know what he wants or what is available so it is up to the one-to-one marketer to listen to the customer's requirements and adapt the product to his or her needs by making suggestions, guiding the customer and adding a personal touch. It is the logical progression from mass to segment to direct and then to one-to-one marketing.

Why implement one-to-one marketing?

- One-to-one marketing allows you to take advantage of new technology. It is a concrete way to capitalize on the benefits of new technology. Technology is evolving at an amazing rate and is becoming more and more interactive. A few years ago the Internet was an unknown commodity to most people but the rate of its adoption into the home has been enormous. The adoption and utilization of new technology and therefore new commerce should not be ignored or under-estimated. Modern technology can lead to quick and powerful marketing; it ignores country boundaries and effectively contracts the size of the world. Traditional methods of mailing have become expensive and slow when compared with the inexpensive, fast and effective new technology of e-commerce. All over the world cyber travel agencies are being developed whereby the customers do the work and have direct access to tour operators and airlines to book their own holiday.
- One-to-one marketing gives you the chance to create new markets, markets of individual customers with diverse needs, which allows you to acquire new customers, but more importantly, sell a wider variety of new products and services to extend to the newly discovered needs of existing customers.
- You will be able to improve customer retention and loyalty dramatically and increase the amount of business you receive from each individual, despite the acquisition campaigns of competitors.
- One-to-one marketing gives you the opportunity to protect and increase unit margins. Let us take, for example, the subscription to a magazine. The second year of subscription often costs more than twice as much as the first. Why? Because presumably you like the magazine. As a result the unit margin of an existing customer is higher than that of a new customer as the company is using profit margins to create customers. Charging regular customers more is a natural consequence of trying to acquire new customers by using discounts but by bettering the product and tailoring it to the customer's specifications the company can retain the existing customers and therefore add to unit margins.

So it becomes clear that one-to-one marketing entails a need to compete using a different set of rules. How does it apply to tourism? Tourism incorporates a wide range of organizations, from destinations (countries, regions, cities and resorts) to private operators such as airlines, hotel chains, theme parks and so on. The need for one-to-one marketing methods applies to all organizations. In the past, it was only travel agents that had any meaningful sales contact with the final consumer. However, owing to the changing structure of the tourism industry and the development of new technology, the destinations themselves, through destination management organizations (DMOs) and tour operators, are encouraging a direct business relationship with the end user.

More and more destinations are using Destination Management Systems (DMS). DMS allow the centralization of all information, including customer information, into one central database. This information can then be used through various channels. Tour operators are also developing their own call centres and using travel agents' databases for a more direct approach. Even transport companies and airlines are going straight to the end consumer; for example, seats on the Eurostar can be booked through on-line sales. All organizations have similar challenges, those of anticipating and responding to the customer's needs, increasing the customer's value and loyalty and encouraging repeat business. As a result, all organizations must adopt a one-to-one marketing strategy to maximize the benefits of their contact with the customer.

The principles of one-to-one marketing

Meeting customer needs individually

Two customers can outwardly seem to be very similar to each-other, they may both want to go to Italy for two weeks, stay in a three-star hotel and have a budget of a thousand pounds but may still want different things from the destination. Nightlife may be important to one visitor whilst the other may only be concerned with museums and art galleries. No two customers are completely alike and this is why one-to-one marketing is especially important to tourism. Differentiating customers by their needs and then catering for those needs individually is a new tendency showing a move from mass marketing to segmentation, to a focus on the individual. In the past customers were put into groupings and marketing towards the clusters was standardized; however, now tourism is moving towards a de-grouping and treatment of the customer as a single entity. One-to-one marketing is also a powerful step towards increasing customer loyalty and as a result, unit margins.

Knowing your customers and their value to you

Customers have different, individual needs, which hold different values to a destination. The collection of customer information is a means to discovering the customer's needs and therefore value. To compete in this, the interactive age we have to treat different customers differently and to do this we must understand customer differences. The value determines how much time and investment should be allocated to that customer, and a customer's needs represent the key to keeping and growing that customer.

Aggregate marketing treats all customers the same. They all receive the same product benefits, are all charged the same price and are not in individualized interactions. However, each customer is unique and some are more valuable than others. The actual valuation of a customer is his or her 'Life Time Value' (LTV), the stream of expected future profits, net of costs, on a customer's transactions, discounted at some appropriate rate back to its net present value. Remember that the profit on a customer's relationship with a destination is not solely derived from the future purchases the customer makes. Customers also benefit the destination or product in other ways such as referrals of other customers, knowledge of other customers' tastes and preferences and help in designing new products or services. Maintaining any sort of relationship with the customer will involve cost – phone calls, faxes, e-mails, personal sales calls and setting up information systems necessary to track and remember; interaction all cost money. Those who call in to customer service the most will cost the company more money to serve. However important LTV is, it is essentially a forecast based on probabilities and we can never know precisely what a particular customer will do in the future. However, what is certain is that keeping existing customers is more profitable than trying to turn new prospects into customers.

The benefits of calculating LTV are not just to understand the *average* customer's valuation but to create an accurate ranking-order system, allowing a company marketing a destination to *differentiate* its customers by their individual valuations and to add more marketing time and effort to retain the most valuable customers. Because one-to-one marketing treats its customers as individually as possible, it aims at understanding the relative valuation of each of them. Customers are individually different, and have individually different values to a company, and the most accurate picture of a customer's value is LTV. It is important to decide which are the most valuable customers and establish a maximum amount of money to be spent on retaining these customers. Those of high value must be invested in; those of medium value must be encouraged to buy other products and services from the company.

Customers of low value should either be dropped or made to pay for the services they receive.

Defining the right strategy

A customer base is characterized by customers who have a diverse set of values and/or a diverse set of needs. The customer base can be highly differentiated on both counts or on neither. The nature of the customer differentiation of a company is a guide to an appropriate marketing strategy. By comparing a company's capabilities with its customer base a new strategy can be mapped out, aimed at improving those capabilities needed to turn the business into more of a one-to-one enterprise. If a business has customers with widely varying tastes and preferences, they must be differentiated by their needs. The more the customers differ from one another in needs, the more benefit can be gained from offering a variety of products and services and customizing right down to an individual level.

Let us take the example of the tourism destination once again. The needs of the customer are incredibly diverse. A back-packer is going to have completely different preferences to an elderly couple, just as honeymooners are not going to want the same package as a family with young children. The destination remains the same but the package must be varied to become customized to the individual's needs. It is a case of examining the customer's needs and tailoring the product to suit those needs, whether it be offering a family hotel with children's activities or a weekend city-break incorporating city tours and cultural visits. Equally, in tourism customers are bound to have different values for the destination. Obviously backpackers on a shoestring budget are worth less than honeymooners who may have been saving for years to fulfil their dream holiday. However, it is important to remember that the backpackers may be opinion leaders, they are often students and will travel again in the future, probably with a larger budget, and therefore have a high potential valuation. Thus, if one-to-one marketing is implemented, contact can be maintained with these potential customers throughout their travelling life.

Implementing one-to-one marketing

One-to-one marketing can be put into place by using several simple capabilities:

Customer tracking

This can be done through databases, which allow a vendor to tell its customers apart and remember them individually. As much information as possible must be obtained about the customer and his or her purchasing habits and needs. The customer's history would be recorded through his or her previous interactions and with each interaction the company will learn more about the client. The customer and company can then collaborate jointly to determine the appropriate product or service for that customer.

It is important to make it easy for customers to specify their needs by asking the right questions and then remembering and recording the specifications so that the customer does not have to re-specify. That way, customers have to go to less effort next time they wish to use the service. For example, most call centre operators will have in front of them the complete history of a particular customer's previous transactions, thanks to sophisticated databases.

Interactive dialogue

Some kind of feedback link is necessary for the destination to learn about the customers individually and therefore make them loyal and improve the company's unit margin. It is absolutely essential to open channels of communication between the consumer and the company. Sometimes it can be as simple as printing a web-site address on the packaging of the product or, in the case of tourism, on the destination brochure. As the computer penetrates more and more homes, and as the various interactive tools available to consumers continue to increase in utility, web-sites that allow the customer to buy on-line will attract the most enthusiastic and therefore valuable customers.

Interaction by telephone is often the first point of contact with the customer. To incorporate one-to-one marketing the company must simply ask one or two questions about the customer's needs and map the customer into a needs-based category. To implement this, the company would need to do research to create the correct needs-based groupings and give its phone sales representatives the necessary scripts.

Written questionnaires are another way of interacting with customers. However, it obviously involves the customer making an effort. An increased use of coupons in order to obtain more information in destination brochures is a way of finding out about the type of client who is really interested in the destination. Another idea is a questionnaire inside a destination brochure, for example, which needs to perform some service for the end user that is actually connected to the user's need for the product. Filling in the questionnaire must also involve as little effort as possible for the customer and all barriers preventing the customer from sending it in must be removed.

Here are some suggestions for removing those barriers:

- Offer a postage-paid envelope.
- Assure the customer that returning the questionnaire will not result in any undesired additional mail or solicitations, or allow the customer to 'opt out' by ticking a box.
- Put the questionnaire at the beginning of the brochure so it is the first thing the customer sees after opening it.
- Allow the customer to reply by mail, e-mail, fax or a free-phone number.

Even after making it as convenient as possible it may still be necessary to offer some sort of incentive to the customer, perhaps a discount at a certain hotel, or on car hire, more information on the product or a free gift.

The collecting of customer information is aimed not at creating summary research but developing a better understanding of each *individual* customer's needs. Every communication and response from a customer has the potential to tell a one-to-one company more about exactly what a particular customer wants. Every single interaction is a priceless opportunity to learn more. Only recently, as information technology has improved, has it become possible for a company to identify and act on customer differences in a cost-effective way.

Customization of products and processes to customer needs

Tourism products are ideal to customize due to their flexibility. One destination can be combined with another, different hotels can be chosen, and all sorts of activities can be decided upon depending on the customer's preferences. Tailor-made holidays are becoming more and more popular due to the amount of choice the customer enjoys. Even the way the product is presented can vary depending on ways of payment, promotion and booking (last minute deals are also increasing in popularity).

Loyalty programmes

Customer loyalty is vital for numerous reasons. It costs more to serve new clients than it does old but surprisingly most companies do not even try to diminish the costs of trying to attract new customers as they are already budgeted. One-to-one marketing aims at reducing these costs by keeping customers instead of constantly looking for new ones. Costs involve advertising, mailings, information packs and, especially, time. The faithful customer is stable, predictable and knows the purchasing process of the company, therefore saving the staff time and bettering the service. The satisfied customers tend to recommend the product to their friends and acquaintances. Recommendation is the best form of advertising to acquire new customers. This is especially the case for tourism, when people talk about the destination they have visited and encourage others to go there. The idea of information days when happy customers meet prospective customers is developing already in the world of tourism. Word of mouth is by far the most convincing advertisement a holiday destination can have as it comes from satisfied customers whose opinions are trusted by their friends. Personally recommended customers tend to be of better value, meaning more profitable and longer lasting than those attracted by advertising or promotions. Loyal customers allow the company to provide them with a more personal product due to the fact that the company has had the chance to learn about the clients' needs and adapt to them – this is what one-to-one marketing is all about. However, despite the obvious benefits of customer loyalty, many companies focus more on gaining new clients than keeping old ones.

Loyalty programmes work differently depending on the company; however, the essential is for the consumer to benefit by repeatedly using the service or company provided. Loyalty programmes can be very sophisticated or very simple, for example the tour operator No Limits has put into place a loyalty system whereby each time customers book or introduce a friend to No Limits they receive 'miles' which equal reductions on travel. The hotel chain Los Paradores has a card system called La Carte Amigos de los Paradores giving regular customers free nights in the hotels as well as numerous other advantages such as the option to choose their room. An example on a larger scale is Club Mauritius, a group of tour operators, hotels and airlines who have come together with the aim of offering a loyalty programme whereby the cardholder receives benefits such as regular information about special travel offers to Mauritius, free parking in the airport car park, free afternoon tea, reductions on sports activities, car rental and in certain shops, and a bouquet of flowers on departure. Depending on the number of visits the customer makes to Mauritius the benefits become more attractive. Eurostar offers a similar system with blue, silver and gold membership cards.

Many airline companies have also implemented 'frequent flyer' loyalty programmes, easily put into place due to the fact that they already have the necessary information in the reservations system. Benefits include easier check-in procedures, use of a private lounge and access to newspapers etc.

It must be remembered that, of course, other companies can set up similar loyalty programmes but the key to retaining the customers is the learning process which will have been undertaken by the company to ensure that the customer is receiving exactly what he or she wants and expects.

Conclusion

In conclusion, one-to-one marketing is about listening to customers, remembering them and providing them with the service each consciously or sub-consciously requires. It is about adapting your marketing strategy to the future and exploiting modern technology to achieve a more personal approach. After a period of mass marketing, globalization, segmentation and lifestyle grouping in tourism, today we have to follow the tendency towards individualization.

24

Perspectives and thoughts on tour guiding

Betty Weiler and Sam Ham

Current perspectives on tour guiding

Guided tours vary widely with respect to the following:

- Length (e.g. a few hours, all day, or several days)
- Seasonality (one-season or year-round)
- Location (e.g. site- or attraction-specific, city, rural or a combination)
- Type (e.g. cultural, environmental, industrial, educational, adventure)
- Transportation (walking, non-motorized, vehicle-based, land-based, water craft-based, bicycle)
- Terrain (land-based, fresh water-based, ocean-based)
- Clientele (general, particular socio-demographic group, special interest group).

As a result, the nature of tour guiding and the skills required by an individual guide can vary widely. For example, specialist ecotour guides require minimal impact skills, while city guides may have less need for these skills. Guides leading extended tours require more complex leadership and group management skills, and may require high-level navigational skills, knowledge of remote area first aid and evacuation procedures. Many guides have activity-specific skills, licences and qualifications that complement their guiding expertise.

However, there are some elements that are common to all types of guided tours, such as:

- Presentation, communication and interpretation skills
- Customer service skills (ability to work with colleagues and customers)
- Cross-cultural awareness and communication skills
- Ability to follow health and safety procedures
- First aid qualifications
- Group management and leadership skills
- Knowledge of local tourism resources and the tourism industry
- Ability to research, develop and update tour content (Canadian Tourism Human Resource Council, 1996; Tourism Training Australia, 1999).

Trends in tourism generally seem to indicate a growth in more specialized tourism products aimed at more focused target markets. There is also evidence of increased environmental and cultural consciousness among travellers, including in some cases willingness to pay more for tourism products that are environmentally responsible (Blamey, 1995: 111–13). If these trends continue, growth areas are likely to be in tours targeted at special interest groups, tours focusing on particular experiences or products (e.g. adventure, nature-based, cultural and indigenous tours), and tours marketed as being environmentally friendly. There may also be a growth in customized tours, in which individuals or groups can hire a guide (or operator) and specify exactly what they want with respect to each of the above.

The current geographical distribution of tour guiding largely mirrors the distribution of tourism, generally. Where there is growth in tourism and an increase in numbers of tourists, there is growth in organized tours and therefore an increase in the demand for quality tour guides. However, the demand may be somewhat greater where there are significant barriers to independent travel, such as in China, Russia and certain countries in the Middle East, Africa, Southeast Asia and Latin America. Some of these barriers include a native language different from that spoken by the majority of visitors to the region, threats to safety and personal security, political barriers and lack of tourism infrastructure. It seems the more exotic and unfamiliar the natural and cultural environments of a destination, the more likely that a visitor will engage the services of a guide.

The regional demand for tour guiding may be affected by many other factors such as the prevalence of visitors who can visit only for a short time, and therefore require the assistance of a guide in order to sight-see. For example, cities that cater to business, educational and conference travellers tend to support a larger number of tour guides.

In the future, guided tours to remote destinations such as Antarctica and some of the new travel destinations opening up in Asia seem likely to continue to thrive because most or all of the visitors to these destinations need a guide to visit the region. Given that first-time travellers seem more likely to seek the comfort and security of a guided experience, destinations near to new tourist markets such as China and India are also likely to experience growth in tour guiding. However, destinations that are experiencing growth in tourism but are not perceived to be 'difficult' to visit may have a stable or declining demand for guided tours. Unless particular actions are taken, it is possible that mature destinations and those in decline will experience a decline in the demand for guided tours.

What's wrong?

Images of guided tours, tour guides and tour guiding

The image of guided tours and clients of guided tours is stereotypical and homogeneous, and at present represents a self-fulfilling prophecy.

Many of us who work or teach in the tourism field and those who have travelled extensively are aware that tourists may choose from a wide range of guided tours that vary in scope, length, group size, target market and so on. However, prospective tourists are often not as informed as they could be. Thanks in part to mass media, the dominant image of the guided tour is often one of a large group of elderly tourists, or perhaps middle-aged Japanese couples, travelling by coach, on a fixed itinerary, with scheduled stops and with a virtually uninterrupted commentary by a tour guide, usually via a microphone, talking about the various sights and features along the way. While reality may be quite different, it is the image that sells, or doesn't sell, the product, and this particular image poses a significant barrier to diversifying the client base and the product range. The image is reinforced partly by tour product marketing, including not only the brochures and other promotional materials used to entice clients, but also by the places and mechanisms by which guided tours are packaged and marketed, e.g. concierge desks at hotels and tour wholesalers. The visitor gets little sense that he or she might have some influence over the content and style of the tour, the size of the tour group, the tour length, or the time of departure. It is little wonder, then, that those who do not feel a 'need' for a guided experience choose to travel independently. Simply put, their stereotypical image of a 'guided' tour does not match their notion of a desirable recreation experience: it is seen as neither voluntary nor enjoyable.

Changing this image could significantly alter tour guiding and the future of guided tours. The perception of flexibility, variety and the option of customization with respect to itinerary, tour content, tour guide and tour clients would widen their appeal. This would eventually lead to an image of tour clients in the future who choose a guided tour not because of need or convenience, but because of an expectation of a quality experience. The product must, of course, also change with the image, becoming more flexible and responsive to client interests and preferences.

Client motivations and expectations about guides and guided tours

Visitors have few expectations of guided tours and tour guides. Generally tour clients expect to spend the day (or hour, or week) safely and with a minimum of discomfort, together with some level of information and entertainment. Their expectations are often dictated by what they read in the tour brochure, which is usually to 'see' and maybe to 'hear' something rather than to 'experience' or learn something or to come away moved by that experience. Not surprisingly, then, most research measuring the satisfaction levels of visitors on guided tours has found that visitors claim to be satisfied with their experiences (Geva and Goldman, 1991; Blamey and Hatch, 1996).

At present, it is assumed that guided tours largely cater to inexperienced travellers who are attracted by the safety and security of travel within a guided tour experience. However, some visitors are motivated by the opportunity to sample a new experience for which they lack either the specialized skills, the local knowledge, or a suitable vehicle and/or equipment (Blamey and Hatch, 1996; Weiler and Crabtree, forthcoming). Examples include guided snorkelling tours, white water rafting, indigenous cultural tours, and boat-based whale-watching tours.

Visitors on specialized guided tours have also indicated that they are motivated not only by the ease and convenience of travelling with a guide, but by the opportunity to learn something (Weiler and Crabtree, forthcoming). In these cases, the reputation of the company and qualifications of the guide may be important factors in tour selection. And finally, as mentioned earlier, some target markets are motivated by the desire to purchase an environmentally responsible and/or culturally sensitive tour.

In the future, a wider diversity of products could extend the client base of experienced travellers who want a high-quality tour experience with a knowledgeable and capable guide, or who want to sample a tour experience outside their normal range of experiences and interests. In other words, visitors would choose a guided tour, not because they have to, but because they perceive the guide and the tour as offering something better than they can experience on their own. This will require target market research, sophisticated product development, packaging and marketing, and an overall shift in consumer and industry perceptions of a guided tour experience, as was discussed in the previous section. In addition, clients may need to be educated to make more informed decisions when choosing a guided tour.

Teaching and research on tour guiding

Guided tours have a negative connotation for many people, including professionals in the industry, educators and the 'enlightened' traveller.

Tour guiding has been the subject of very little scholarly enquiry, let alone rigorous research. This may be due to the tour guide's lack of profile and status and therefore visibility to researchers, in comparison to the impacts of large-scale tourism developments, which are conspicuous and therefore widely debated by academics, industry and the general public. Similarly, there has been considerable research on tourist accommodation, tourist attractions and, more recently, tourism events. The contribution and impacts of tour guides and tour guiding are usually glossed over by researchers, planners and managers.

Tour operators have certainly been the subjects of research, but often in the form of surveys and inventories of where they are based and what they deliver, rather than any critical analysis of the experiences that they offer (cf. Cotterill, 1996). Some research has been conducted on the marketing of guided tours and on specific guided tour market profiles (Wight, 1996a, 1996b). As discussed in the previous section, there has been some research on the motivations and expectations of tourists on guided tours and, more recently, the tourist experience. Again, however, it has tended to be descriptive rather than explanatory or predictive. As a result, the concepts and models used to educate tourism students about tourist motivations and the tourist experience are largely untested and may serve to reinforce stereotypes and possible misconceptions of the guided experience. For example, Pearce and Caltabiano (1983) argue that as the tourist becomes more experienced as a traveller, he or she moves 'up' what they call the *travel career ladder* and away from certain needs. There has been a tendency to assume that packaged tours and guided tour experiences fulfil the needs of travellers on the 'lower' rungs of the ladder. Without strong data to support this theory, educators who use this model may thus teach implicitly that those who join guided tours are somehow lesser travellers than those who travel independently. An alternative view, which is grounded in research on guided interpretive activity attendance in US parks (Ham, 1982; Mullins and Hanna, 1981), is that selecting a guided activity merely represents a regularity or pattern in tourists' leisure tastes and preferences. Extended to tour selection decisions, those who select guided tours over independent travelling may do so not because of uncertainty or the need for a 'chaperone', but simply because a guided tour promises to deliver the type of experience the tourist desires. More research is needed in this area.

Another example is the concept of authenticity, with considerable debate in the literature as to what exactly constitutes an authentic experience and how much of modern tourist behaviour is a quest for authenticity (Dann, 1996). As with the travel career ladder, there is a tendency to want to oversimplify and compartmentalize tourists and touristic experiences. Here independent travel is labelled as something more 'authentic', an ideal to strive for, and at the opposite end of the continuum the guided tour is seen as a contrived and therefore lesser form of travel. Some view the use of a local, as opposed to a foreign, guide as a step in the right direction, providing a more authentic experience for visitors. Empirical testing of what constitutes a quality experience and an authentic experience for the visitor, and the role of the tour guide as a cultural broker and facilitator in that experience, is required in the future.

And finally, most educators know of and teach about the impacts of tourism, but how many recognize the pivotal role that a guide plays? Particularly important in this role is the interpretive function of guiding. A central defining principle of sustainable tourism is its focus on conservation and perpetuation of the natural, cultural and physical values inherent in a place. How tourism achieves this lofty goal is often debated, but there is increasing evidence that what a guide *says* to her or his clients can influence how they think and behave with respect to the places they visit. In other words, what messages a guide imparts to a group of tourists relative to the natural and cultural values of a place may in large part determine what they will think, feel and do both in the short term (on-site) and possibly even in the long term (once they have returned home). According to Ham and Krumpe (1996) and others (see, for example, Knapp and Barrie, 1998), one of the most important things guides can do is to facilitate a bonding between their clients and the places they lead them; connecting people and places in powerful ways that nurture respect and caring about those places. As we have argued elsewhere (see Weiler and Ham, 2000), the guide's role in this process is central. If research begins to document this role, it is likely that a clearer understanding of the guide's importance in sustainable tourism will be achieved.

Professionalism in tour guiding

Tour guiding is a low-status profession, characterized by low pay, poor working conditions, and seasonal and casual employment conditions.

Tour operators and tour guides vary with respect to a number of attributes:

- Size of company, number of offices, number of employees
- Commercial (private) vs. non-profit vs. public-sector funded operation
- Generalist vs. specialist operators and guides
- Paid vs. volunteer guides
- Freelance vs. contract vs. regular employees
- Local vs. foreign guides
- Professional vs. casual vs. part-time guides.

In most cases, qualifications are not required, those with qualifications are not remunerated or rewarded in any special way, and there is no career path, so that in time good guides may be inclined to move on to something else. In Australia, for example, the tour operations industry has no industrial awards, i.e. there are no industry-wide legal specifications regarding the rights and obligations, qualifications, working conditions and rates of pay, for either tour operators or guides. Some of the larger tour companies have enterprise agreements, which specify such conditions, but there is no government or regulatory body requiring an individual to be qualified or licensed in order to work as a guide.

For practising tour guides, there is also little incentive for individuals to actively upgrade their skills or qualifications or improve the quality of their tours. To date there has been no evidence that qualifications or skills lead to preferential treatment either in gaining employment or in career advancement.

It then falls to the wider tourism industry, educational institutions, protected area managers and other government bodies to find ways, first, to raise the awareness of what is 'good practice' in tour guiding, and secondly, to provide incentives to improve the standard of guiding practice throughout the industry. To date, this has been mainly by way of professional associations and codes of conduct. The future may bring accreditation and certification of guides, if not initiated by industry, then imposed by governments. If linked to education or training programmes, these could have significant repercussions for those already working in the industry, especially those without formal qualifications.

A final mechanism for recognizing and rewarding good practice is by way of an employee or tourism industry award scheme that recognizes outstanding guiding. These can co-exist with some of the other initiatives already mentioned, and are truly 'best practice' awards that complement the minimum standards approach of the other initiatives, while simultaneously serving to motivate and educate guides as well as to regulate the practice of guiding.

Tour guide training

Tour guides and guided tours are falling short of what they could be delivering, a high quality experience that excites, changes people, motivates and rejuvenates them, while maximizing the benefits for operators, host communities and the environment. Although marketplace competition has sometimes led to innovations designed to give a company a competitive edge, aggressive experimentation with new guided tour products seems lacking. This may be due to a degree of complacency in the industry that derives from tourists' low expectations, as well as from an inherent lack of imagination on the part of guides themselves, and the companies they work for. To some extent, such forces may stem from the preparation of professional guides.

Guides, like many professionals, can be prepared for their work in several ways. First, they can be *trained technically* with skills presumed to be germane to delivering the kind of products and services needed and wanted by clients. Secondly, they can be *educated* as to the *how, why and what if* of applying their knowledge and skills to the workplace. And finally, they can be *socialized* into their profession via formal and informal processes that mould and shape how they see themselves, and how their employers, clients and peers see them. Current prevailing perceptions and self-perceptions of guides sometimes conjure up images of semi-robotic message repeaters who carry out rigidly orchestrated itineraries and faithfully regurgitate carefully memorized scripts, leaving little to the guide's creative imagination and ingenuity. These perceptions are, in turn, reflected in unimaginative technical training programmes that are designed to produce guides who match the perceptions. Training and education in how guides can use their skills to excite and motivate visitors, and in how their work can produce benefits to society, is lacking.

References

Blamey, R.K. (1995) *The Nature of Ecotourism.* Occasional Paper No. 21. Canberra: Bureau of Tourism Research.

Blamey, R. and Hatch, D. (1996) *Profiles and Motivations of Nature-Based Tourists Visiting Australia.* Occasional Paper No. 25. Canberra: Bureau of Tourism Research.

Canadian Tourism Human Resource Council (CTHRC) (1996) *National Occupational Standards for the Canadian Tourism Industry: Heritage Interpreter.* Ottawa: CTHRC.

Cotterill, D. (1996) Developing a sustainable ecotourism business. In H. Richins, J. Richardson and A. Crabtree (eds), *Taking the Next Steps.* Brisbane: Ecotourism Association of Australia, pp. 135–40.

Dann, G.J.S. (1996) *The Language of Tourism . A Sociolinguistic Perspective.* Wallingford, UK: CAB International.

Geva, A. and Goldman, A. (1991) Satisfaction measurement in guided tours. *Annals of Tourism Research*, 18 (2): 177–85.

Ham, S.H. (1982) Familiarity and adaptation: A study of family attendance at interpretive activities. PhD dissertation, University of Idaho, USA.

Ham, S. and Krumpe, E. (1996) Identifying audiences and messages for nonformal environmental education: a theoretical framework for interpreters. *Journal of Interpretation Research*, 1 (1): 111–23.

Knapp, D. and Barrie, E. (1998) Ecology versus issue interpretation: the analysis of two different messages. *Journal of Interpretation Research*, 3 (1): 21–38.

Mullins, G.W. and Hanna, J.W. (1981) Participation in interpretive activity subgroups. *Journal of Interpretation*, 6 (1): 25–31.

Pearce, P.L. and Caltabiano, M.L. (1983) Inferring travel motivation from travellers' experiences. *Journal of Travel Research*, 22: 16–20.

Tourism Training Australia (1999) TTA Web site: http://www.tourism-training.com.au.

Weiler, B. and Crabtree, A. (forthcoming) Assessing ecotour guide performance: findings from the field. Proceedings of the 1998 Heritage Interpretation International Conference, Sydney.

Weiler, B. and Ham, S. (2000) Tour guides and interpretation in ecotourism. In D. Weaver (ed.), *The Encyclopaedia of Ecotourism.* Wallingford, UK: CAB International.

Wight, P. (1996a) North American ecotourism markets: motivations, preferences and destinations. *Journal of Travel Research*, 35 (Summer): 3–10.

Wight, P. (1996b) North American ecotourists: market profile and trip characteristics. *Journal of Travel Research*, 35 (Spring): 2–10.

25

National tourist offices

Walter Leu

It is quite feasible to regard tourism as a kind of theatrical performance, directed by National Tourist Offices (NTOs) and played out on a stage called 'destination', but in a relationship between host and visitor which pays regard to human dignity, as it is not the role of the host to play the part of the 'dancing bear' for the benefit of tourists. Nevertheless, the question must be asked: will Europe still be attractive enough to be able to count on a faithful audience for its tourist performance in the 21st century? Will Europe have the courage and creativity to face up to its ever-more aggressive competitors throughout the world? What will be the role of the NTOs in this context? A millennium turning point is an invitation to every kind of prophecy and hypothesis. In the 19th century Europe invented tourism and in the first 70 years of the 20th century achieved world leadership in tourism. Since the 1970s it has more or less been on the defensive. The 21st century will effectively be the moment of truth for 'Destination Europe'.

Amongst a number of defining factors there are four to which I will especially draw attention here and which, in my opinion, will decide whether Europe can – or indeed must – continue to play in the Champions' League and even take the lead again. The question is whether this is to be achieved with or without the contribution of the NTOs.

The European Union route

I imagine it to be generally agreed that the political, economic, monetary and defence unification of Europe must not be equivalent to uniformity of European cultural and gastronomic identity. McDonalds may be present everywhere but that does not mean that we want to convert Euroland into Hamburgerland. However, if we still believe that a product is easier to market the more clearly it can be defined and the more it possesses the attribute of becoming an instinctively recognized brand, then it is obvious that the development of ever-closer ties within Europe offers considerable advantages for marketing tourism. Here I am mainly thinking of marketing tourism overseas. The European Travel Commission (ETC) credo to position Europe as 'One Destination' is thus increasingly seen as a matter of course. The awareness of Europe's internal and external clientele in this respect is significantly enhanced by the fact that European political development features constantly in the international media. The publicity effect of this presence is greater than the sum of all reports on individual countries.

A further positive factor for European tourism is the creation of the Euro and the growth of the European Monetary Union (EMU). This makes travel easier, makes tourist offers more transparent, and acts as a restraint on prices. One can envision a future, therefore, when it will be possible to visit every corner of the world without constantly having to change money and with only two currencies: the US Dollar and the Euro (at a rate of 1:1?).

The progressive unification of Europe strengthens its presence in world tourist markets and basically makes the destination more attractive. But in the presence of the customers' unstable behaviour, this message is only effective if it is supported by decisive marketing within individual markets, by an excellent quality product, acceptable prices (meaning not low prices but value for money), plus continuing and coherent public relations and advertising using modern information technology. Technology must, however, remain an auxiliary and not replace people as providers of services and sympathy. Today all too many promoters of tourism make the mistake of treating technology itself as a strategic objective instead of an instrument for achieving objectives.

Therefore, if Europe follows the path from a confused multiplicity to a comprehensible variety within unity, it is obvious that this change also requires an adjustment to advertising strategy. This means that the ETC will tend to become ever more indispensable and that its role as an umbrella organization for European destination marketing should be considerably strengthened. It is ironic that this fact is perceived more clearly by tourist professionals outside ETC than by the ETC itself. Dr Ralf Carsten, President and CEO of Turistik-Union International, has made a plea recently for a much stronger ETC, which ought to become the marketing agency for Destination Europe. He was even bold enough to say that national marketing could be reduced in importance overseas and should be replaced by increased European activities. It would appear that some of the European solidarity, which was the driving force in founding the ETC in 1948, has faded to be replaced by a more strongly nationalist perspective.

Sustainability – the moment of truth for tourism

'Sustainability' has become for me a negative provocation, the label for a culture of dishonesty, the ultimate in lip service. No speech, no article, no statement from politician or tourism professional does not repeat this word over and over again – though not unfortunately in accordance with its real meaning and content. It serves as a fig leaf to disguise the continuing and dominating obsession with quantitative growth on the principle of '*après moi le déluge*'. In the 21st century we who work in tourism must find our way back to a policy of 'qualitative growth'. This means that we must once again recognize that the capital assets of European tourism consist of elements that are easily destroyed, namely our human capital, our culture, nature and the environment. We must learn to use these assets – but not to use them up. It must be a strategic objective to live on the interest from tourism but not to consume the capital. Tourism can only create long-term employment if the environment is tolerable for the local inhabitant and the visitor alike. In this who other than the NTOs can dare to play the role of the 'devil's advocate'?

Sustainability is a long-term concept, which creates added value by the law of optimization, and not maximization of income, that is to say, it does not want the hen to lay the eggs and at the same time to be served up on plate as '*poulet rôti*'. Europe's volume share of world tourism is not so important as its share of the worldwide potential of good and cultivated visitors who realize that a good product cannot be acquired at dumping prices. Europe is too small to maintain its relative share of what appears to be an unstoppable growth market. Let me say once again: we must improve the quality of our market share so that the following definition of mass tourism will not apply to Europe: 'Mass tourism is the occupation of a country by an unarmed army for a limited period.'

A new tourism ethos for the 21st century

Tourism is not one but all industries. This indicates not only tourism's high multiplication factor, but also that tourism is the substratum of many policies – economic, regional, social and cultural. Not everything that seems profitable to the individual businessman is desirable for the national economy. Shareholder value taken to the extreme is poison for the social contract and is the cultivation of mere egoism. George Soros (who certainly cannot be described as a follower of Keynes!), recently said: 'The markets are obsessed with greed and fear and therefore react to all economic theory not rationally but emotionally.' What does this mean in relation to tourism? The globalization of the economy is a reality and this calls for a global framework of order based on a globalization of ethics. Obviously I don't want a flood of regulations; that just exchanges one evil for another. Whatever is desirable in the fundamental supporting pillars of the state and the economy must to an ever-greater degree be valid for tourism. Tourism is in fact an emanation of culture and one of its vehicles of transmission. I link a new ethos for world tourism to the following hopes in the form of a realistic vision:

- The last traces of the 'master and servant mentality' in tourism must vanish.
- Every guest is a king – but every king is only a guest.
- The relationship between supplier and customer must change to a partnership with parallel interests. In this way, it will be possible to arouse support on both sides for genuine sustainability and to convert exaggerated hedonism into a rational pleasure in consumption.
- The interests of shareholder and stakeholder must not conflict, but must be complementary.
- Tourism should not only talk of the visitors' rights, but also of their duties.
- Friendliness is not just something to be expected on the hosting side. Visitors, too, should show more respect for other people, cultures and identities.
- Development policies for tourism must be discussed from the start with the local population, so that they too support them. Representatives of hospitality are not just the professionals but the whole population. This will avoid tourism becoming a ghetto culture.

- The social standing and conditions of employment of workers in the European tourist industry must be improved.
- The necessary improvement of the ethics of tourism will unavoidably result in a competition of ideas in the 21st century. Concept marketing will be more important than product marketing.

And what about the future of the NTOs?

Soon after the first NTOs were established more than 80 years ago, sceptics were questioning what the chances of survival were. The mere existence of any business or organization, such as an NTO, gives it no right to survive. Whereas human life has a value in itself, an NTO must face up to the constant challenge as to whether its usefulness to society, the state and the economy gives it the right to exist. This is all the more the case since the budgets of European NTOs are still financed to between 50 and 100% by the taxpayer. So the question can only be answered in the general context of political interests.

From the beginning and until very recently the mandate of many of the NTOs was approximately as follows:

- **Phase 1:** To promote a general awareness of its own country, of its historical and cultural strengths and the beauties of its landscape etc. with the objective to create a climate of sympathy. This also led to non-commercial collaboration with groups within the export economy who were similarly interested in an active presence in the markets – which was a first, if unconscious step toward destination marketing.
- **Phase 2:** To arouse tourist interest. Phase 1 was only a first step towards the objective of arousing a concrete interest in travel, to convert the 'friendly' country into a target destination for tourists. This was done with the classic means of advertising and public relations.
- **Phase 3:** To make the potential visitor decide to convert his or her wish into reality. Customers were brought to this point by sales promotion and targeted information.
- **Phase 4:** The task of the NTO ended with Phase 3, and reservations and sales were in principle to be left to the industry.

It was also thought that this procedural concept provided a clear division for financial responsibility: phases 1 and 2 were to be financed out of public funds, phase 3 was to be financed from both public and private sources, and finally phase 4 was the responsibility of the private sector.

This was the basic model in that happy world, now past, where there was no globalization, deregulation, shareholder value and so on! Today we are confronted by new parameters without there being a final and reliable new model for action available. NTOs are more than ever searching for a new definition of their task and their identity: they vacillate between the demands of the public sector for strategic return on investment and the private sector requirement of immediate operating profit.

As already mentioned, the share of the public sector in the financing of NTOs is substantial and without this funding they could not exist. Their continued existence is, however, dependent on future state economic policy and the further development of the separation between tasks that will continue within the public domain and those that are to be left to the private sector. This is a dynamic process which is far from being complete, whereas the arguments involved are in part ideological. Many governments are still not sure whether it is sensible or necessary to pursue a strategic policy for tourism in order to optimize the exploitation of economic growth potential. If so, then NTOs are essential. Nor can you do without them in countries where the creation of tourist demand is a means to develop economically disadvantaged regions – few private investors would be prepared to invest money for reasons of social and regional policy.

Conceptual destination marketing

As part of location competition between countries, regions and cities conceptual destination marketing will have a much greater significance than in the past. Conceptual destination marketing implies the summation of all the characteristics that give a location or a region a positive profile: culture, political stability, the economy, natural beauty, population, education, but also non-quantifiable aspects such as reputation, image, sympathy, reliability etc. It goes without saying that the strong positioning of a destination, which must be accompanied by the creation of a brand image, can only succeed through long-term measures based on consistency, coherence and continuity. It is in this aspect of strategic targeting that the NTO is an appropriate institution to achieve strategic effectiveness at national level for tourism as a whole. In the rapidly changing environment of supply and demand, the resources of the private sector are too quickly absorbed in the fluctuations of day-to-day tourist business. The growing prominence of the Satellite Account System for assessing the multiplication effect of tourism shows more clearly than ever before that tourism is very much a cross-section discipline for which destination marketing at national level performs an umbrella function.

The criteria cited here to justify – indeed to demonstrate the necessity of – the NTOs existence, are similarly valid for maintaining the effectiveness of the European Travel Commission (ETC), which must also fulfil an umbrella function for Destination Europe.

If we agree that tourism:

- is part of national and regional and local area planning,
- is often the only effective instrument for the economic improvement of disadvantaged regions,
- is a strategic linking element within national economic policy,
- is a factor for job creation *par excellence*, particularly for young people, in an environment of high rates of unemployment,
- is an excellent image builder and sympathy-promoter for a country, unparalleled by any other industrial sector,
- is a conduit for cultural exchange between one country and another,
- smoothes the path for the entire export economy,

then there should be no dispute that in this new century NTOs will not just play the part of the Sleeping Beauty or the stop-gap, but will take a leading role in tourism strategy. The public sector will certainly not be able to abandon its role as principal shareholder and stakeholder.

Nevertheless, shareholders lose interest in their company when it fails to yield a return. For this reason, the political pressure on NTOs to re-position themselves is increasing and governments will subject them to a permanent fitness programme. In the age of globalization, tourism finds itself in a situation of hyper-competition. Not too long ago, both the number of destination countries and the number of people who could afford travel and holidays were small. Today every country on earth is a national destination and in the year 2000 some 700 million international tourist arrivals are expected. Such a growth in extent and, alas, in bulk makes it increasingly difficult for customers to keep their heads above water and choose sensibly. Modern information technology is a help, but it too could well drown itself in the flood of information. The NTOs are challenged to take on a new leadership role in an environment of innovatory and creative marketing methods – in the New Information Technology Age they must act as information brokers and contribute to the intelligent sifting of information that shows customers the way to go from trash that stifles and blinds them. We have to overcome the fact that tourists are 'over-newsed' but under-informed.

The result of this trend will be that NTOs have to get even closer to the market and collaborate more closely with the private sector, but always with the backing of the public sector in order to preserve them from becoming completely dependent and losing their ability to act at the strategic level. NTOs must become particularly professional with regard to more effective support of small and medium-sized enterprises (SMEs), since in Europe some 80% of tourism turnover is earned in small and medium-sized businesses, who also account for more than 85% of all jobs. A specially challenging task is the improvement of profitability in this sector, which today is frankly unsatisfactory – added value is just too low.

It is my conviction that the NTO has a future. Its role as nothing more than a PR instrument in the hands of governments and politicians is, however, over: on the other hand, it must not become merely the messenger boy of the tourist industry and lobbyists. The 21st century NTO will be an organization operating in the public interest but run as a business. Through closeness to, and knowledge of the market, it will achieve quantifiable results by retaining old customers and attracting new ones. Its marketing must become more selective, because it is not just the tourist statistics that count, but the effect of tourism on the profitability of the economy as a whole. The successful supplier is not blinded by statistical growth, but impressed by the increase in the number of satisfied visitors and by adequate added value return from each overnight stay.

26

Public–private sector partnerships in tourism

John Heeley

Introduction

The intention of this chapter is to examine the origins and development of public–private sector partnerships in England, with particular reference to the tourism industry. The chapter puts forward the challenging proposition that, based on the English experience, public–private sector partnerships in tourism are best undertaken at the local level, where 'arms-length' local destination marketing bureaux provide a model organizational form to address the challenges and opportunities raised by tourism. This argument for the primacy of the local level runs counter to the conclusions that others have reached (e.g. Thomas and Thomas, 1998). Differing academic and practitioner perspectives were aired at a seminar organized by the Confederation of British Industry (CBI, 1999). My views reflect over a quarter of a century's work, both as an academic specializing in UK tourism and latterly as the head of city and tourist promotional agencies for Sheffield and for Coventry and Warwickshire. The primacy of the local level is something for which, over the years, I have consistently argued (see, for instance, Heeley, 1981).

Context

> We are in a field of co-operation and co-ordination . . . there are, if anything, far too many cooks concerned with tourism and I would like to say that there always will be, and so our biggest problem is how to resolve the old difficulty that when you have too many interests and too many helpers, each one of whom can contribute a little, how do you get them all to work together? (Leonard Lickorish, British Travel Association, 1968; cited in Heeley, 1975)

Tourism, as an industry, has its public and private sector components. This has always been the way of things, as detailed in several excellent historical texts (e.g. Neale, 1981). There is an inevitability about the involvement of both sectors – even if there are shifts of emphasis over time (see, for instance, Cannadine, 1980), as well as widespread variations between and within nation states. As a generality, however, private sector bodies are central to the provision of hospitality, transport and entertainment services, and they also support the marketing of destinations, as can be seen, for instance, with tour operators and airlines. Public sector intervention is brought about by a variety of factors, foremost amongst which are the needs to regulate private sector activities, to provide non-remunerative infrastructure and superstructure, to remove obstacles to more effective private sector performance, and to redress market failures. Walton's account of the historical development of Blackpool, for example, exemplifies all four modes of intervention as they gained palpable expression in promenades, illuminations, print and bylaws, and much else besides (Walton, 1978).

Over and above intervention, the rationale for public sector involvement in tourism has another, important dimension, that of leadership. For everywhere, tourism administration provides a conundrum. Whether looked at from the vantage point of the national, regional or local levels, the tourism sector is fragmented, being dominated by small firms, and is ill defined, inasmuch as many operations, public and private, do not depend solely on tourism. A chronic need therefore exists for some or other institutional mechanism to represent, co-ordinate and advance the interests of the sector. The above quote from Lickorish captures this exigency. Nearly always, it is the public sector that steps into the breach.

A feature of the past 40 years has been the creation of 'hybrid' public–private sector mechanisms. These mechanisms are referred to here as public–

private sector partnerships, defining them formally as organizations which are constituted, managed and funded as 'independent' partnerships to exercise the classic intervention and leadership roles of the public sector. Within the English context, such agencies are alternatives to traditional and by no means extinct forms of tourist organization, namely, the central department, the quasi-non-governmental organization (quango) and the local authority.

The public–private sector partnership in tourism is premised on the public sector 'letting go' of some or the whole of its traditional intervention and leadership accountabilities. Crucially, in 'letting go', it seeks to increase the participation of other key players and stakeholders, particularly the private sector. Not surprisingly, however, the participation of all stakeholders in the new partnerships venture is premised on 'pay-back'. In exchange for financial and other support, each public and private sector stakeholder is looking for its *quid pro quo*, which invariably is an ability to influence the policies and programme of the partnership agency and ultimately to benefit from its operation.

'Letting go' and 'pay back' therefore exist side by side in the public–private sector partnerships. Independence is woven into the philosophy and constitutional fabric of the public–private sector partnership. In contrast, independence of operation in policy and managerial senses is negotiated against a backdrop of expectations about payback, and as such is unlikely ever fully to obtain.

Despite or in spite of this ambiguity, and notwithstanding that conventional forms of tourist organization still predominate, there is now no doubt that the growth of public–private sector partnerships is a world-wide trend, manifest at all territorial levels – international, national, regional, sub-regional and local.

The World Tourism Organization (WTO, 1996) cites numerous examples, from Penang to Amsterdam, and ranging across Partnership Australia, the Polish Tourist Authority and the Canadian Tourist Commission, through to the privatization of US state tourism departments and the Maison de la France project. Fundamentally, the WTO report relates these initiatives and experiments to a political climate of disengagement, in which a mixed but related set of considerations have come to the fore – from 'best value' to concerns over 'displacement' effects and 'red tape', to a doubting of continuing subsidy and a passion for the 'free' market.

As well as disengagement, other important politico-administrative trends alluded to in the WTO report are those of decentralization, regional policy and regionalism. What it would all seem to boil down to is that however much the precise form and content of a particular public–private sector partnership may reflect its unique historical, political and cultural setting, an overarching template is set by the sometimes conflicting forces and demands of disengagement, decentralization, regional development and regionalism. So how does England fare in all of this?

The genesis and development of public–private partnership arrangements in England

In Plymouth, the Marketing Bureau is seen as the vehicle to provide the solution. It acts as a catalyst between the City Council and the myriad of large and small companies that make up the tourist industry. The mutual mistrust has been overcome. (Roger Matthews, Director, Plymouth Marketing Bureau, 1989)

Traditionally, in the period up to 1970, local authorities in England were pivotal to meeting the public sector intervention and leadership challenges to which tourism gives rise. They did so at the local, destination level, where so much of tourism takes place. The development of tourism in England has traditionally been delivered by a combination of local government and the private sector (Heeley, 1980). This has been true of the physical and marketing requirements, as well as the policy and planning dimensions. Typically, utilitarian motives of private gain and wider economic benefit to the community have underpinned this coming together of commercial and local government agencies.

What utilitarianism has in practice meant is captured in this statement by the Chairman of the Harrogate Wells and Baths Committee in his evidence to a Parliamentary select committee at the turn of the century: 'although we have a loss directly in working the undertakings, the indirect gain to the town in attracting the additional number of visitors is sufficient to compensate us for any direct loss on the establishments. Of course, as a corporation we can do that whereas under private companies it would be altogether impossible' (cited in Heeley, 1980).

The above quote illustrates how tourism development took place at the local level, with local government helping trader interests to promote and develop the tourist product. In the case of Victorian and Edwardian Harrogate, this amongst other things meant the Royal Hall, the Pump Room, the Winter Gardens and the manicured lawns of the Stray and Valley Gardens. Trader interests and local government complementing one another in this way implied that a genuine 'community of interest' existed, one in which local government regulation and provision of non-productive infrastructure and superstructure sustained private sector wealth production. This, in turn, gave rise to local prosperity and employment gains.

Against the backdrop of this classic model (and ultimately as a departure from it), public–private sector partnerships in tourism have unfolded in two successive and overlapping waves. The first wave occurred in the wake of the 1969 Development of Tourism Act which established a national tourist organization, comprising the British Tourist Authority (BTA) and separate country tourist boards for England, Scotland and Wales respectively. Soon after its formation, the English Tourist Board (ETB) resolved to set up a nationwide structure of regional tourist boards, taking advantage of enabling powers contained within the 1969 Act.

Interestingly, in shaping up the Development of Tourism Bill, mandatory statutory regional tourist agencies had been rejected by national government on the grounds that 'tourism will only make progress in an area in which the interests involved really want to work together' (cited in Heeley, 1975). Again, classic 'community of interest' stuff is here being reflected, and an indication of why ETB were to encounter difficulties in establishing regional agencies for areas where little such community of interest was apparent.

In the event, it took ETB some two years to set up a nationwide system of 11 regional tourist boards (RTBs), during the course of which the Board's original motive of administrative decentralization and its ideal of 'tripartism' were diluted to accord with political realities, especially the winning of local authority support and involvement. ETB's 'tripartite' model for the regional tourist boards was premised on equal one-third funding and representation by the constituent local authorities, private sector operators within each region, and the 'parent' English Tourist Board. Tripartism, as such, foundered on the rock of accessing financial support from the private sector, so much so that a decade after their creation only about 10% of RTB funding derived from commercial members.

So the RTBs became 'independent' (but in reality local authority dominated) regional marketing consortia, thanks to a combination of the power and influence of the local authorities, of sales and marketing-minded chief executives, and of minimalist private sector funding. This contrasted sharply with ETB's original intentions, which had seen the Boards as regional offshoots, mechanisms to facilitate the discharge locally of ETB national campaigns.

The second wave of public–private sector partnerships can be dated to the late 1970s, unfurling in the 1980s and 1990s. It reflected an upsurge of interest in tourism by local authorities, coinciding with a period when local government itself was experiencing radical change. While some authorities responded in the traditional manner to the opportunities and problems raised by tourism by setting up committees and departments, others (especially the larger cities) took to creating arm's-length destination marketing bureaux, drawing on some of the terminology and practice of US visitor and convention bureaux.

These joint ventures of the local public and private sector interests were pioneered in Plymouth, where in 1978 the Plymouth Marketing Bureau was established as a company limited by guarantee, governed by a Board of Directors of whom six were nominated by the local authority and nine elected from local tourist trader interests. A decade later, nearly half of the annual expenditure of the Bureau was derived from non-local authority sources and cost effectiveness was being trumpeted (Matthews, 1989).

Similar financial and efficiency imperatives, as well as the need fully to capitalize on investments in the National Exhibition Centre, led to the formation of the Birmingham Convention and Visitor Bureau (BCVB) in 1982. In Liverpool, an urban development agency, the Merseyside Development Corporation, was the catalyst and core funder of another 1980s experiment in joint venturism, the Merseyside Tourism and Conference Bureau. In this decade, the perceived success stories of the Liverpool and Birmingham bureaux, and of the Greater Glasgow Tourist Board and Visitor and Convention Bureau (established 1983), contrasted with failure elsewhere, especially in the so-called 'heritage towns'. Here, local authority indifference to the tourist industry meant that marketing bureaux were essentially private sector forums. Denied the succour of local authority support and core funding, such bureaux tended to have a chequered history, with more failures (e.g. Chester) than successes (e.g. York). The York Visitor and Conference Bureau, formed in 1987 and backed by local firms such as Portakabin, Rowntrees and Terry's, could in 1990 boast that all of its £200 000 annual turnover was derived from commercial membership and trading activities (York Visitor and Conference Bureau, 1990).

Into the early 1990s Birmingham, Liverpool and Glasgow were used as role models for the creation of local destination bureaux in Manchester (1990) and in Sheffield (1991), the latter styling itself Destination Sheffield and the former revamping and re-launching itself some six years later as Marketing Manchester. Both Destination Sheffield and Marketing Manchester were notable as prototypes of the integrated destination marketing communications exercise. Here, in addition to the normal visitor and convention bureaux (i.e. tourism) functions, were the related fields of city imaging and festivals management. This wider remit was also evident in the establishment of subsequent bureaux, e.g. Leicester Promotions in 1993, Coventry and Warwickshire

Promotions in 1997, and in the BCVB's re-emergence as Birmingham Marketing Partnerships. Elsewhere, the narrower tourism remit remained (e.g. the South Warwickshire Tourism Company, established in 1997). Profile Nottingham, launched this year, combines tourism and city imaging programme areas, but not festivals.

However, discharge of destination marketing accountabilities direct by the local authorities is still common in England. It characterizes spa and seaside towns, and remains the favoured delivery mechanism in many provincial cities, e.g. Leeds and Newcastle. Indeed, regions and sub-regions of the country typically exhibit a mixture of the 'arm's-length' and local authority modes of tourism administration, set within the official regional and national tourist board framework.

This is exemplified for the 'old' county of Warwickshire in Table 26.1. It can be seen that there are four local destination marketing bureaux, with combined budgets of approximately £5 million pounds per annum. In addition, two borough councils (Solihull and Rugby) have dedicated tourism officers, while the councils of North Warwickshire and of Nuneaton and Bedworth assign tourism responsibilities to a leisure officer and to a marketing manager, respectively. The existing county has excluded Birmingham since a nation-wide reorganization of local government, which took place in 1974.

In Warwickshire the work of these tourism structures is supported by the Heart of England regional tourist board, and by the tourist-related inputs of several other agencies, including the county council, the government's regional office, regional arts boards, and the new regional development agency, Advantage West Midlands.

Strengths and weaknesses of public–private sector partnership arrangements in England

> The regional level is not one that relates well to either tourism demand or to the suppliers of tourist services. (Airey and Butler, 1999)

Any tourism structure – be it national, regional or local – is effective only inasmuch as it produces customers. Only by doing so will the structure generate significant and sustained levels of industry support. Public–private sector partnership arrangements in tourism should ultimately be evaluated by reference to these criteria of visitors and industry support generated. However, conclusive assessment of public–private partnerships in this way is constrained by several factors.

Table 26.1 Tourism organizations in Warwickshire: budgets and main sources of funding

	Annual income (£000)[a]	English Tourist Board (%)	Local authorities (%)	Commercial sector (%)	Earned (%)	External grant (esp. EC) (%)
Heart of England Tourist Board	2759	20	9	8	63	–
Birmingham Marketing Partnerships	2956	–	36	3	46	15
Coventry and Warwickshire Promotions	1065	–	61	4	21	14
South Warwickshire Tourism Co.	929	–	51	11	38	–
Rugby Tourism	13	–	67	15	18	–
Total	**7722**					

[a]Annual income given for financial years as follows:
Heart of England Tourist Board 1997/8
Birmingham Marketing Partnerships 1996/7
Coventry and Warwickshire Promotions 1998/9
South Warwickshire Tourism Company 1997/8
Rugby Tourism 1997/8.

Performance assessment has been an unknown term and practice for much of the 30-year period that these bodies have been undertaking their pioneering partnership roles. In a more general sense, measuring the impact of marketing work is notoriously difficult because of the complexity of the customers' decision-making processes, the multiplicity of causal factors at play, and the need to disentangle discretionary visits and spend from those that would have in any case occurred. On the industry support side, comparative analysis of private sector contributions throws up major computational issues and imponderables. What is the best measure of industry support? Is it commercial subscriptions and/or media advertising revenues and/or exhibition partner income? How do we treat in-kind, 'off-the-balance sheet' contributions? At the present moment, industry support is difficult to interpret in any statistically meaningful, comparative sense.

All these anomalies, caveats and qualifications notwithstanding, there is a *prima facie* case to conclude that the operation of regional tourist boards in England from 1972 to 1999 has been by and large unsuccessful in attracting tourists and industry support. Taking a lead from Airey and Butler, the regional level is manifestly unsuited to marketing, and is not one that is conducive to the development of close working relationships with the tourist industry. The Tourism Society, a prominent forum of industry academics and practitioners, has even gone as far as saying that promotion should only be undertaken at the national and local destination levels, and 'never at the regional level' (cited in Airey and Butler, 1999). Regional tourist boards, the Society says, 'have performed very patchily'.

The view here echoes those of the Tourism Society. The regions the RTBs represent provide insufficient marketing focus and are not themselves brands, while the Boards themselves have been bureaucratic as opposed to entrepreneurial, erring to the lowest common denominator as opposed to the competitive strength. They are coherent tourist destination areas neither in name nor reality and are not genuine communities of interest.

Localized joint venture arrangements, on the other hand, have in the main arisen to represent real communities of interest. Their respective territories are more or less the basis on which customers visit and the industry is organized. Working to full potential, they enable a destination to be presented in a co-ordinated way, engendering a flexible and entrepreneurial approach. Typically, they operate within a framework where targets are set and the success or failure of every project is measured and reported upon.

'Arm's-length' bureaux have proved adept at enlisting the support of large and small private sector operators and at winning external grant income, especially the European Regional Development and European Social funds. The weaknesses of destination marketing bureaux are that they can be parochial, and that they do not readily embrace inter-destination partnerships. Moreover they can all to easily become the victims of their own success. The vagaries of local authority tourism finance are such that a bureau's ability to lever trade monies and external grant may lead to core funding being withdrawn! Functions inappropriate to a bureau's core business(es) may also be off-loaded on to the 'successful' bureau.

Finally, arm's-length can quickly become off-shore and unloved, unless there is painstaking communication back to the stakeholders (especially the local authority), supported by influential champions of the bureau's cause drawn from the ranks of local government and the business community. The secret of success for an arm's-length bureau is all about communication and championing.

References

Airey, D. and Butler, R. (1999) *Tourism at the Regional Level*. Portoroz, Slovenia, International Association of Scientific Experts in Tourism, Reports, 41, pp. 71–90.

Cannadine, D. (1980) *Lords and Landlords: the Aristocracy and the Towns, 1774–1967*. Leicester: Leicester University Press.

Confederation of British Industry (1999) The New Regional Dimension to Tourism Delivery. Seminar, London, 30 September 1999.

Department for Culture, Media and Sport (1999) *Tomorrow's Tourism*. London: DCMS.

Heeley, J. (1975) A study of organisations concerned with tourism in the UK. MSc thesis, Scottish Hotel School Glasgow, University of Strathclyde.

Heeley, J. (1980) Tourism and local government, with special reference to the county of Norfolk. PhD thesis, Centre for East Anglian Studies, Norwich, University of East Anglia.

Heeley, J. (1981) Planning for tourism in Britain: an historical perspective. *Town Planning Review (Journal of the Royal Town Planning Institute)*, 52 (1): 61–79.

Jeffreys, E. (1999) England – a new framework for action. *Tourism,* Issue 102.

Matthews, R. (1989) *Marketing Bureaux*. London: English Tourist Board (Insights).

Neale, R.S. (1981) *Bath: A Social History 1680–1850 or a Valley of Pleasure, yet a Sink of Iniquity*. London: Routledge and Kegan Paul.

Thomas, H. and Thomas, R. (1998) The implications for tourism of shifts in British local governance. *Progress in Tourism and Hospitality Research*, 4: 295–306.

Walton, J.K. (1978) *The Blackpool Landlady: a Social History.* Manchester: Manchester University Press.

World Tourism Organization (1996) *Towards New Forms of Public–Private Sector Partnerships: The Changing Role, Structure and Activities of National Tourism Administrations.* A Special Report for the World Tourism Organization. Madrid: WTO.

York Visitor and Conference Bureau (1990) Annual Report for the year ended 30 June 1990.

27

Coastal resorts and climate change

Martin Lohmann

Introduction

This chapter offers a framework for the analysis of climate change impacts on tourism in coastal resorts: How can a change in climate affect tourism? Where are the 'interfaces' between climate change and tourism and how do they work? Which kind of information do we need on climate change and its effects (e.g. from meteorology, biology, geography) in order to assess the impact on tourism? How do social processes (social perception, impact of media, political decisions) in a society facing a climate change process modify the pure effect of climate change?

In October 1999, the 5th UN conference on climate change met in Bonn, Germany. One of the main topics was how to organize a reduction of, for example, carbon dioxide emissions in a way that national economies will not suffer. Looking at this discussion, there seems to be little doubt that there is a significant risk for society connected with climate change.

Climate change and climate change impacts

Results of climate change research (Houghton *et al.*, 1996) show that man has intensified the greenhouse effect by increasing the concentration of carbon dioxide in the earth's atmosphere. According to the prediction of climate models, this development is accompanied by a rise in global average temperature. This has a number of further consequences, which are the subject of climate change impact research. Possible effects are, for example, the rise of sea level or changes in vegetation. As far as the magnitude of these effects or regional effects is concerned, no reliable data are yet available. In addition to physical, geological and ecological changes, it is also necessary to consider sociological and psychological aspects, such as *who* perceives climate change, *how* individuals and/or societies perceive climate change, and how they respond to their perceptions of changes (for example, adaptive behaviour, avoidance strategies), in order to assess societal effects of climate change (cf. Stehr and von Storch, 1995). In order to gain some insights into how this complex system may influence tourism, we need a model of how tourism works to see where climate change impacts can affect tourism.

How does tourism work?

Five factors are a prerequisite for tourism: attractiveness, amenities (or facilities) and accessibility on the side of the destination (cf. Holloway, 1994: 6–9) and ability to travel and motivation to travel on the demand side (Lohmann *et al.*, 1998).

Attractiveness refers to physical features (e.g. the beauty of mountains), but may also be used in connection with some kind of event. Amenities are those essential services the tourist needs such as accommodation, food, local transport etc. Finally, accessibility refers to means of transportation to the destination as well as the psychological distance (to be reached easily) and the possibility of booking a trip to that specific destination (distribution channels). The assumption is that a region becomes a potentially successful tourist destination (i.e. is able to attract a large number of tourists) only when the region has all these three characteristics. On the other hand, a person becomes a potential tourist only if he is able to travel (usually a question of time, money and health) and if he has the motivation to do so.

We have developed a simple structural model to describe which central factors determine whether and how tourism takes place (Figure 27.1) (Lohmann *et al.*, 1998).

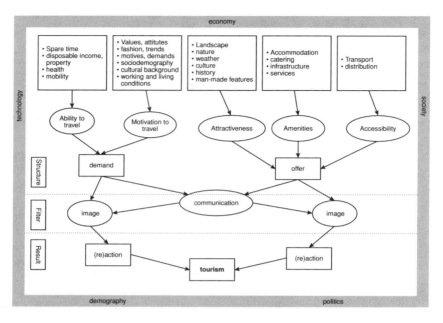

Figure 27.1 Tourism – framework and prerequisites

How can climate change affect tourism?

Naturally, climate change will first have an impact on the tourist supply, e.g. through changed weather patterns (Lohmann and Kaim, 1999) or through impacts on the 'hardware', like reduction of landmass, destroying infrastructure. The supply of goods and services may also change through reactions of the tourism industry with respect to a real or feared climate change (e.g. more indoor facilities offered for bad weather conditions). In a second step, all this may lead to a change in tourism demand for a given area.

Nevertheless, as tourism is an economic activity mainly defined by demand (cf. Smith, 1995: 35), we will look at climate change effects on tourism starting from the demand side. One crucial aspect is the way in which climate change effects can influence the ability and the motivation to travel (cf. Figure 27.1) in general and, more specifically, for a certain coastal area. In view of the uncertainties in climate research (cf. Krupp, 1995; Hasselmann, 1997; Maxeiner, 1997; Tenbrock, 1997), something like a prognosis cannot be expected.

We have identified three possible 'interfaces' between climate change and tourism (Figure 27.2):

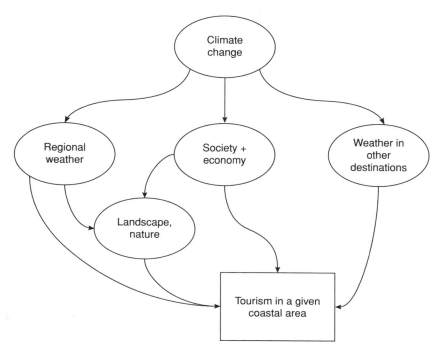

Figure 27.2 The interfaces between climate change and tourism

1 Regional weather patterns (temperatures, clouds, amount of precipitation. etc.), including change of landscape due to changed weather, (e.g. dry summers, floods).
2 Perception and evaluation of climate change in society and political, administrative and economic reactions (like environment politics, attitudes of politicians, leisure time and its distribution over the year, disposable financial means, prices, e.g. for transport and insurance).
3 Weather conditions in competing destinations.

Thus, we distinguish between direct and indirect effects of climate change impacts on tourism demand.

Direct effects

One of the most important factors influencing the attractiveness of a destination and the motivation of people to go there is weather (i.e. the perceived weather or the psychological representation of some of the meteorological/ physical variables defining the weather). Both the industry itself and tourists

287

give this factor – the weather – some explanatory value for success or failure in tourism (e.g. Braun and Lohmann, 1989; IHK Kiel, 1998). Other relevant studies include Clawson (1966), De Freitas (1990), Adams (1973), Lohmann and Kaim (1999).

Another important factor influencing tourism directly is the weather in competing destinations. A change here may alter the relative position of a given coastal area and thus lead to a new ranking of destination preferences of tourists.

Referring to the described model in Figure 27.1, weather as a 'materialization' of climate change may change the attractiveness of a destination and influence the motivation to go there.

Indirect effects

Among indirect effects are the 'classical' climate change effects like rising sea level, infrastructure destroyed by storms, etc.; the kind frequently talked about in the public media (Christiansen, 1997; Hansen, 1997; Hasselmann, 1997; Lean, 1999; McCarthy, 1999; Anon., 1998; Reynolds, 1999). The impact of these on the destination is a decrease in attractiveness, on the supply side the difficulty (or impossibility) to continue the business, and on tourism demand a weaker motivation to travel to the destination.

Less frequently mentioned, but probably rather powerful, are impacts on tourism demand via social and economic effects. For example, in a society showing high public awareness concerning environmental issues, the possibility of a future climate change may result in rather strict environmental legislation which influences the costs of mobility (making among other things travelling more expensive). This may lead to reduced production of cars with a consequent reduction of the number of jobs and reduced incomes (decrease in tourism demand). Considering the close relationship between economic situations and leisure travel (Aderhold, 1999; Lim, 1997) such processes can influence – via ability to travel (Figure 27.1) – tourism to some extent.

In order to determine possible impacts of climate change (and related effects) on coastal tourism, these are the important questions:

- Do climate change effects affect a coastal area in such a way that tourism in the traditional locations is no longer possible?
- Does climate change include changed weather patterns and how do they affect the natural and man-made environment on the one hand and tourism demand for this coastal area on the other?

- Do climate change impacts affect the ability to travel, e.g. by generating social and economic processes, which may be part of an avoidance or adaptation strategy?
- Does climate change influence the situation in competing destinations and how will this affect tourism demand for a given region?

A development perspective of tourism in a destination under climate change conditions has to incorporate different approaches and sciences. In most cases, it will be close to impossible to arrive at a valid and reliable forecast, besides perhaps some extreme cases like disappearing islands in the Pacific Ocean (cf. Lean, 1999). However, even in these cases one cannot be sure whether it should be considered a climate change effect or a natural variability. Uncertainty seems to be an escort of climate change. Therefore, social research (with tourism research being a part of it) on climate change issues has to incorporate uncertainty in its research programme, as a barrier and challenge to decision-making.

The case of North German coastal resorts

Coastal areas on the North and Baltic Seas in Germany are among the most important tourist destinations in Germany (Aderhold, 1999; Lohmann *et al.*, 1998) and tourism is the most important source of income for the region (Feige *et al.*, 1999: 61).

NIT, the Institute for Tourism and Recreational Research in Northern Europe, Kiel, in co-operation with the Meteorological Institute at the University of Hamburg, the DWIF (Deutsches Wirtschaftswissenschaftliches Institut fur Fremdenverkehr) in Berlin and the Department of Psychology at the University of Koblenz–Landau conducted a multidisciplinary research project as an extensive social scientific research programme 'Coastal Tourism and Climate Change', commissioned by the German Ministry of Education, Science, Research and Technology. The focus of this research was on the question of which direction tourism in the German coastal regions would take under various climate change development scenarios (fictitious, but possible and in line with the International Panel for Climate Change (IPCC) data; cf. Bray, 1998: 19, 52).

In the course of this research project we have developed a preliminary conceptualization of how climate change can influence tourism in general and gained some insights with specific relevance for the destinations in Northern Germany (Bray, 1998; Feige *et al.*, 1999; Lohmann *et al.*, 1998; Braun *et al.*, 1999; Lohmann and Kaim, 1999); similar research has been carried out for other types of destinations, e.g. the Alps (Abegg, 1996, Buerki, 2000).

A complex set of methodological approaches was used in this project: scenario techniques, representative surveys of the German population, focus groups with representatives of the tourism industry and administration, psychological experiments, and others. These are described by Lohmann *et al.* (1998).

To give an example of the empirical parts of the project: within a series of psychological studies (cf. Braun *et al.*, 1999) we researched the possible impact of climate change scenarios and of the reactions of the tourism industry on the expressed destination preferences of tourists. Scenario 1 described a moderate warming accompanied by both more hours of sunshine and stronger precipitation. The industry reaction was a combination of air-conditioned hotels and more outdoor activities. In Scenario 2 the climate was described as significantly warmer, with much more precipitation, sometimes sultry and – during the wintertime – heavy storms; higher dikes and reduced fauna and flora completed the picture. The industry reaction consisted of more and better indoor facilities, both cultural and sports activities/events, shopping malls etc.

We presented these scenarios to possible tourists and then asked for their interest in spending a holiday at the German coast. The results showed a decrease in the number of interested people, especially under the conditions of Scenario 2, which can be partly (Scenario 2) or more than (Scenario 1) compensated by appropriate industry reaction.

These are some of the main findings of the project as a whole:

1 *Tourism at the German seaside is sensitive to climate change and its effects* Sensitivity is high in those cases, where climate change impacts lead to a substantial change in attractiveness, facilities, and/or accessibility on the supply side or the ability to travel on the demand side. But even then climate change will be only one factor among others influencing tourism.
2 *The evaluation of the effects as positive or negative depends at least partly on the developing philosophy of tourism* Climate change effects may lead to a stronger or a weaker demand or to a high variability in tourist flows as well. In every case the tourism industry will try to adapt to the new situation, but the reactions will be quite different under the different conditions.
   Thus, climate change impacts are not necessarily harming tourism in the coastal resorts. In some cases – depending on the amount and the

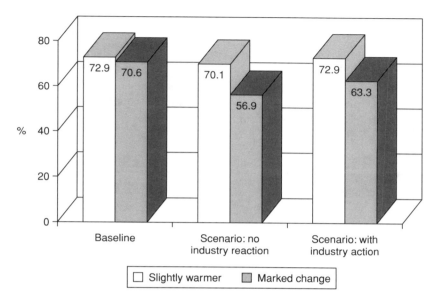

Figure 27.3 Change of interest in spending a holiday at the North German coast under different climate conditions

direction of climate change itself and on the prevailing development philosophy *('Leitbild')* of tourism in the area – they may even be helpful. For example, a tourism strategy of growth may find support through climate change leading to warmer daytime temperatures during summer, whilst a tourism strategy of limitation/restriction will face a challenge under the same climate change condition.

3 *Environment policies for slowing down/reducing climate change and its impacts will influence coastal tourism as well, independently of the 'real' climate change*   Induced by economics and/or policies these effects may be the result of rising costs, lower wages, higher unemployment rates or restrictions in transport, heating or others.

4 *Climate change effects and political (re)action may be an additional challenge for the tourism industry; however, within the next 30 years tourism at the coast will still be possible*   Within the next two decades climate change and its impacts in the North of Germany are supposed to be not too dramatic (cf. Bray, 1998: 96). The development of tourism will be more dependent on the (global) activities of the industry. Climate change will play the role of an additional, modifying factor.

5 *In some cases, adaptation strategies may be useful or necessary, including a repositioning of the destination*   The related activities have to be

appropriate; for example an over-reaction using the new opportunities of a slight warming to attract lots of new tourists may turn into a boomerang effect, with a reduced demand due to overcrowding at the end.

6 *Adaptation can be expensive* This is a crucial aspect: Tourism will still be possible, but someone has to pay for the adaptation to the new circumstances.

7 *Climate change is a process* What in some of the scenarios looks like a not too uncomfortable situation in the next few decades may be nothing but a transition stage to a less desirable future.

Discussion

Our results show – in line with the international literature (e.g. Buerki and Elsasser, 1999) – that as long as a destination is able to satisfy the basic needs of the tourists and as long as the tourists have sufficient financial means, the tourism industry in a region will be able to adapt to climate change effects.

We could not identify a specific need for immediate action for the coastal resorts in northern Germany related to climate change. More interesting is the question of the possibilities of action. Are there any 'no-regrets' strategies (cf. Abegg *et al.*, 1997: 110) at hand? That is, could actions be taken to improve the position of the coastal tourism in Germany regardless of which way climate change may turn, for example, better and more reliable financing of tourism allowing for a flexible response whenever needed, less bureaucratic structures in tourism administration and marketing and a flexible consumer-oriented product design. Such strategies would create a sound basis for a rather uncertain future.

We must face the fact that we will have to live and plan with a great deal of uncertainty. In order to reduce this uncertainty to a manageable amount, future research is needed. Our approach, described here briefly, may be an additional tool to many others to gain a clearer picture of the possible future of tourism in coastal areas under climate change conditions. For a better understanding we need more detailed data on possible weather characteristics. The availability of climate change data on a smaller geographical scale would also be very helpful. And finally, we urgently need more research on the role of social processes (perception, impact of media, political decisions etc.) in a society facing a climate change process with a great deal of uncertainty.

The somewhat limited threat of direct climate change impacts for tourism at the coast in northern Germany within the next two or three decades is a result not to be transferred to other places in the world without checking the specific situation there. Other destinations, with a different geographical situation and a different structure of tourism, may be hit by climate change much harder. But our methodological approach may serve as a guideline for future research projects in other areas.

Tourism as a whole, a global phenomenon, is a field that will be easily influenced by climate change, but will not be made impossible. Tourism can switch to other destinations if one is swept away, dried out or hit by some other severe impact of climate change. Tourism is more flexible than the local population.

Acknowledgement

The Bundesministerium für Bildung, Wissenschaft, Forschung und Technologie (German Federal Ministry for Education, Science, Research, and Technology) supported this research. The author thanks Johanna Danielsson, Kiel (Germany) and Lynn Lohmann, Munich (Germany), for their comments on an earlier draft of the manuscript.

References

Abegg, B. (1996) *Klimaänderung und Tourismus – Klimafolgenforschung am Beispiel des Wintertourismus in den Schweizer Alpen.* Zurich: VDF Hochschulverlag der ETH Zurich.

Abegg, B. *et al.* (1997) Climate impact assessment in tourism. *Die Erde,* 128: 105–16.

Adams, D.L. (1973) Uncertainty in nature, cognitive dissonance, and the perceptual distortion of environmental information: weather forecasts and New England beach trip decisions. *Economic Geography*, 4: 287–97.

Aderhold, P. (1999) *Kurzfassung der Reiseanalyse '99.* Hamburg: Forschungsgemeinschaft Urlaub und Reisen.

Anon. (1998) Malediven – Bedroht durch wärmeres Kiima. *Fremdenverkehrswirtschaft International*, 26: 88.

Braun, O.L. and Lohmann, M. (1989) *Die Reiseentscheidung: Einige Ergebnisse zum Stand der Forschung.* Starnberg: Studienkreis fur Tourismus.

Braun, O.L., Lohmann, M. *et al.* (1999) Potential impact of climate change effects on references for tourism destination: a psychological pilot study. *Climate Research*, 11 (April): 247–54.

Bray, D. (1998) Visioning Event Horizons – Global Warming, the German Coastal Region and Tourism. Abschlussbericht zum Projekt Klimawandel und Küstentourismus. Hamburg (Meteorologisches Institut der Universitat Hamburg) (unpublished).

Buerki, R. and Elsasser, H. (1999) Nachfragetrends und Umweltueränderungen an der Schwelle zum 21. Jahrhundert – Das Beispiel Wintertourismus in den Alpen. Manuscript (Zurich).

Buerki, R. (2000) Climate change – adaptations of tourists and tourism managers. Paper presented to the International Millennium Conference: Tourism and Hospitality in the 21st century, University of Surrey, Guildford, England, 11–14 January 2000.

Christiansen, T. (1997) Ist Sylt noch zu retten?, *Kieler Nachrichten*, 12 June.

Clawson, M. (1966) The influence of weather on outdoor recreation. In W. Sewell (ed.), *Human Dimensions of Weather Modification*. Department of Geography, University of Chicago, Research Paper No. 105, pp. 183–93.

De Freitas, C.R. (1990) Recreation climate assessment. *International Journal of Climatology*, 10: 89–103.

Feige, M., Seidel, A., Kirchhoff, M. and Smetan, C. (1999) Entwicklungspfade des Küstentourismus. Abschlussbericht zum Projekt Klimawandel und Küstentourismus, Berlin: (DWIF, Deutsches Wirtschaftswissenschaftliches Institut für Fremdenverkehr) (unpublished).

Hansen, J. (1997) A warming world needs human remedy now. *International Herald Tribune*, 19 June, p. 10.

Hasselmann, K. (1997) Die Launen der Medien. *Die Zeit*, Nr. 32, 1 August, p. 311.

Holloway, J.C. (1994) *The Business of Tourism,* London: Pitman.

Houghton, J.T., Meira Filho, L.G., Callander, B.A., Harris, N., Kattenberg, A. and Maskell, K. (eds) (1996) *Climate Change 1995. The Science of Climate Change.* Cambridge: Cambridge University Press.

IHK Kiel (1998) *Wirtschaftslage und Erwartungen in Schleswig-Holstein: Tourismuswirtschaft Sommersaison 1998.* Kiel: Industrie- und Handelskammer.

Krupp, C. (1995) *Klimaänderungen und die Folgen.* Berlin: Herausgegeben vom Wissenschaftszentrum Berlin für Sozialforschung.

Lean, G. (1999) They're going under. *The Independent*, 13 June, p. 15.

Lim, C. (1997) Review of international tourism demand models. *Annals of Tourism Research*, 24 (4): 835–49.

Lohmann, M. and Kaim, E. (1999) Weather and holiday preference – image, attitude and experience, *Revue de Tourisme*, 2: 54–64.

Lohmann, M., Kierchhoff, H.W. *et al.* (1998) Entwicklungspfade des Tourismus unter Einfluss des Klimawandels. Abschlusseicht zum Projekt Klimawandel und Küstentourismus. Kiel, NIT (unpublished).

Maxeiner, D. (1997) Die Launen der Sonne. *Die Zeit*, Nr. 31, 25 July, p. 38.

McCarthy, M. (1999) Beachy Head cliff collapses into the sea. *The Independent*, 12 January, p. 5.

Reynolds, P. (1999) Mother Nature's wrath. *Time*, 22 February, p. 54.

Smith, S.L.J. (1995) *Tourism Analysis: A Handbook,* 2nd edn. Harlow: Longman.

Stehr, N. and von Storch, H. (1995) The social construct of climate and climate change. *Climate Research*, 5: 99–105.

Sterr, H. (1997) Die Problematik des Klimawandels für das integrierte Küstenzonen Management. *Schriftenreihe für Landschaftspflege und Naturschutz*, 52: 87–98.

Tenbrock, C. (1997) Die Stunde der Schwarzmaler. *Die Zeit*, Nr. 43, 17 October, p. 23.

28

Conclusions – problems, challenges and solutions

Richard Butler and Peter Jones

The previous chapters in this book have addressed many aspects of tourism and hospitality in the 21st century. This concluding chapter begins with a discussion of what we regard as over-riding problems of tourism and hospitality in the new century, followed by a review of major challenges which the industry will face. We conclude the chapter with some thoughts on the likely nature of tourism and hospitality in the future.

Problems

While the world faces many problems, most of which affect tourism and hospitality to a greater or lesser degree, there are four significant general problems that emerge from the chapters to be of particular relevance to tourism and hospitality.

The problem of definitions

Despite the fact that the terms 'tourism' and 'hospitality' are widely used, there continues to be a lack of agreement as to exactly what each of these encompasses and as to the relationship between them. In this discussion, we take tourism to be an all-encompassing term covering every aspect of people staying away from home, and hospitality to be a specific aspect of this, dealing with accommodation and feeding tourists. One difficulty, of course, is that the hospitality industry also feeds and accommodates many people who are not tourists.

In reality 'tourism' is often interpreted quite narrowly, i.e. as the flow of visitors from one country to another. This is because, like many of the authors of chapters in this book, academics and researchers generally rely heavily on the World Tourism Organization (WTO) as their principal source of data. Yet in many parts of the world, particularly the United States and China, there are very high levels of domestic tourism. Even today only about 10% of the US population has a passport.

This problem of differentiating between international and domestic tourism is likely to become even more severe. If the European Union should become the United States of Europe, intra-regional travel within the Union will cease to be international tourism regardless of its purpose. (Travel between Hong Kong and PRC has already ceased to be international tourist travel, although the volume of traffic has increased and the purpose changed little.)

It is clear there is also a great deal of inconsistency between data, which is largely due to the problems of definition. Purpose of visit is one such definitional problem. When tourism is not defined it generally means pleasure tourism, people on holidays, but formal definitions (like that of the WTO) tend to include anyone travelling. Witt and Song state in this volume that 70% of worldwide trips were holidays, 15% were business and 10% were related to visiting friends and relatives (VFR). Yet the most recent Horwath International global hotel study (1999) identifies only 50% of occupancy deriving from the leisure traveller and 46% from business guests. From the hospitality and airline industries' point of view the business traveller is extremely important and often the major focus of attention and effort.

The apparent inconsistency in figures is partly because so many pleasure tourists stay in less conventional accommodation. In Scotland, for example, Scottish Tourist Board figures published in 1999 show that hotel accommodation makes up only about 40% of total tourist accommodation, excluding VFR beds. Rather too many surveys concentrate solely on hotel guests, thus much less is known about other staying visitors. Domestic tourists are more likely than international tourists to use accommodation other than hotels as they are better placed to know about alternatives. Until the problems relating to the definitions of tourism and hospitality are resolved and the definitions become all-encompassing, applying with equal validity to all regions, there are likely to be continued difficulties and inconsistencies in understanding tourism and travel data and statistics.

The problem of forecasting and predicting growth and change

A feature of this text has been the forecasts about tourism's future. Witt and Song are clear about which methods work, and Frechtling (also in this volume) makes some telling points about which factors will influence tourism in the next decade. But most econometric and statistical trend projections are based on the principle of *ceteris paribus* – all things remaining equal. What if they do not? A feature of the 20th century, especially the second half of the century, was relative stability in many aspects of tourism, but this may not be true for the 21st century.

Global tourism is forecast to grow, but overall growth forecasts hide tremendous differences between regions and countries. According to Teye (this volume) Africa receives only 4% of all international tourists and only 2% of total international tourism receipts. He shows that many African countries are economically worse off now than they were 40 years ago, still over-reliant on agricultural and/or mineral production, with tourism presenting both cultural and environmental challenges. He concludes that there have been and still are a myriad of obstacles to tourism development, such as political instability, economic restructuring, human resource constraints, lack of regional co-operation and a lack of basic infrastructure.

An optimistic view of Europe and North America is that at best their tourism industries are stable. In their respective chapters, Cook states that short-term growth in US arrivals will be slow, whilst Cleverdon suggests tourism in Europe is growing at a rate of 3% compared with a global rate of 4%, and its market share is forecast to decline from 59% (1995) to 47% by 2020. On the other hand South America looks set for a period of sustained tourism growth. Arrivals have been growing at an annual rate of 9% and receipts at 12%. It has some tremendous advantages, including its relative proximity to lucrative North American markets, historic and language links with Europe, and excellent natural resources (rainforest/Andes/beaches).

Asia Pacific also seems to be on an upturn. Chamberlain (this volume) quotes the WTO as forecasting that this region will 'grow faster than any other' and will pass the Americas to become second to Europe in the number of visitor arrivals. This means five times as many visitors in 2020 as in 1998 – admittedly a low year – although there may be some difficulty in accommodating that number of visitors and it might pose strains on the infrastructure in the region. Asia Pacific illustrates perfectly how vulnerable these industries are to unexpected events. The recent financial crisis in this region led to dramatic falls in arrivals, hotel rates and hotel occupancies, not only in the Pacific region but globally . This kind of event makes forecasting tourism performance in some regions almost impossible. No one can predict what might happen in the Middle East, the Indian sub-continent and the Russian Federation. Political instability, economic turbulence and religious differences could all have negative effects on potential tourism development and growth.

Overall there is evidence of extremely rapid growth in some regions, that this growth will continue, and that other regions will begin to attain a greater share of tourism in the years ahead. But there is really no such thing as a 'fair share' despite what ministers and NTOs say. Not everywhere needs or can expect to attract large numbers of tourists. Those places that have not grown significantly or do not have major tourism industries generally are in that position for good reasons. Cetron (this volume) identified some of these reasons – a lack of perceived attractions compared to other areas, relative or absolute inaccessibility, unsuitable climate, political regimes which discourage tourism, problems of security, health and safety, relatively high cost and often a combination of several of these.

What is needed is an examination of which, if any, of these elements are likely to change significantly in the short- to medium-term future, to understand if those regions are likely to see major increases in tourism. Even then, should such a change in situation come about, we need to see whether the region is appropriately equipped to handle such an increase effectively. Rapid percentage growth is rather easy from a low base, but long-term sustained growth is what is important, if indeed it is growth that is desired. If the world is serious about sustainable development and living within the limits of the resources available, then growth, especially rapid growth, may not be the pattern desired or acceptable in all regions. This aspect is rarely tackled in forecasts, where the focus is normally on growth.

The problem of industry characteristics

It seems clear there is going to be continued growth of global brands such as McDonalds and Burger King, Hilton and Holiday Inn, British Airways,

One World Alliance, Thomas Cook and American Express, Avis and Hertz. Despite the fact that the Internet makes some people suggest the brand is dead, big firms will continue. There are still economies of scale to be achieved by being big, even in a world of e-commerce, as the AOL–Time Warner merger demonstrates. But the industries will continue to have many small operators managing unique operations on a local basis. One of the comments frequently made about tourism is its fragmentation and the difficulty this poses for instituting controls, particularly self-regulation by the industry. It often results in multiple, sometimes opposing, objectives among different players, which require different solutions in different locations. This is one of the reasons for the frequent lack of application and success of national master plans. Despite the globalization trends to which Chamberlain and others refer in this volume, there is likely to remain a large element of the tourism industry made up of very small players. The web should encourage and assist the maintenance of some of this diversity.

The tourism workforce is typically described as having low ability and few skills. Large numbers of young people are employed in these industries, expected to work long, unsociable hours, paid below average wages resulting in extremely high levels of staff turnover. This pattern may not be able to continue, if only because in many countries in the developed world there will be fewer young people to be employed under these or any conditions because of changing demographics. Changes in the composition of populations, nationally and globally, are likely to have major, if still uncertain effects on all aspects of tourism and hospitality in the coming century.

The problem of climate change

A key problem that tourism and hospitality has to face is climate change. This issue could have greater effects on tomorrow's world and tourism and hospitality in particular than anything else discussed so far. Two islands have disappeared already because of rising sea levels, and the effects of El Nino and weather instability throughout the world have been terrible in recent years. The most worrying aspect is that very little is known about the full nature or level of these effects. To all intents and purposes the tourism and hospitality industries appear to have buried their heads in the sand and seem intent on ignoring what could be *the* major problem of the century.

Some of the likely effects as well as rising sea levels, include negative effects on ski areas with fewer days of snow-cover, increased cloud and rainfall in some areas, and increased temperatures and greater sun exposure in other parts of the world, with general increased turbulence and unpredictability of weather. Lohmann (this volume) showed that many of these are serious enough to at least threaten, if not change, the patterns of tourism and to have significant impacts on hospitality operations.

If sea levels do rise significantly as forecast, many world cities including London, Tokyo, Los Angeles, Washington, Sydney and Singapore would be under water, as well as Bangladesh, the Maldives, the Seychelles, the Netherlands and Florida among others. There would be economic, political and social turmoil. Tourism depends on global economic well-being and this would not exist if this scenario became reality.

At this time, however, it seems that only the insurance and banking industries have begun to take real notice of what is likely to be a significant problem, not just for our industries but the world as a whole. Even if serious steps are taken to reduce the problem, it will be decades before the process is reversed, if indeed, it can be reversed.

It is worrying that in general the problem is being ignored by forecasters and by planners. It seems rather naive, for example, to produce a tourism master plan for a place that might be under water by the time the plan is ready to be implemented.

Challenges

The tourism and hospitality industries face a large number of challenges caused by the general nature of global dynamics, as well as the specific problems noted above.

The challenge of demographics

There is considerable evidence that tourism is linked to population size and GDP, so in some respects the future of tourism would seem assured. Demographics is a key element of most forecasting models of tourism. Throughout the 20th century trends were clear and predictable. It was a period during which the average life expectancy of people living in the developed world increased from 47 years to 75. This was due to improved economic conditions, to advances in medicine, especially antibiotics and vaccines, health care and better diet generally and, in the past 50 years, a decline in mass conflicts and wars.

Some believe that our exponential growth in knowledge will accelerate this trend. Mapping the human genome could lead to advances in gene therapies, such as cell replacement and gene scrubbing, so that human life might be extended almost indefinitely. The development of human stem cell technology may enable individuals to grow in a laboratory their own spare parts – already blood vessels are produced in this way. Some experts are predicting that human life span could certainly be extended to 150 years of age, or even indefinitely.

On the other hand, while science has solved many problems, a great many still remain and others are being created. Only one virus – smallpox – has been eradicated to date, although polio may become the second very shortly. Antibiotics, while allowing a reduction in disease, are becoming less and less effective. Antibiotic-resistant TB is now commonplace. In the UK and the United States patients who fail to follow the strict, complex and long-term regime required to cure this disease are forcibly hospitalized to ensure they do so. There are already restrictions on food exports and we may well see restrictions on people who have certain symptoms or illnesses from travelling.

In addition, new infections and diseases, such as Ebola, Lassa, AIDS and CJD, have developed to which there are no known cures. Forty million people worldwide have HIV. In 20 years, AIDS has moved from being undocumented to being one of the largest causes of death in the world. The origin of these diseases is often unknown, although it is increasingly recognized that viruses can cross the species barrier. The world has yet to see another pandemic like the flu outbreak in 1918/19, which killed at least 18 million people, but such a pandemic is almost certain according to academics. The 1918 flu pandemic spread globally through the movement of large numbers of troops following the end of the First World War. Today the travel industry, along with a global food distribution system, could have the same effect.

The challenge of the Internet

The Internet is changing the way many businesses are conducted. The appearance of e-commerce could be as significant an event in this century as the agrarian revolution of the 17th century, the industrial revolution of the 18th century, and the information revolution of the late 20th century. Shares in e-businesses are the fastest growing stocks on the stock market, even though many have yet to make a profit. Currently only 2% of the world's population has Internet access, but this is changing rapidly.

One scenario is that demand for goods and services will increase as distribution costs come down, entrepreneurship will thrive as individuals are given access to global markets, and overall economic growth will raise living standards and wealth everywhere. But there is a downside to the Internet. It is not only a tool for empowering entrepreneurship and businesses, but also a tool for empowering and informing the dispossessed, the outsiders, the have-nots and the extremists. Bombs exploded by Basques in Spain, Tamils in Sri Lanka and Hesbollah in the Middle East can all be made by following instructions available on the worldwide web. Instructions for making weapons of mass destruction – chemical, biological, atomic – will soon be available to any such individual or group. If used, such weapons would create a world that would be in economic chaos as industrial output was disrupted by events affecting energy supplies, production, labour and likely political stability. In such a world tourism and hospitality would suffer more than most industries.

New technology could make moving around the world much safer. Microchips on credit cards can store millions of bits of information about their owner and their owner's preferences. Currently these are used mainly to facilitate transactions, but they can just as easily facilitate personal interactions. These microchips, and even cellular phone technology, will become implantable beneath the skin, which could greatly facilitate security scanning and passport control at airports. It also enables people to use voice commands to interact with their surroundings, controlling items of electrical equipment such as doors, curtains, lights and thermostats by voice alone. Of some interest is the extent to which resort accommodation should become a haven of respite from this 'wired world' or be as technically sophisticated as other living environments. They will probably have to be wired, leaving the choice with the guest as to what use is made of the technology.

The challenges of travel and leisure

Even if e-commerce thrives, the Internet may have an adverse effect on business travel. In the so-called 'wired-world', business travel may actually decline. A global infrastructure of low orbit satellites, asymmetric digital subscriber lines (ASDL) and other new technologies will enable business people to interact, rather than just communicate, in real time, thereby negating the need physically to travel. In many large cities the speed of ground travel has remained almost unchanged in the past 100 years as the advantage of the internal combustion engine over the horse has been confounded by the problem of congestion. Whilst technology will allow business travellers to 'work' on trains and aeroplanes, it is possible to foresee the day that using a mobile phone in public will become as distasteful, both socially and medically, as smoking is now, thus removing this 'benefit' of travel.

Indeed, firms may wish staff to avoid travelling on grounds of efficiency and security and may come to see travel as undesirable for other reasons. First, travel to other countries may be a health risk. Travel to some countries has always required vaccination or protection against established diseases such as hepatitis, typhoid and malaria, but new diseases for which there is no protection and no cure have raised the stakes. Second, business travellers who represent wealthy global firms may be the target of criminals or extremists. Bodyguards already accompany business people travelling in certain countries due to the risk of kidnapping or worse.

The Internet could, therefore, be bad for business travel, but what about leisure travel? These customers differ from business travellers in two main ways. First, they are spending their own disposable income which makes them particularly value conscious, so the Internet driving down prices is something that will stimulate such demand. Second, they have an ever-wider choice as to where they can go and what they can do when they get there. The Internet provides much more information about destinations, facilities, infrastructure and transport options, although already there appear to be signs of information overload for some consumers.

It can be argued that the technologies that make it unnecessary for the business person to travel, will also enable the leisure traveller to stay at home. Virtual reality offers a high degree of stimulation and simulated danger without any of the actual physical risk. Egyptian and other tourism industries have been devastated by the impact of terrorism. Such fears and concerns are likely to heighten demand for holidays in apparently secure environments such as cruise ships and closed integrated resorts combining timeshare, hotels, self-catering, restaurants and leisure facilities such as South Seas Plantation, Club Méditerranée and Center Parcs.

The challenges of perception and awareness

Despite the real risks noted above, human behaviour is based less on actual risk and more on the perception of risk, a feature we are very bad at calculating. The effects of a disaster seem to take about 18–36 months to be forgotten at a national level. Acts of terrorism or health scares tend to be viewed as one-off events and providing they do not appear with great regularity in the same place, seem to be accepted by tourists as being unpredictable and unlikely to happen at the destination to which they are going at the time they are going. This philosophy views Egypt is one of the safest places immediately after the last terrorist attack. A single occurrence, however bad, seems to slip memories fairly quickly, a feature the tourism and hospitality industries assist if they can.

Reality is that such events as terrorist acts are of high magnitude but low frequency. For any individual, while results could be fatal, the odds are rather small if one is sensible and does not go to obvious problem spots. On the other hand, potential disasters like climate change are of low personal magnitude but of high or constant frequency, that is, the specific effects are not life-threatening, but the overall likelihood of being affected by the phenomenon is very high or constant. If tourists worry, they seem to worry more about the disasters least likely to affect them in probability terms. The industry does not seem to worry, or does not want to be seen to worry. Air safety is a good example – a lap belt will not significantly increase one's chance of surviving an air crash compared to where one sits in an aircraft but it is given great attention, while the most valuable and highest paying passengers are normally placed in the most dangerous part of the plane!

As well as perception of risk, there is the question of perception and awareness of opportunity for leisure, tourism and travel. The influence of the Internet and new forms of communication in this area have already been noted. Changes in cost and availability of services will also have significant effects on what is perceived of as opportunity and potential destinations for many tourists and travellers.

The challenge of the 'dark side' of travel

The tourism and hospitality industries are generally poor at catering for disabled populations. Figures in the United States suggest that the disabled or challenged sector is a very large one, and despite difficulties, is travelling more and likely to place specific demands on all elements of the tourism and hospitality sectors. There is a great deal of money to be made by meeting the demands of specific groups, and these sectors are no exceptions. Security and user-friendly infrastructure is not cheap, but is not only necessary and fair, but also good business sense. The disabled rarely feature in any forecasts or predictions as a specific group, but it is a large group and one which is likely to get larger and more vocal in expressing its needs and commenting on the industry's shortcomings as members of this group travel or try to travel more in the future.

Tourism also has other dark sides. Tourists can be attracted by the macabre to locations associated with tragedy and death, such as sites of massacres, death camps and war in general. The weird, the extreme, the bizarre also attract visitors in considerable numbers. There are contemporary destinations that have a reputation for sex tourism of all kinds, some extremely undesirable and illegal. Sex tourism is just one aspect that tends to be ignored by most respectable, middle-class academics and industry professionals. It is also one example of the economic activity derived from tourism that is not captured by the statistics. It is unlikely that anyone has any idea of what the true economic value of tourism and hospitality would be if all the undeclared, untaxed activity was included.

The challenge for research

Finally, there is the state of tourism and hospitality research, a subject that should be of concern to all involved in these industries. Both Weiler and Olsen were critical in this volume of the state of the art. Weiler claimed that tourism researchers had removed themselves psychologically and physically from research consumers, i.e. industry. She argued that much research is not meeting industry needs, there is too much low quality research published, much of the output is written in a way that makes it difficult for industry to access and/or understand, and there are huge gaps in the body of knowledge. Olsen identified hospitality research as being eclectic, the body of knowledge poorly defined, journals having a very mixed review process and conferences being even worse. He claimed there is too much replicative work and too much theory-building, with very few people, especially doctoral candidates, answering the 'so what' questions. These charges are serious and if correct, have major implications for the future of the industries since inadequate research is likely to lead to inappropriate or incorrect decisions about investment, development and operations. The tourism and hospitality industries have poor reputations with respect to investing in research, compounding the problem.

Conclusions

A level of agreement emerges from the chapters with respect to some likely characteristics of the tourism and hospitality industries in the coming century. It seems clear that there is going to be greater polarization in the industries in all kinds of ways:

- the 'haves' vs. the 'have nots' in terms of consumers as well as destination areas
- large, global firms vs. small, niche players

- increased mass tourism vs. increased elite tourism
- domestic vs. international tourism
- business vs. pleasure tourism, often with extremely different requirements
- full service vs. no frills commodity service/products.

There may be less seasonality for many reasons:

- congestion and supply saturation in peak periods will reduce attractiveness
- growth in self-employment will drive low-cost and thus off-peak demand
- increased numbers of retirees free of work-related time constraints
- changes in patterns of leisure time – short breaks
- climate change, altering climatic seasonality in some locations.

The notion of 'blur' will apply not only to e-commerce but also to the world generally:

- between business and leisure (travel, activity, time)
- between provider and consumer
- between operational types.

There is likely to be increased homogeneity in many areas of travel:

- no frontiers and hence no need for passports,
- countries will become less distinguishable from each other
- urban architecture and imagery will be increasingly uniform (golden arches syndrome)
- many more tourism products – airline seats, bookings, rooms – will become sold as perishable commodities.

These predictions have to be placed in the context of a lack of knowledge about a number of things. We really do not know about:

- key tourism sectors – religious, business, sex, medical, shopping
- the true economic value of tourism
- tourist motivations – whether they are tribal, or spiritual
- the real reasons for travel and destination choice, rather than simple market research categories
- environmental forces – how green will society have to be, or choose to be?
- e-commerce and the 'wired world', in particular its penetration and level of acceptance

- climate change, its magnitude, its effects and its time scale, as well as possible solutions.

Industry has to take a number of steps in response to these factors. First, to satisfy the business traveller tourism providers – airlines, car hire, hotels, restaurants – must become completely 'wired'. They must make it possible for their customers to interface with every type of global communication system at the fastest speed possible with utter reliability and meeting all of their needs.

Second, suppliers must provide a totally secure environment, free from both health and security risks, in light of the culture of fear Todd speaks about in this volume. This may involve the necessity to develop a totally integrated service that protects the customer from their point of arrival at a destination to their point of departure, even if this means even more tourist ghettos for those who place a high importance on peace of mind.

Third, industry is going to have to become more flexible. Short breaks will be even more popular and maybe more common than long holidays. Most of the growth in intra-regional travel arrivals in Europe will be due to this. This will place an enormous strain on the travel industry, even though it may be good for hospitality and may become heavily dependent on the web to facilitate this.

Fourth, brands and branding will need to be rethought. We need to determine if and for what elements brands are still important, whether brand loyalty is still important, and how to constantly renew the attraction of a brand.

Fifth, there will be some real issues with regard to labour supply and quality, not the least being where the cleaners, waiters and chefs will come from in the future. More importantly perhaps, whether they will be able to deliver the ever-more consistent and high standards that customers will expect.

Sixth, the industries are very bad at understanding risk and managing crises, and if tomorrow's world is more unstable, with increased storms, catastrophic flooding and increased terrorism, insurance companies and legal necessity will require tourism and hospitality providers to become sophisticated crisis managers.

Finally, there is clearly a need for academics to do relevant work and share the findings with industry colleagues in a way they can be understood. However, both Weiler's and Olsen's comments also apply equally to research done in the private sector and the government sector. Academics are often justifiably critical of research in tourism and hospitality undertaken by non-academics. However much we might try to educate and train our students in appropriate research methodologies and techniques, once they leave university they are often unable to use the knowledge they have gained. Many of the Terms of Reference for projects mean consultants and others have to conduct research under unrealistic time scales and with unachievable objectives, which they feel unable to criticize if they want to stay in business or keep their jobs. The results often include unusable National Tourism Plans as several contributors have noted, and inaccurate predictions. The need for quick and simple answers to complex problems for government political decisions or short-term industry planning makes this sort of situation far too common to be acceptable.

Olsen said that because research in our field is so diverse and applied 'it demands visionaries from across the spectrum of industry and academic stakeholders who are capable of taking it to the next level'. That is a mighty challenge, but it might be possible. All it takes is getting all the best minds in the field to recognize the need for improvement and create the will for it to happen. This text, and the conference on which it was based, has tried to do just that.

Index

Authors

Places

Subjects